*the
development
of
american
political
science*

D0931906

the
development
of
american
political
science
FROM BURGESS TO BEHAVIORALISM

Albert Somit
STATE UNIVERSITY OF
NEW YORK AT BUFFALO

Joseph Tanenhaus

Irvington Publishers, Inc.
551 Fifth Avenue
New York, NY 10176

Library of Congress Cataloging in Publication Data

Somit, Albert.
  The development of American political science.

  Includes bibliographical references and index.
  1. Political science—United States—History.
2. Political science—Study and teaching—United States.
I. Tanenhaus, Joseph, joint author.   II. Title.
JA84.U5S63 1980   320'.0973   80-17120
(original LC 67-17759)
ISBN 0-8290-0122
ISBN 0-8290-0122-0
Printed in the United States of America

preface

Like most prefaces, this one contains little that is central to the argument in the text itself. Hence these comments can be safely ignored.

Nevertheless, this may not be an inappropriate occasion on which to account for a collaboration which has now extended over a decade. As indicated below, we disagree on numerous aspects of our common discipline, although not really violently. Disagreement has frequently resulted in a joint inquiry designed to demonstrate which of us was most in error—inquiries in which both sides usually emerged triumphant. This volume is another product of these years of vigorous though fundamentally good-natured squabbling.

We hope our friends—and here is where the real danger lies —will not ask which section is the primary responsibility of which author. Several years of service in the central administration of a large university has conditioned each of us to accept full blame for whatever causes displeasure and to be totally self-effacing whenever merit is involved.

Over the past several years we have discussed so many elements of this book with so many of our fellow social scientists that we could not adequately acknowledge our individual debts to them if we tried. Where scholars have published their views, we have, of course, done our best to indicate what has proved useful to us. On a subject like this, though, the most intriguing ideas are as apt to be tossed about in informal conversation as they are to appear in print. More often than not we have only the vaguest notion of what is borrowed—and from whom.

To those colleagues who have commented on draft chapters, our obligations are clear and heavy. We owe our best thanks to Vernon Van Dyke, John C. Wahlke, Evron M. Kirkpatrick, Albert Lepawsky, Bernard C. Hennessy, Walter F. Murphy, and Donald G. Tacheron for their generous and valuable efforts to make this a better book. Needless to say, none of them agrees with us on every point, major or minor.

We are also indebted to our research assistants, Roosevelt Ferguson, George Beckerman, Harrell Rodgers, and above all, David Atkinson, for their part in developing the quantitative data on which much of this study is based. We are no less indebted to Dean D. C. Spriestersbach of the University of Iowa and to Professor Sidney Roth of New York University for help in providing the wherewithal which made these excellent assistants possible. A word of recognition is also due to our respective offspring, Jed Lawton Somit and Harlan and Beth Tanenhaus, who assisted in some of the more routine but no less essential tasks.

A final word of appreciation is owed our wives. For their interest, encouragement, assistance, and patience we are grateful.

contents

*the
development
of
american
political
science*

I

the
present
and
the
past

*T*his volume is not offered as a full-blown history of American political science; it is not even intended as a well-rounded *short* survey. Instead, we have deliberately limited our attention to those aspects of the past which bear directly on the present "state of the discipline." Toward this end we pursued three closely related objectives: to trace the rise of political science as a profession; to examine the manner in which political scientists have traditionally defined their professional responsibilities and goals; and, probably most important, to describe how political scientists have viewed the "scope and method" of their field since its emergence as an independent area of scholarly inquiry in the late nineteenth century.

We arrived at these objectives and, in fact, at this study itself, by a rather circuitous route. We initially set out to write only a brief historical sketch which would serve as the opening chapter of a long-projected textbook. Such a sketch was an indispensable prerequisite, we felt, to any meaningful treatment of contemporary American political science. The past was thus to be handmaiden to an understanding of the present—and this understanding was and still is our central concern.

Once embarked on the enterprise, we became increasingly aware that the subject demanded a far more detailed and systematic explication than we had originally anticipated, and that the task we had set ourselves simply could not be handled within the alloted space. With bemused incredulity we watched the proposed chapter expand into the volume now in hand. This enlarged framework makes it possible, however, to set the issues currently facing the discipline in proper perspective.

As this study progressed, we gradually formed a number of conclusions about both the history and the present condition of political science, although blithely to speak of a "history" and of "conclusions" is to say either too much or too little. History does not write itself but entails a deliberate selection and organization of "facts." Nor are conclusions necessarily inescapable, being often as much a function of personal predilection as of the evidence on which they are ostensibly based. Still, these conclusions—or judgments—should be stated explicitly at this point, for they bear directly upon issues now being controverted in the profession and have undoubtedly influenced our discussion of these issues. They can be summarized as follows:

First, most American political scientists are largely unfamiliar with the origins and early evolution of their discipline. It could hardly be otherwise. The time has long passed when the recollections of even our senior practitioners can be a reliable guide to what has transpired; an adequate history of the field has yet to be written; and the available literature, although often of high quality, affords at best a fragmentary and partial account.

Next, despite—or more likely because of—this unfamiliarity, the profession is very much the product and prisoner of its past. As William Anderson once remarked,

No body of knowledge springs into existence full-blown and perfect. Each is the result of a long and fumbling process, a groping toward light and perfected form and scientific method. Each bears upon its body the marks of labor at birth and the scars of wounds incurred in later accidents and in arduous struggles for assured position and self-improvement.[1]

From the beginning, American political science had to face that untidy package of questions which inevitably confronts all new fields: What were its boundaries, i.e., its legitimate subject matter?

[1] Anna Haddow, *Political Science in American Colleges and Universities 1636–1900,* New York, 1939, p. ix.

Within these boundaries, what tasks or goals should its members pursue? By what methods could these objectives most readily be attained? The 'manner in which these questions were met in the formative years (1880–1903) had a pervasive effect on the discipline's subsequent development. Where a problem was resolved, that solution influenced the thinking of succeeding generations. To the degree that the answers put forth sanctioned diverse courses of behavior, political scientists still lack a common purpose and objective. And where the questions evoked fundamentally irreconcilable responses, these rival philosophies became a central and enduring component of the discipline's intellectual heritage, and the unsettled issues a chronic and prolific source of discourse and dissension.

Third, American political scientists have paid a heavy price in time, effort, and controversy for their failure to attend more closely to their past. The problems which today trouble the discipline give point and poignancy to the maxim that those who will not learn from history are condemned to relive it. An example will suffice here. For the past twenty years political science has been rocked by the behavioralist controversy. Now, it is one matter to regard the quest for "rigor"—and the angry debate over the merits and feasibility of this quest—as reassuring evidence of a maturing and advancing discipline; it is quite another to recognize it as the latest manifestation of an aspiration as old as the profession itself.

Lastly, the discipline has in several instances overlooked truly significant contributions made in earlier periods. Again, a single example: How many persons remember John W. Burgess other than as a ridiculously fanatical Germanophile?[2] Yet, on re-examination, Burgess ranks not only as the "father" of American political science, but among the truly great figures in its history. His aspirations for a scientific politics, grasp of scientific method, insistence upon broad interdisciplinary training, and concern with systematic theory set a standard rarely surpassed from his day to the present. One of the most satisfying aspects of this study has been the opportunity to re-discover and to acknowledge the

---

[2] The one recent study in which Burgess is taken at all seriously is Bernard E. Brown, *American Conservatives: The Political Thought of Francis Lieber and John W. Burgess,* New York, 1951.

achievements of scholars long neglected by an unknowing and ungrateful posterity.

Obviously, some of these judgments will evoke a mixed reaction, as the phrase goes, from our fellow political scientists. In the course of our narrative it will be necessary, moreover, to comment on other matters where divergent views are more often than not the rule. Under these circumstances, the reader may reasonably demand that the authors make clear their own ideological commitments so that the judgments expressed can be weighed accordingly. A word or two on this score would seem to be in place.

One of us took his doctorate in what was then generally considered to be the leading behaviorally-oriented political science department. Although sympathetic to the objectives of behavioralism, he is skeptical that anything approaching a hard science of politics can ever be attained. Hence he regards himself as mildly anti-behavioral. The other received his training in a department thoroughly traditional in outlook. Naturally enough, he considers himself pro-behavioral. That is to say, he is both partial to the objectives of the behavioral movement and moderately optimistic about the likelihood that major portions of political science can be studied as rigorously as economics and social psychology.

In writing this volume we have had to treat a number of touchy subjects, an exigency on which joint authorships tend to flounder and founder. With very few exceptions, the opinions expressed are held in common and do not represent, so far as we are consciously aware, a compromise or midpoint between conflicting beliefs. Such happy agreement would probably have been impossible were it not for our basic differences of outlook.

Finally, a brief comment on the organization of this book.

In presenting our analysis, we have found it useful to employ five time periods. These are: "pre-history" (before 1880); 1880 to 1903; 1903 to 1921; 1921 to 1945; and from 1945 to date. Within each period, however, the treatment is essentially topical and analytical, rather than chronological. While the reasons for selecting these particular dates will be explained in greater detail at appropriate places in the text, a preliminary comment is in order.

Although we regard these chronological subdivisions as fitting and convenient, we do not wish to suggest that political science changed radically during each of these eras. On the contrary, the interests, problems, and characteristics of the discipline manifest a remarkable persistence and continuity. This is, in fact, one of our major themes. Thus, were it not that the American Political Science Association was founded in 1903—an event of great professional importance—the four decades from 1880 to 1920 might conceivably be treated as a single span, for the other substantive aspects of political science which most concern us changed relatively little over this forty years. Even the post-1920 push for a "science of politics" represents less a total break with the past than the revival of a dormant aspiration and a renewed interest in matters hitherto largely ignored. And, as already suggested, many of the topics so bitterly debated since 1945 are indubitably the lineal descendants of issues argued in the profession not only in the 1920's and 1930's, but in the 1880's and 1890's as well.

Still, the foregoing notwithstanding, political science has also altered significantly over the years. Each of the periods has its distinguishing features and discontinuities with the past. Change and growth accordingly constitute a second major theme. In short, persistent and enduring characteristics invest these periods with an underlying continuity, unique and special characteristics demarcate and identify the successive stages of development. A knowledge of both aspects is the key, we are convinced, to an appreciation of where the discipline stands today.

part 1
a
discipline
is
born

*P*olitical science, as a discipline demanding intensive graduate training for its practice, did not exist in the United States until the last quarter of the nineteenth century. Not until then was serious post-baccalaureate work offered at American schools. The resulting transformation of higher learning profoundly affected practically all of the arts and sciences, rather than political science alone.

As late as 1875, higher education in the United States was typified by the residential four-year college with "a largely ministerial faculty, a classical and tradition-centered curriculum, a recitative class session, a small student body highly selected for gentility and social status, and an unearned Master's degree given to alumni for good behavior after graduation."[1] For real graduate study Americans journeyed abroad, especially to Germany. Nearly ten thousand of them enrolled in German universities by the end of the century. At first these fledgling scholars were mainly interested in law, theology, medicine, and chemistry. After the Civil War, however, students of history and politics were increasingly represented.

[1] Bernard Berelson, *Graduate Education in the United States,* New York, 1960, p. 16.

The political science taught at the German universities was known as *Staatswissenschaft*. To later generations this term came to connote dusty, multi-volumed tomes, interminable German sentences in search of a verb, arid abstractions, terminological distinctions without a difference, and vast composts of pedantic trivia. But young Americans in the 1870's and 1880's were of another mind altogether. For them, *Staatswissenschaft* was like a breath of fresh, spring air. It was characterized by carefully defined concepts and a comparative, systematic, and highly professional analysis of data. In stark contrast to the ethically oriented, didactic political science of their undergraduate experience, *Staatswissenschaft* encouraged the belief that inquiry akin to that of the natural sciences could ultimately uncover the laws underlying political evolution and development.

Quite naturally, Americans who had been educated abroad made repeated efforts to set up doctoral programs based on the German model. Although Ph.D.'s. were granted at Yale as early as 1861, the graduate school did not take firm root here until the latter decades of the century. Particularly prominent among those successful in establishing doctoral training in this country was John W. Burgess, who organized the School of Political Science at Columbia in 1880.

Once rooted, Ph.D. programs grew like a jungle vine. In 1890, less than 200 earned doctorates were awarded by American institutions; a decade later, the figure had doubled. Within a single generation (1876–1900), the Ph.D. became the mark of academic respectability and competence. Hardly had the doctorate taken hold than it was subjected to the first of what would be an unending series of attacks. Best known of the earlier diatribes was William James' scathing "The Ph.D. Octopus" (1903). "The truth is," James charged, "that the Doctor-Monopoly in teaching, which is becoming so rooted an American custom, can show no serious grounds whatsoever for itself in reason. As it actually prevails and grows in vogue among us, it is due to childish motives exclusively. In reality it is but a sham, a bauble, a dodge, whereby to decorate the catalogues of schools and colleges."[2] Innumerable critics would ring the changes on this theme in succeeding years.

[2] Reprinted in William James, *Memories and Studies,* New York, 1911, pp. 329–47, at p. 338.

8

Part I (i.e., chapters 2–4) of this volume deals with the development of American political science up to the creation of the American Political Science Association in 1903. Chapter 2 describes the nature of American higher education prior to 1880 and relates the circumstances leading to the founding of Burgess' School of Political Science. Chapter 3 examines the structuring of the discipline during its formative years, 1880–1903. The extra-scientific interests and activities of practitioners during the formative era are treated in Chapter 4.

II
pre-history
and
origins

*A*t about five o'clock in the morning of June 8, 1880, John W. Burgess, Professor of Political Science and Constitutional Law at what was then called Columbia College, was awakened in his Paris "sleeping room" by someone pounding on the door. Responding to the summons, he was confronted by a messenger bearing a cable. Suddenly wide-awake, Burgess tore open the envelope and read the terse communication, "Thank God, the university is born. Go ahead."[1] These two sentences told the now exuberant professor that the Trustees of Columbia College had finally adopted his proposal for establishing a graduate school of political science and that he could proceed with his plans for engaging its faculty. The Trustees' action was a great personal triumph for Burgess. It was also to prove epochal for Columbia, for graduate education in the United States, and for American political science. Only the latter, of course, directly concerns us here.

Any appreciation of the momentous nature of this decision requires some understanding of American colleges and universities at the time. A quick retrospective glance is therefore appropriate.

AMERICAN HIGHER EDUCATION BEFORE 1880

During much of the nineteenth century, higher education in the United States was conducive to neither productive scholarship nor

[1] John W. Burgess, *Reminiscences of an American Scholar*, New York, 1934, pp. 194–95.

11

inspired instruction. Religious sectarianism, local pride, the absence of a national policy, and the sheer difficulty of physical communication in a land so vast and undeveloped, led to an educational system made up of literally hundreds of small colleges.[2] All too often these were shoestring operations, perpetually on the verge of bankruptcy and collapse, with pitifully barren libraries, hopelessly inadequate laboratories, and grossly overworked and badly underpaid faculties. More or less modelled on the English pattern, most were residential institutions with rigidly prescribed curricula which cut the student, whatever his talents or interests, to fit a Procrustean bed.

Actually, the formal course of study was not the main source of trouble, for at the better schools (and at those which aspired to this status) the usual requirements included instruction in Latin, Greek, mathematics, rhetoric, ethics, logic, metaphysics, political economy, constitutional history, and "natural philosophy." What was mean about this program was less its scope than its superficiality. Advancing knowledge in the natural sciences found slow and imperfect reflection in the classroom. Instruction was rarely carried beyond an elementary level even in the most traditional subjects. Purporting to offer a "classical education," the colleges not only failed to instill an appreciation for the classics—they did not even produce competent Latinists.

The inadequacy of the system was in good part a consequence of incredibly stultifying pedagogy. Instruction seems to have been basically catechetical. Recitation and drill, stereotyped questions and equally stereotyped responses, prevailed. Even at Yale, Andrew D. White wrote,

. . . to the lower classes the instruction was given almost entirely by tutors, who took up teaching for bread-winning while going through divinity school. Naturally most of the work done under these was perfunctory. There was too much reciting by rote and too little real intercourse between teacher and taught. . . . In the junior year matters improved somewhat; but though the professors were most of them really distinguished men . . . they were fettered by a system which made everything of gerund grinding and nothing of literature. . . . Professor Hadley had charge of the class in Thucidydes; but with every gift for making it a means of great good to us, he taught it in the perfunctory way of that period;—calling on each student to construe a few

2 Richard Hofstadter and Walter Paul Metzger, *The Development of Academic Freedom in the United States,* New York, 1955, pp. 114–51.

lines, asking a few grammatical questions, and then, hardly with ever a note or comment, allowing him to sit down. . . . It was always the same mechanical sort of thing. . . .[3]

White may have painted the picture darker than it was, but, the evidence suggests, not by much.

Instruction also tended to be remorselessly didactic. Even the advanced courses in ethics, philosophy, religion, economics, and politics—often taught by the president himself—were manifestly designed to ensure that the students developed into God-fearing, morally upright, sound-thinking citizens. When the data so painstakingly assembled by Anna Haddow[4] are placed in proper context, it becomes all too evident that much of the early collegiate instruction in political science was of this homiletic character. What then passed as political science would be called "education for democratic citizenship" by a later and more sophisticated generation.

In addition to the oversight of their students' mental and moral development, the faculty was charged with quasi-custodial responsibilities. These duties were demeaning and time-consuming; on occasion they were downright hazardous. White's description of life at Hobart College, a "little 'church college' of which the especial boast was that, owing to the small number of its students, it was 'able to exercise a direct Christian influence upon every young man committed to its care' " is instructive. At Hobart, he wrote,

It was my privilege to behold a professor, an excellent clergyman, seeking to quell a hideous riot in a student's room, buried under a heap of carpets, mattresses, counterpanes, and blankets; to see another clerical professor forced to retire through the panel of a door under a shower of lexicons, boots, and brushes. . . . One favorite occupation was rolling cannon-balls along the corridors at midnight, with frightful din and much damage: a tutor, having one night been successful in catching and confiscating two of these, pounced from his door the next night upon a third; but this having been heated nearly to redness, and launched from a shovel, the result was that he wore bandages upon his hands for many days.[5]

[3] Andrew D. White, *Autobiography*, 2 vols., New York, 1905, vol. 1, pp. 26–8. White was both a distinguished political scientist and an outstanding educator. See below, p. 46.

[4] *Op. cit., passim.*

[5] White, *op. cit.*, vol. 1, pp. 19–20.

It may be unfair to suggest that conditions at Hobart were typical. But, on the other hand, neither was Hobart unique. As the eminent political scientist Francis Lieber wailed after tripping over a pile of bricks while pursuing some wayward South Carolina College students one evening—"Mein Gott! All dis for two tousand dollars!"[6]

Whether the system induced students to act as irresponsible and malicious boys rather than as gentlemen and fledgling scholars, or their behavior induced the system, is hard to say. Either answer would have been of slight solace to the harassed (and sadly underpaid) professors. Everything considered, it is not difficult to understand the rapid turnover of teaching staffs or to sympathize with the readiness of many instructors to move into less trying occupations.

The picture was equally bleak at the graduate level, though for different reasons. True, the students were older and hence less boisterous, but of systematic education and formal training there was virtually none. Some young B.A.'s would hang on at their college for a while and, if there were enough of them to warrant a class, they would occasionally be offered special instruction. Yet they were not graduate students in any serious or meaningful sense. To "earn" an M.A., little more was required beyond ". . . staying alive and out of trouble for three years after graduating from college and by giving very modest evidence of intellectual attainments."[7]

This system had scant need for faculty with advanced training in the various academic specializations. Indeed, the typical don was a "generalist" with a Bachelor's degree and, possibly, some additional work in theology. There was little incentive for him to extend his knowledge, for even the mediocre instructor already

[6] Hofstadter and Metzger, *op. cit.*, p. 230. Leiber may have been particularly unfortunate. Burgess, among others, described the students at Amherst as hard-working and well-behaved. He also spoke approvingly of the decorum of Columbia's students, though they were so lazy (deeming it uncivilized to attend early classes, or to use the afternoons and evenings for other than gentlemanly forms of pleasure and relaxation) that he preferred to teach in the School of Law.

[7] Richard J. Storr, *The Beginnings of Graduate Education in America,* Chicago, 1953, p. 1.

14

knew far more than he was in a position to impart. What is perhaps most surprising is that, despite the frustrations of an order so geared to dulling the minds of teachers and students alike, a few colleges did manage to retain on their staffs a handful of able scholars.

THE GERMAN UNIVERSITY AS MODEL

From time to time during the nineteenth century, dissatisfaction with American higher education resulted in efforts to establish graduate programs basically emulative of the German universities. Although Johns Hopkins University (1876) was the first of these to succeed, there had previously been similar attempts at Harvard, Pennsylvania, Michigan, Western Reserve, New York University, Columbia, and elsewhere.[8] Spearheading this movement were the Americans who had gone to Germany for their advanced study. Initially, these migrants were mainly interested in medicine, law, theology, and chemistry; by 1870, though, increasing numbers sought training in the social sciences. A small trickle before the Civil War, visiting students formed a steady stream thereafter. At Göttingen, for instance, only 34 Americans were recorded in attendance for the entire second quarter of the nineteenth century; by the 1870's there were over 160 taking work in one field or another. Berlin was even more popular, enrollment totalling some 1300 for the 1880's.[9]

What drew these throngs from abroad? Above all, the reputation of German scholars. Here, few Americans were disappointed. At Berlin alone, the social science faculty included such distinguished teachers as Ranke, Droysen, Mommsen, Treitschke, von Gneist, Curtius, and Adolph Wagner. Once enrolled at a German university, the Americans were even more favorably struck by the educational arrangements that seemed to foster this academic eminence—the twin concepts of *Lehrfreiheit* and *Lernfreiheit*.[10]

[8] *Ibid., passim.*

[9] Jurgen Herbst, *The German Historical School in American Scholarship. A Study in the Transfer of Culture,* Ithaca, New York, 1965, chap. 1.

[10] For a fuller discussion of these concepts than appears below, see Hofstadter and Metzger, *op. cit.,* pp. 383–497, and Herbst, *op. cit.,* pp. 19–22, 163–73.

For the professor, *Lehrfreiheit* meant the opportunity to pursue his chosen research without restriction as to subject, direction, or method. Not only was he free to engage in research; it was his major responsibility; and academic reputation turned primarily on research attainments. Certainly, the atmosphere was conducive to scholarly inquiry.[11] The professor was relieved of tutorial duties and liberated from the confinements of prescribed syllabi; his research techniques and findings often afforded the materials for his lectures and seminars, the university provided well-equipped laboratories, excellent libraries and, on occasion, research assistants. If life was somewhat less pleasant and more laborious at sub-professorial levels, this was small price to pay for such impressive results.

For the student, fresh from the strictly supervised and intellectually regimented existence of the average American college, the second freedom, *Lernfreiheit,* was an even headier potion. There were virtually no administrative restrictions on his freedom to learn. He could travel from university to university enrolling for courses as he chose and attending them as he liked. Except for a final examination, taken when he felt adequately prepared, there were no tests at all. The university supplied lecture halls and research facilities, but the student's private life and personal conduct were his own concern. He was treated, in short, as a mature adult responsible for his own affairs. The university's sole obligation was to make it possible for him to pursue truth for its own sake and to prepare himself, if so he elected, for a profession or an academic career. The rest was up to him.

ENTER JOHN W. BURGESS

Among the young Americans who journeyed to Germany during the early eighteen seventies was John W. Burgess. Following service in the Civil War, a baccalaureate at Amherst, and a brief

[11] As Herbst points out, the German professors, as civil servants, were expected to exercise their freedom with the restraint and discretion appropriate to their station, though "more often than not they viewed this as a merely theoretical and therefore negligible restraint on their freedom." *Ibid.,* pp. 166–69.

period of legal training and active practice, he accepted a position at Knox College in Galesburg, Illinois. After two years there, Burgess decided that he needed advanced training. When an examination of "the catalogues of all the American colleges" revealed "no adequate provisions for the study of history, public law, and political science anywhere," Burgess wrote for advice to the distinguished historian George Bancroft, then U.S. Minister to Prussia. Almost by return mail came "a reply from Mr. Bancroft offering himself to guide my studies and recommending that I come immediately to Germany." So, in the summer of 1871, Burgess and a young friend named Elihu Root, "steamed away from Boston with our faces set for Göttingen, hoping there and in other German universities to acquire the education which would fit us for the life work which each of us had chosen for himself."[12]

Göttingen, and subsequently Berlin, proved all that Burgess had hoped for and more. He was profoundly impressed by the professors under whom he studied. The superiority of German scholarship, Burgess became convinced, stemmed from the intensive research training which was an integral aspect of German higher education. Failure to provide this training explained the inadequacy of American political science.

On his return to the United States, Burgess joined the Amherst faculty and, shortly thereafter, sought to institute a program of graduate instruction patterned on the German model he so admired. Encountering stormy opposition from his Amherst colleagues, he reluctantly left his alma mater in 1876 for Columbia. There, too, his proposal for a graduate school elicited determined resistance, and a long and bitter struggle ensued. At Columbia, though, Burgess had powerful allies. After four years of debate, persuasion, and gentlemanly coercion, his labors came to fruition.

In June, 1880, as previously noted, the trustees of Columbia College authorized the creation of a School of Political Science. A month later, Burgess met at Vevey, Switzerland, with the three young men he had invited to join him as colleagues—Munroe Smith, Richmond Mayo-Smith, and Clifford Bateman.[13] At

---

[12] *Reminiscences, op. cit.,* pp. 85–86.
[13] All three had been Burgess' students at Amherst. Two were quickly to establish outstanding reputations, Smith in comparative jurisprudence and

Vevey, Burgess and his junior associates laid the ambitious plans which guided the School during its first years. There will be subsequent occasion to consider the outstanding features of the Columbia undertaking. Nonetheless, three aspects merit comment at this juncture: the students, the curriculum, and the method of instruction.

One of the most important innovations of the School of Political Science was that at least three years of undergraduate work was required for admission. Candidates who successfully completed the first year of the School's program would be awarded a baccalaureate; those who finished all three years would, on the submission of a satisfactory dissertation, receive the Ph.D. By limiting enrollment to advanced students, Burgess achieved his aim of establishing a true graduate program in political science.

The curriculum of the School, even a cursory inspection reveals, contained several remarkable features.[14] First, it covered a goodly share of the social science of its day—economics, history, geography, and politics. Sociology was promptly added in 1891 when Franklin Henry Giddings was called to the School from Bryn Mawr College. Although Burgess may not have used the term, he strove mightily to make political science (sometimes, following the French practice, he used the plural, political sciences) thoroughly interdisciplinary.

Another characteristic was the extent to which subjects were treated comparatively, an approach now again fashionable. Burgess utilized comparative analysis both in handling nation-states and in dealing with the several states of the American union. Still another feature worthy of note is the broad training required in political theory, bibliography, and statistics. How many graduate departments today insist upon as much?

The legal emphasis of the program is also significant. This emphasis was only natural, for Burgess and most of his associates

---

Mayo-Smith in social statistics. Bateman, who died less than three years later, was replaced by still another of Burgess' Amherst proteges, Frank J. Goodnow. And Goodnow, of course, was to make an enviable mark in comparative administration and comparative administrative law.

[14] The entire curriculum is reprinted in Ralph Gordon Hoxie (ed.), *A History of the Faculty of Political Science, Columbia University*, New York, 1955.

18

had been trained in law at home and exposed to the legal approach in France and Germany. Personal inclination coincided, moreover, with the realities of the moment. A substantial proportion of the students enrolled in the School of Political Science had just completed the two-year program at Columbia's School of Law. They brought with them a hunger for the theoretical and philosophical treatment of public law and jurisprudence almost completely lacking in the required course work at the practically oriented law schools of the day—a hunger already evidenced by the popularity of the elective classes in public law and political science which Burgess had previously offered in the School of Law.

A last feature should be mentioned, albeit an unintentional one. Although Burgess was in principle committed to the freedom of choice for graduate students which had so deeply impressed him in Germany, budgetary considerations forced him to compromise. The faculty of the School was so small during these early years that, for all practical purposes, the entire program of study was prescribed: the student had no alternative but to take whatever was offered at any given time for his class. A range of options became possible as the School grew.

The curriculum gives a pretty fair notion of the scope of political science as Burgess viewed it, but tells little about the School's instructional philosophy. The best source for this is an essay he wrote in 1883 for a volume on *The Methods of Teaching and Studying History*.[15] We must keep in mind that he is there discussing subjects of a fundamentally historical nature and that the emphasis might have been somewhat different had his remarks been intended for an audience of political scientists. Nevertheless, the thrust of the School's approach is unmistakable. The training of graduate students, he declared, involved several stages or steps. The first, or "outward" form, related to the method of classroom instruction. This, he insisted, must be accomplished chiefly by original lectures. The graduate student "must learn among his first lessons that truth, as man knows it, is no ready-made article of certain and objective character, that it is a human interpretation, and subject therefore to the fallibility of human insight and reasoning,—one-sided, colored, incomplete."

The printed word, Burgess argued, was all too readily ac-

[15] G. Stanley Hall, ed., Boston, 1883, vol. I, pp. 215–21.

cepted as authoritative and posed the danger that memorization would be substituted for the process of critical evaluation. On the other hand, the student could more readily assess the worth of original lectures where "he has the person of his author before his eyes" and "observes his weaknesses as well as his strength." Under these conditions, Burgess argued, "true scholastic skepticism and belligerency will be aroused, and criticism, judgment, reasoning, insight, be developed." No doubt, this critical capacity was one of Burgess' primary objectives. But he was aware, and had no intention of permitting his readers to forget, that such lectures could only be given by a research-oriented "productive" faculty—on the German model.

The second stage in graduate education at the School of Political Science concerned itself with what Burgess termed "internal principles or purposes." This entailed training in the handling and evaluation of historical data. The School sought to teach the student

> . . . how to get hold of a historical fact, how to distinguish fact from fiction, how to divest it as far as possible of coloring or exaggeration. We send him, therefore, to the most original ·sources attainable for his primary information. If there be more than one original source upon the same fact, we teach him to set these in comparison or contrast, to observe their agreements and discrepancies, and to attain a point of view from which all, or if this is not possible, the most of the evidence may appear reconcilable.

During the second stage, too, the student was taught how to derive causal relationships from the data developed. Here, comparative analysis, as well as sound logic, was imperative. Burgess and his colleagues insisted upon ". . . a critical comparison of the sequence of facts in the history of different states or peoples at a like period in the development of their civilizations." When this was done "with patience, care, and judgment," he held, "the student who possesses a moderate degree of true logic will soon learn to distinguish, to some extent at least, antecedent and consequent merely from cause and effect."

The third and last stage of graduate work smacks of what we would today call "theory building." It is best put in Burgess' own words:

After the facts have been determined and the causal *nexus* established we endeavor to teach the student to look for the *institutions and ideas* which have been developed through the sequence of events in the civilization of an age or people. This I might term the ultimate objective of our entire method of historical instruction. With us history is the chief preparation for the study of the legal and political sciences. Through it we seek to find the origin, follow the growth and learn the meaning of our legal, political, and economic principles and institutions.

Clearly, it was in method rather than in scope—a topic to which we will shortly return—that Burgess and his Columbia associates were most directly influenced by their German experiences and mentors.

THE IMPORTANCE OF THE COLUMBIA SCHOOL OF POLITICAL SCIENCE

A final word about why we have described the Columbia School rather than other programs which got under way at The Johns Hopkins University and elsewhere at about the same time.

Burgess' School offered the first, and for many years the most ambitious, graduate program of political science in the United States. But beyond this, it did not evolve gradually. Although the period of gestation may have been long and painful, the School sprang almost fully formed at birth from the minds of Burgess and his young associates. The Columbia School of Political Science was the formative institution in the development of the discipline, since its program was the one that other universities consciously emulated or deliberately deviated from in setting up their own graduate work in political science. It was the one early program, furthermore, that displayed anything like the range of interests and emphases encountered in contemporary departments. In fine, when the School opened in the Fall of 1880, American political science as a learned discipline was born.

III
the
formative
years,
1880–1903:
the
discipline
is
structured

*S*een in proper context, the emergence of political science as an independent discipline was part of a wholesale transformation which occurred in American higher education during the concluding decades of the nineteenth, and the opening years of the twentieth centuries. In almost every area of scholarship, graduate training was reconstructed along Teutonic and, to a lesser degree, Gallic, lines. At the same time, and as part of this reconstruction, the traditional sciences were sundered into a multitude of separate, if not always equal, fields.

Nowhere were the consequences more apparent than in the social sciences. The fragmentation of what had previously been "social science" or "political economy" or "history" into discrete, increasingly specialized disciplines was evidenced by the appearance of a whole family of new professional associations. There were founded, in quick order, the American Historical Association, 1884; the American Economic Association, 1885; the American Statistical Association, 1888; the American Academy of Political and Social Science, 1889; the American Sociological

Society in 1903; and the American Political Science Association in 1903. In each case, the birth of the association was accompanied, either immediately, or shortly thereafter, by the establishment of an official scholarly journal.

For political science, as for its sister fields, this was a time of steady, if not spectacular, expansion and growth. The number of political science departments gradually increased; the number of persons devoting "all or most of their time and attention to what we now call political science" rose to somewhere between fifty and one hundred by the turn of the century.[1] It was, moreover, an era in which there were "giants in the earth." The prestige of the discipline soared as Woolsey, Wilson, Burgess, Willoughby, Lowell, Dunning, and Goodnow turned out works regarded then, and some still today, as classics.

Above all, it was a formative period. During these initial decades, political science, like all new disciplines, had to grapple with a number of critical questions. What was its proper subject matter? In what sense was it to be—or attempt to become—a "science"? Could political scientists, *qua* political scientists, legitimately seek other goals besides the pursuit of knowledge? If so, what should these be? Toward what ends should doctoral training be directed—and how could they best be achieved? The manner in which these questions were resolved was to influence, for better or worse, the nature and course of the discipline for academic generations to come.

THE SUBJECT MATTER OF POLITICAL SCIENCE

Every discipline must define its boundaries—the subject matter or types of problems with which it will deal. Reading through the early literature, one often gets a disconcerting sense of familiarity. As early as 1886, Munroe Smith complained that the term "political science" was being loosely used by experts and laymen alike; there even was uncertainty whether the singular or plural form should be employed.[2] A few years later the English historian,

[1] William Anderson, in Haddow, *op. cit.,* p. 258.

[2] In "The Domain of Political Science," *Political Science Quarterly,* vol. I (1886), p. 1.

Morse Stephens, then teaching at Cornell University, expressed similar puzzlement. Despite persistent questioning during his two-year stay in the United States, Stephens reported, he had not been able to find anyone who could tell him precisely what political science was.[3]

To be sure, the founding fathers did not devote an inordinate amount of energy to definitional problems. Many were quite content to cite Bluntschli's dictum that political science was the "science of the state" and to pass on to more engrossing topics. When, occasionally, other definitions were ventured, there was less than complete agreement. Crane and Moses, in a popular text, held that political science was composed of two branches. The first, analytical politics, or politics as a science, dealt with the development and structure of the state as "an organism for the concentration and distribution of the political power of the nation." The second, practical politics, or politics as an art, was concerned with political motives and aims, i.e., the determination of what the state *should* do.[4] Woolsey, in another widely used volume, also employed a two-fold distinction in defining the content of political science. One branch, political theory, considered the "nature and functions of political communities, the fundamental relations between a government and a people." The other, practical politics, was concerned with the ways in which the "ends" contemplated in the existence of the state may be best attained."[5]

Burgess, in keeping with his systematic separation of what are today commonly referred to as political community, regime, and administration in power, preferred a tripartite division. He distinguished political science proper (dealing with the political community) from constitutional law (dealing with the regime and the rules of the game) and from public law (dealing with the legislation and policies of particular administrations).[6] W. W. Willoughby also thought political science fell into three divisions:

[3] American Historical Association, *Report* (1896), vol. I, p. 211.

[4] William W. Crane and Bernard Moses, *Politics*, New York and London, 1883, pp. 1–2.

[5] *Political Science*, New York, 1877, vol. 1, p. 431.

[6] *Political Science and Comparative Constitutional Law*, 2 vols., Boston, 1890.

. . . first, the determination of fundamental philosophical principles; second, the description of political institutions, or governmental organizations considered at rest; and third, the determination of the laws of political life and development, the motives that give rise to political action, the conditions that occasion particular political manifestations. . . .[7]

On the whole, this generation of practitioners was less troubled by the need formally to define political science than by the more practical problem of distinguishing it from related disciplines which professed similar concerns, history in particular. For Herbert Baxter Adams the distinction was temporal: political science was simply contemporary history.[8] Both Adams' seminar room and each volume of the Johns Hopkins *Studies in Historical and Political Science,* which he edited for so long, flaunted Freeman's motto "History is past Politics and Politics present History." It is reasonable to infer that Jesse Macy and Simeon Baldwin agreed with Adams and Freeman.[9] This conception of the intimate ties between the two fields was poetically stated in Seeley's oft-quoted aphorism that "History without political science has no fruit; Political science without History has no root."[10]

Munroe Smith, on the other hand, denied the alleged affinity with history. For him, the content of political science largely overlapped that of law and economics. The three were so interdependent that the "investigation of any one of the three implies the investigation of both of the others" and the difference was of viewpoint rather than subject matter. In Smith's opinion, history was not a discipline in itself but, like statistics, primarily a method to be used in establishing, assembling, and comparing facts.[11]

It was just this notion of history as handmaiden to the study of politics that Professor Stephens, however mistakenly, perceived as dominant among American political scientists. Astonished and dismayed, he prevailed upon Burgess to address the American

---

[7] *The Nature of the State,* New York, 1896, pp. 382 ff.

[8] Hall, *op. cit.,* p. 126.

[9] American Historical Association, *Report* (1893), pp. 181–88, and 1896, vol. I, p. 218.

[10] Sir John Robert Seeley, *Introduction to Political Science,* London, 1896, p. 4.

[11] Smith, *op. cit.,* pp. 3–4, 8.

Historical Association and, hopefully, to clarify the proper relationship between the two disciplines. The result, it would seem, was not quite what Stephens expected.

In his 1896 paper Burgess first defined history (with characteristic modesty he insisted that it had never before been properly defined) and then political science as he saw them. After developing the implications of both definitions, Burgess concluded that the "two spheres so lap over one another and interpenetrate each other that they cannot be distinctly separated. . . . Separate them, and the one becomes a cripple, if not a corpse, the other a will-o'-the-wisp."[12] Yet, if closely related, they were neither identical nor equal. Political science went beyond historical analysis because it provided a theoretical basis for the organization of data. As he put it:

> Political science consists of something more than facts and logical conclusions from facts. It contains an element of philosophical speculation, which when true and correct, is the forerunner of history. When political facts and conclusions come into contact with political reason they awaken in that reason a consciousness of political ideals not yet realized. Thrown into the form of propositions these ideals become principles of political science, then articles of political creeds, and, at last, laws and institutions.[13]

Given this difference, Burgess went on, it was obvious that political science had a superior claim to most areas of common concern. Then, no doubt mindful of his position as invited guest, he gallantly assured his hosts that political scientists would probably not press their claim in all matters.

W. W. Willoughby seems to have been the only one to anticipate a later mode of thought by arguing that the discipline's closest ties were with sociology, rather than history. For Willoughby, sociology embraced the "systematic treatment of all those interests that arise from the life of man in social aggregates." Economics and law, as well as political science, were all subdivisions of the larger study. Still, he saw no difficulty in differentiating political science from the other social sciences. It alone dealt "with society solely from its organized standpoint,—that is, as effectively orga-

---

[12] American Historical Association, *Report* (1896), vol. I, p. 209.
[13] *Ibid.*, pp. 407–08.

nized under a supreme authority for the maintenance of an orderly and progressive existence."[14]

Despite the manifest shortcomings of these several definitions, and the consequent failure to draw a clear-cut line between political science and its sister disciplines, there the matter rested. There, everything considered, it still rests today. The founding fathers undoubtedly did as well as the problem permitted, for subsequent efforts to delineate the scope of political science have not been notably more successful. To say, as would a subsequent generation, that political science is concerned with "power, authority and influence" or that it deals with the "authoritative allocation of values for a society" is to advance a modest distance beyond what earlier practitioners had in mind when they spoke of "government," "state," and "society."[15]

THE PROPER STUDY OF POLITICS

Two intimately related, if logically separate, issues have been chronic bones of contention in American political science: (1) Is political science capable of becoming a *science* in the stricter sense of that term? (2) By what *methods* can the discipline's subject matter be best handled? The treatment of these issues during the formative period foreshadowed much of what was to be said later.

POLITICAL SCIENCE AS *Science*

By the last quarter of the nineteenth century, a form of scientism[16] had attained considerable popularity among American

---

[14] Willoughby, *op. cit.*, pp. 1–2.

[15] The topics dealt with in the pre-1900 texts, it is also instructive to note, do not differ radically from those considered appropriate and relevant for discussion by political scientists today.

[16] By scientism we mean the belief that the methodology generally associated with the natural sciences can be fruitfully used to attack problems of fundamental concern to a given discipline. This belief rests, in turn, on a cluster of value commitments, the most central of which is the conviction that regularities or laws can be developed which have explanatory and predictive utility. Among the other values frequently associated with scientism are: (a) the necessity of avoiding confusion between facts on the one hand, and what is good or desirable on the other; (b) the importance of

PART 1: A DISCIPLINE IS BORN

social scientists. Certainly, some of the most eminent figures of
that day—e.g., Lester Ward, William Graham Sumner, Franklin
Giddings, and Albion Small—were "scientistic" in outlook.[17]
What is less clear is whether many political scientists shared their
views. A systematic examination of the literature suggests that
relatively few practitioners in the formative era gave much attention to the relationship between science and the study of political
phenomena. Nevertheless, the available data persuasively show
that some early members of the profession were firmly convinced
that the discipline would ultimately become a science in more than
a broad and figurative sense.

The most outstanding advocate of scientism was Burgess
himself. He believed that political science should be studied by the
method of inquiry "which has been found so productive in the
domain of Natural Science." Burgess was sure that there existed
fundamental laws governing the growth and behavior of political
institutions and that a meticulous comparative historical analysis
would reveal what they were. His researches convinced him that a
systematic theory built upon clear and precise definitions of three
distinct but interrelated concepts[18] could be used to analyze a
polity at any given stage of its evolution, to assess the soundness of
its policies, and to predict the future course of its development. In
his major work, *Political Science and Comparative Constitutional
Law* (a book which Burgess, not without some justification,
claimed was widely misunderstood), he attempted to set forth this
theory and demonstrate its utility.

As might be expected, Munroe Smith shared Burgess' scientistic views. For Smith, a discipline which sought to be a science
had to satisfy two requirements: first, that it "aims at the discovery

maintaining a close and continuous interrelationship between data and
theory; and (c), the need to use the utmost precision in collecting and
analyzing data. See also the discussion of behavioralism below, pp. 176–82.

[17] Albert Lepawsky, "The Politics of Epistemology," *Western Political
Quarterly,* vol. 17 (1964), Supplement, pp. 31 ff.

[18] As mentioned above, in modern terminology these three concepts
are commonly referred to as political community, regime, and administration in power. Previous students of political science, among them Aristotle
and the German publicists, had made some progress, Burgess conceded, in
working out such a theory. Ambiguities in the treatment of the basic
concepts, however, had impaired the usefulness of these earlier attempts.

of truth"; second, that it demonstrates the existence of fundamental laws. Political science met both of these conditions: it pursued the truth; and its practitioners had already established, he felt, some basic regularities in the area of political behavior.

Another political scientist with scientistic leanings was Jesse Macy of Iowa (later Grinnell) College (like Burgess, Macy had shown a bent for mathematics as an undergraduate). A careful reading of Darwin's *Origin of Species* persuaded him that extraordinary benefits to mankind would accrue if scientific method were applied to the study of politics. By this he meant the substitution of "experiments, demonstrations, and cooperation" for "acrimonious debate." As Macy put it:

> The State is composed of a series of institutions which may be objectively defined and studied. Our federal system readily adapts itself to the laboratory method. Each school district, each town, city, county and State is a station for conducting experiments in government. To keep all one's faculties at their best in ascertaining and performing all one's duties respecting the conduct of any part of the government is a scientific experiment quite as much so and it may be quite as beneficial to the human race as to exercise the same care in respect to the use of those faculties in studying and reporting upon the action of a jelly fish under exposure to the influence of a certain gas, or the light of electricity.[19]

What especially vexed Macy was that most political scientists seemed to prefer the approach he associated with Machiavelli rather than the far more productive one used by Darwin.

We should also note that even during this early period a leading textbook called attention to the need to separate fact from value. It was important, Crane and Moses warned their readers, to draw "the line between what the state *is,* or, under given circumstances, *must be,* and what the state *should be,* and *should do.* A very common fault in much of the current writing on politics, is the mixing up of the treatment of such subjects."[20]

At least one political scientist of the formative era was skeptical that the discipline could tread the path of the natural sciences. Sheldon Amos, after a rather extensive treatment of the

---

[19] *Jesse Macy: An Autobiography,* edited and arranged by his daughter, Katharine Macy Noyes, Springfield, Illinois—Baltimore, Md., 1933, p. 34.

[20] *Op. cit.,* p. 3.

requirements of scientific inquiry in his *Science of Politics*, concluded:

> There is a vast difference between calling a branch of knowledge a science . . . and [it] being, as yet, scientifically cultivated, or advanced in outward form to the full proportions of a maturely developed science. It may be, indeed, that, from a number of causes. . . . Politics will always present an appearance neither homogeneous nor . . . exact.[21]

One suspects that a number of other political scientists shared his views.[22] But just who they were is a matter about which we can only speculate.

THE METHODS OF INQUIRY

As the history of political science abundantly evidences, there is no necessary relationship between scientism and any particular mode of inquiry. The reason is simple. Scientism, like belief in a Supreme Being, is a matter of faith, whereas method, like theology, entails the question of how to relate that belief to the problems of the real world. Those who agree on the former may, and customarily do, differ considerably about the latter.

Barely had its birth pangs subsided when the profession was embroiled in the first of the methodological controversies which were to absorb much of its energies over the ensuing decades. Within a quarter-century not one but two methodological revolutions were attempted. As might be expected, Burgess at Columbia and Adams at Hopkins were the architects and victors of the first. Not surprisingly, they were the targets and vanquished of the second.

The earlier assault was upon the so-called "deductive" approach—an approach which confused mathematics with science and mistook the latter to entail the logical deduction of "laws" from *a priori* first principles, much in the grand tradition of Hobbes and Locke.[23] This conception of science and scientific

---

[21] London, 1883, p. 4.

[22] Cf. Edmund J. James, *Annals* (1897), pp. 361–2.

[23] An example of this would be Henry Sidgwick's contention that "the study of Politics" was "concerned primarily with constructing, on the basis of certain psychological premises, the system of relations which ought to be

method, sadly obsolete, fell speedily before the contemptuous disdain of those trained abroad. With Burgess and Adams leading the way, there rose next to pre-eminence the historical-comparative approach taught by the German publicists. Historical-comparative analysis stressed, first, the necessity of going back to original sources, the older the better. So conceived, sound scholarship required a mastery of the techniques for disinterring, verifying, and evaluating documents. It also encouraged, among its less sophisticated devotees, an unfortunate tendency to rely heavily upon the formal, written record.

The Teutonic methodology had a second salient characteristic —comparison. To this idea both Columbia and Hopkins were committed. Burgess carefully reminded readers of his *Political Science and Comparative Constitutional Law* that

> If my book, however, has any peculiarity, it is its method. It is a comparative study. It is an attempt to apply the [comparative] method, which has been found so productive in the domain of Natural Science, to Political Science and Jurisprudence.[24]

The Columbia faculty planned to apply the historical-comparative method to broad areas of political science and related fields in a proposed ten-volume series collectively entitled "Systematic Political Science." Well-known products of this enterprise were Burgess' aforementioned book, Goodnow's *Comparative Administrative Law,* and Dunning's *History of Political Theories.* Other projected volumes, e.g., Munroe Smith's *Historical and Comparative Jurisprudence* and Seligmann's *Historical and Comparative Science of Finance,* never survived gestation.[25] In like fashion, Herbert Baxter Adams at Hopkins saw the historical-comparative approach as the touchstone to general laws of political behavior and development, a conviction which led him into a curious body of studies intended to prove that the wellsprings of New England local government were to be found in medieval Germany.

---

established among the persons governing, and between them and the government, in a society composed of civilized men, as we know them." *Elements of Politics,* London (1891), p. 15.

[24] *Op. cit.,* vol. I, p. vi.

[25] Plans announced in several volumes of the Columbia Studies series, viz., volumes V, VI, & VII.

Hardly had this methodology captured the leading graduate schools when it, too, came under fire. The criticisms centered less on the merits of comparative analysis than on the notion that the assiduous perusal of records and manuscripts would somehow lead to an understanding of political behavior. By the middle of the 1880's Woodrow Wilson, who had his fill of document "rummaging" under Adams, sounded the clarion of revolt.

Wilson agreed that the comparative or the more strictly historical approach afforded "the only thorough method of study in politics."[26] But political scientists should deal with more than documents and records: they should deal with real events, real people, real political life. Citing Bagehot and de Tocqueville as models, Wilson urged a "man of the world" approach. The student of politics "must frequent the street, the counting-houses, the halls —yes and the lobbies—of legislatures." This did not mean, however, that the political scientist was to abandon his books and spend all his time "in wiseacre observation among busy men." Books were to be the "ballast"—not the total cargo.[27]

In a letter to Adams, Wilson explained how he, personally, hoped to combine the two methods. "As you know," he wrote,

What I "go in for" is the *life,* not the texts, of constitutions, the practise (sic!) not the laws of administration: and I can get at these things only by cross-questioning systems at their homes. I have learned, for instance, all that is necessary to be known about what that autocratic person, the French *Prefect may do* and what the law has to say about his appointment:—*anybody* can find such things out and make long-headed remarks about them. What I want to know is, what the Prefect *does* do and under what influence he is appointed. I must know the live prefect before I can feel that I know anything about French administration.[28]

[26] *The State,* Boston, 1889, cited by Haddow, *op. cit.,* pp. 243–44.

[27] "The Study of Politics," *New Princeton Review,* vol. III (1887), pp. 188–89. Adams had already yielded considerable ground the year before by accepting as Wilson's doctoral dissertation an essay essentially devoid of the prescribed documentary research. In addition, Adams himself had somewhat earlier published, in the Johns Hopkins *Series,* several studies based less on documents than on observation and interviews. Cf. Johnson, *Rudimentary Society Among Boys,* Series 2, #XI; Shein, *Land Laws of Mining Districts,* Macy's *Institutional Beginnings in a Western State* and *Local Government in Iowa,* Series 2, #XII, Series 2, #VII.

[28] W. Stull Holt, ed., *Historical Scholarship In the United States, 1876–1901: As Revealed in the Correspondence of Herbert B. Adams,* Baltimore, 1938, p. 92.

Not unlike later advocates of "realism," Wilson was not altogether successful in applying his preachings to his own research. *The State* is hardly a monument to "live" political science and, as Bernard Crick rather maliciously observed, Wilson "never even sat for an afternoon in the gallery of the Senate" in doing his *Congressional Government.*[29]

Yet, Wilson undoubtedly influenced the thinking of his colleagues. By the end of the period there were few practitioners who would deny that the political scientist should, in principle, concern himself with life as well as with literature. A very small number even carried the principle into practice. Within a decade or two, then, the comparative approach had been recast to include a comparison of living people, real events, and functioning governments, as well as of documents, charters and constitutions. The precise balance between the two, and the specific means by which "reality" could best be grasped, were left for future generations to debate.

DOCTORAL TRAINING

Acceptance as a full-fledged practitioner in an academically oriented profession normally calls for the Ph.D. or its equivalent. The acquisition of this degree requires a long and intensive program of study formally designed to transmit the appropriate knowledge and skills. What also occurs, though, is a process of "professional socialization" whereby a body of beliefs, standards, and concerns is concurrently passed along from the older to the younger generation. The activities and accomplishments most esteemed by the teachers acquire prestige in the eyes of the students; the issues and tendencies which loom large for the masters are almost certain to be stressed in training the apprentices. Doctoral programs consequently mirror in miniature, as it were, the discipline's accepted values and concerns.

From the outset, American doctoral programs, as did their German prototype, sought to turn out political scientists capable (and, hopefully, desirous) of doing "original research"—and the

[29] Bernard Crick, *The American Science of Politics,* Berkeley and Los Angeles, 1960, p. 104.

"productive scholar" is still the ideal pursued today. This research orientation no doubt contributed substantially to the advance of the profession. It also spawned some problems' for which neither political science nor any of the other disciplines so afflicted have been able to find satisfactory solutions.

DOCTORAL TRAINING AT COLUMBIA AND HOPKINS

The only American Ph.D. programs of consequence before the end of the nineteenth century, it is safe to say, were those at Columbia and Johns Hopkins. Seventeen persons holding American doctorates were nominated for office or committee appointment at the first (1903) meeting of the American Political Science Association; of this group, seven had taken their degrees at Columbia, five at Johns Hopkins. By 1900, Hopkins had turned out at least 30 Ph.D.'s who would shortly become members of the Association; Columbia had been almost half as productive.[30] To these two schools came a steady stream of requests for teaching personnel; from them went out a steady flow of newly minted instructors. A partial list of the departments so staffed would include Chicago, Illinois, Indiana, Michigan, Minnesota, Missouri, Pennsylvania, Princeton, and Texas.[31]

Given the pre-eminence of Adams' and Burgess' departments, it was only natural that they profoundly influenced thinking elsewhere. Since what was done at Columbia and Hopkins set the pattern for other institutions (see the appendix to this chapter) we can focus our attention accordingly. At an earlier point certain features of Burgess' School of Political Science were described. It would be useful now to consider the major similarities and differences between the training offered there and that afforded at Johns Hopkins under Herbert Baxter Adams.

The similarities are perhaps more striking. Both programs were specifically designed to train professional scholars; both were

[30] The sources for these data are the lists of Ph.D.'s for the period published by Columbia and Hopkins. These persons were subsequently checked out in *Who's Who in America,* and against membership rosters published in the APSA *Proceedings.*

[31] As early as 1883 Adams claimed some hundred faculty placements at some fifty colleges. Many, of course, were not in political science.

founded and directed by men who had taken their own graduate work abroad and who had been very favorably impressed by what they had seen. The School of Political Science, Burgess frankly admitted, sought to incorporate "as models of university teaching the methods of the German universities, of the Sorbonne and College de France, and the Ecole Libre des Sciences Politiques."[32] And Adams, though disavowing any intention of "slavishly following foreign methods" at Hopkins, "did not hesitate to adopt the best results of European experience to American educational wants."[33]

At both institutions, too, the programs were heavily research oriented. The seminar, espoused by Adams as the only real "training school for doctors of philosophy,"[34] was also employed at Columbia to provide "close control and acquaintance between teacher and pupil." Almost from the beginning, Burgess was able to provide a few fellowships for "men who should manifest in their graduate work the highest powers of research."[35] Although each fellow was given a teaching assignment, these duties were carefully limited "so as not to take the time of the fellow from his research work." Columbia required, furthermore, "that the instruction in every case should be the product of his own research." By the end of the century, the School had more than fifty such appointments (in the several fields of social science) with which to entice prospective students.[36]

The critical importance of research was driven home in other ways. For instance, Columbia required that all Ph.D. dissertations be published, at the student's own expense, if necessary. Adams believed this practice worthy of emulation.[37] Other universities did not long hesitate before adopting the Columbia-Hopkins publication requirement.

[32] *Reminiscences,* p. 198. "The English model," Burgess reported after an inspection trip, was not one from which he was "able to learn much."

[33] Johns Hopkins *Series,* vol. 2, #2, pp. 97–98.

[34] *Ibid.,* p. 64.

[35] *Reminiscences,* p. 199.

[36] See advertisements in vol. X of Columbia *Series,* 1898–99.

[37] He felt, however, that a broader purpose would be served if privately published dissertations were distributed at least to major libraries. *Study of History in American Colleges and Universities,* Washington, D.C., 1887, p. 84.

The establishment of the *Political Science Quarterly* also stemmed from Columbia's commitment to scholarly publication. Dissatisfied because graduate students "were obliged to read their magazine literature in the political sciences in foreign journals," Burgess had proposed, in his 1880 plan for the School of Political Science, to found a scholarly periodical which would meet the need for a "distinctively American literature in this domain." Soon realizing that there was not a "sufficient number" of Americans competent to "furnish the contributions for such a publication," he temporarily shelved the idea. By 1886, however, the necessary reservoir of talent had been trained and the *Political Science Quarterly* came into being. For at least a quarter-century the major American outlet for scholarly articles in political science, the *Quarterly* did much to shape and to reflect the development of the profession.

In two other stimuli to research, Adams was the innovator. He founded (1877) the Johns Hopkins Historical and Political Science Association, a group made up of advanced students in his seminars, faculty members (President Gilman included) actively involved in historical-political research, and seminar graduates seriously pursuing creative scholarship. Each member was obligated to prepare an original research report for delivery to the Association's membership and, when Adams liked a paper (like Browning's Duchess, he had "a heart too soon made glad, too easily impressed"), he would try to arrange for its publication.

Adams' ability to place articles improved remarkably with the appearance (1883) of his second innovation, *The Johns Hopkins Studies in Historical and Political Science*. Whatever Adams' original aim, this series was soon transformed into little more than a vehicle for publishing Hopkins doctoral dissertations. The virtues of such a device so impressed other institutions that rival series were soon inaugurated. Even Columbia was swept along. In 1891 dissertations by its learned doctors began to appear as *Studies in History, Economics and Public Law*.

An examination of the various publications undertaken or sponsored by the graduate faculties at Hopkins and Columbia not only reveals their understanding of sound academic scholarship, but also points up the main differences between their approaches. At Columbia, the subject matter of inquiry ranged far and wide across history, law, economics, and politics. Methodologically, comparative analysis was stressed, with a liberal use of quantitative data where relevant.

At Hopkins the thrust was quite different. Adams concentrated on the study of "American Institutional and American Economic History . . . beginning with local institutions, and extending ultimately to national institutions.[38] With few exceptions, the items in the Hopkins *Series* during its early years center on American colonial and early state affairs. The Columbia *Studies,* on the other hand, had no dominating purpose other than to "create a school of American political philosophy and a distinct American literature of these sciences."[39] The heterogeneity of its topics reflect a greater breadth of interest—and conceivably the greater latitude permitted Columbia candidates at this time.[40] Part of the explanation may be, aside from Adams' grand design, that the Columbia faculty had simply moved further away from history and a basically historical approach than had the Johns Hopkins staff.

One more aspect of graduate education during the formative period, and another difference between Columbia and Hopkins, deserves specific mention. This involved the practice of taking all or part of one's graduate work abroad.

Burgess' experiences in Germany convinced him, as we have seen, that such a *wanderjahr* was essential for the proper development of a research scholar.[41] After his return to Amherst, and for many years thereafter, his students were sent abroad to round out their training. All of the original faculty of the School of Political

[38] The inspiration for this gigantic undertaking came to him, he proudly related, in the "Seminary of Professor Erdmannsdoerffer at the University of Heidelberg." (Johns Hopkins *Series,* no. 1, #2, p. 40.)

[39] *Reminiscences,* pp. 201–02.

[40] In principle, Johns Hopkins sought "to encourage independent thought and research" (Johns Hopkins *Series,* Series 2, #1, p. 5); in practice, as Woodrow Wilson found to his dismay, students were dragooned into "cooperative class work"—i.e., drafted as laborers for one of the many research projects designed to further Adams' objectives (Haddow, *op. cit.,* pp. 194–95).

[41] Burgess frankly admitted that he could ". . . not have composed the chapters on 'The Nation' [in his *Political Science and Comparative Constitutional Law*] except for the help I received from the notes on [Prof. Wappaus'] lectures, which I had preserved." *Ibid.,* 103–04.

Science, and five of its seven Ph.D.'s mentioned above, emulated his example. So, Dunning, taking his degree in 1885, went to Germany to study, just as Burgess had done fifteen years before; so, a decade later, Merriam, for whom Dunning in turn was intellectual "mentor and sponsor,"[42] journeyed to Paris and Berlin.

At Hopkins, on the other hand, the European sojourn was little stressed, Adams' oft-expressed enthusiasm about his own odyssey notwithstanding. Only one of the five Hopkins Ph.D.'s referred to earlier crossed the Atlantic for this purpose. The difference in practice reflected, perhaps, the Hopkins concern with American rather than foreign institutions.

Early in the twentieth century Columbia, too, began to deemphasize the importance of study in Germany and France. Whereas some half of those who made up what might be regarded as the profession's first "Establishment"—i.e., the persons nominated for office at the first Association meeting—had pursued formal training abroad, twenty years later it was exceptional to have embellished one's preparation in this fashion. Whatever the reasons, and the increasing doctoral output and growing self-confidence of American political science departments were undoubtedly contributing factors, the consequences of the change were soon apparent. Previously, a sizable number of American practitioners had first-hand contact with continental scholars. They were familiar with the German and French literature, and the experience of living abroad encouraged a cosmopolitanism in professional matters. Once American political scientists lost direct personal touch with their European counterparts, they became increasingly parochial in outlook as well as in training.

RESULTANT PROBLEMS

By the close of the formative period, doctoral work in political science had pretty well crystallized into the form it presents today —a program aimed at turning out persons with a demonstrated capacity to carry out original research. Beyond question, the emphasis on productive scholarship served to raise the level of expertise within the profession and to afford American students a

[42] Charles E. Merriam, *The Future of American Government in the United States: Essay in Honor of Charles E. Merriam,* Leonard D. White, ed., Chicago, 1942.

training comparable in intensity and rigor to that offered at European universities. At the same time, it gave rise to two problems which have haunted not only political science but all of American higher education to the present day.

Given the orientation described above, graduate programs paid little attention to the fledgling Ph.D. as prospective teacher. Since the great majority of new doctorates went into academic life, they were admirably unprepared for the pedagogical duties promptly thrust upon them. A few were equipped by nature or prior experience for this task; the others made do as best they could. Under these circumstances, the resulting quality of instruction was hardly calculated to satisfy students, college administrators, or even the hapless teacher himself. What, then, should be done about a system which produced learned scholars who often lacked the most rudimentary conception of how to transmit their knowledge to others? Graduate and undergraduate faculties gravely debated this question in the 1890's and 1900's. With undiminished gravity and concern, they do so today.[43]

This basic problem was aggravated by a professional value system which defined scholarly competence and academic achievement in terms of publication. All but the most obtuse graduate students quickly realized that books and articles, rather than scintillating lectures, paved the road to advancement. Deans and presidents, to be sure, solemnly voiced their abiding concern with the proper instruction of the young and the importance attached to good teaching at their own institutions. Still, promotions and raises somehow had a closer relationship to the length of one's bibliography than to the quality of one's pedagogy. Faced by this reality, the young instructor was sometimes forced to choose between his responsibilities as a teacher and an academic code whereby advancement was frequently contingent upon publication. Teaching, understandably enough, occasionally lost out.

In the long run the compulsion to appear in print did not always advance the interests of the discipline. Where everyone must do research, a good deal is done that would have been better left undone; where everyone must publish, a good deal is written that would have better been left unsaid. Here, too, the events of the formative period profoundly affected the subsequent development of the discipline.

[43] Berelson, *op. cit.*

APPENDIX

For a time it seemed that Michigan would also become an important center of graduate work in political science. The School of Politics at Michigan opened its doors in 1881 with Charles Kendall Adams as Dean, and with a faculty that included Thomas E. Cooley, President Angell, and Henry Carter Adams. Similar in structure to Burgess' empire at Columbia, the Michigan School admitted students who had completed two years of undergraduate work. Three more years of satisfactory performance and the submission of an acceptable thesis qualified the student for the Ph.D. Course offerings covered American politics, European politics, international law, diplomacy, forestry administration, administrative law, taxation, political economy, and the social and sanitary sciences. The School sponsored the Michigan Political Science Association (patterned after the Academies at Hopkins and Columbia) to promote and to publish scholarly studies by its staff, advanced students, graduates, and others. By 1883 the Michigan School of Politics had some twenty students, including several Ph.D. candidates. But Adams departed for Cornell University shortly thereafter, and the decision to close the school was officially announced in 1887. Nor did Michigan quickly revive its ambitions. When political scientist John A. Fairlie came to the University in 1900, he was assigned to the department of history. Not until 1911, a year after Jesse S. Reeves was called from Dartmouth, did political science at Michigan regain departmental status.

The University of Pennsylvania might have developed a strong doctoral program in political science during this period had not its distinguished specialist in public administration, Edmund J. James, shifted his interests from politics to economics. This shift was already evident in the direction taken by the University of Pennsylvania *Publications in Political Economy and Public Law,* which James edited from its inception in 1885 until his departure for Chicago in 1896. By the time that the Academy of Political and Social Science was founded in 1889, with James as its President and moving force, his commitment to political science had already become quite secondary. From its inaugural volume in 1890, the Academy's *Annals,* also edited by James during its first few years, emphasized economics and sociology rather than political science and history. Although James joined the American Political Science Association in 1905, he did not play a leading part in the organization. On the other hand, he was centrally involved in the American Economic Association, ultimately being elected to its presidency. Graduate work in political science did not receive much attention at Pennsylvania until James T. Young returned there with a German Ph.D.

40

Little in the way of doctoral training was available elsewhere until the very end of the formative period. Brown University had almost nothing of a formal program, even though it had awarded a brace of Ph.D.'s to political scientists before the turn of the century. One went to George Grafton Wilson in 1889, and the other to James Q. Dealey in 1895. The former was from the beginning, and the latter soon to become, active in the affairs of the discipline. Not until almost the end of the nineteenth century did Wisconsin and Chicago foreshadow their eventual importance as breeding grounds for political scientists. Wisconsin started late, but strongly, with degrees to George Henry Alden and Samuel E. Sparling in 1896 and to Paul S. Reinsch in 1900. Alden soon left political science for history, but Sparling and Reinsch became members of the profession's first Establishment (see above, p. 39). The University of Chicago did not open its doors until 1890 but then moved quickly. Between 1898 and 1902, Ph.D.'s were granted to six persons, two of whom (Lawrence Boyd Evans and Jeremiah Simeon Young) remained in the discipline.

Harvard showed almost no interest in training political scientists despite the presence on its faculty (from 1883) of Albert Bushnell Hart, a leading figure in the early days of the Association. The first prominent member of the discipline to hold a Harvard Ph.D., William Bennett Munro, did not obtain it until 1900. (College President C. A. Duniway, Ph.D., Harvard, 1896, became moderately active in the affairs of the Association late in the Emergent Period.)

Princeton's commitment to doctoral work in political science was even less noteworthy, despite, or perhaps because of, the presence of Woodrow Wilson who, as we have seen, was hardly enthusiastic about his graduate experiences at Johns Hopkins. It is relevant to recall that during Wilson's presidential tenure at Princeton he called there two senior political scientists who had been spared the trauma of doctoral training at home or abroad. They were Harry A. Garfield (who showed excellent judgment in his choice of a father) and Henry Jones Ford.

IV
extra-scientific
responsibilities
of
the
profession

*J*ust as each discipline must determine its subject matter, so too must it decide the activities and interests appropriate to its practice. This choice is the conjoint product of "official" doctrine and the sort of enterprises in which its members actually become involved. We must look, therefore, both at what is done and what is said.

From the very beginning, political scientists saw scholarly inquiry and the systematic accumulation of knowledge as a major objective. From the beginning, though, many of them regarded two other activities as also falling within their sphere:—first, educating the young for citizenship and civic affairs; second, personal involvement in public policy. Both were accepted as correlative responsibilities during the formative years. Both, sporadic dissents notwithstanding, have since absorbed much of the profession's attentions.

PERSONAL INVOLVEMENT IN PUBLIC POLICY

American political scientists who studied abroad were often surprised by the extent to which continental academicians, especially those in Germany, participated in governmental and political activities.[1] As Andrew D. White enviously reported, "in every great nation of Europe it will be seen that in these faculties there is a considerable number of professors who, while carrying on their university duties, take an active part in public affairs."[2] Yet there was no need to turn to the old world for precedent. Ever since its founding, in 1865, the American Social Science Association, whose membership included many prominent academicians, had been heavily policy oriented. This orientation, amply evidenced in the writings of E. A. Ross, Lester Ward, William Graham Sumner, Franklin Giddings, and Thorstein Veblen, was one of the important intellectual tendencies of the time.

Whatever the source of inspiration, many early political scientists were busily engaged in public questions. The character of their participation ranged wide indeed.[3] All told, perhaps two-thirds of those initially appointed to the offices and standing committees of the American Political Science Association had already been, or were soon to become, more than casually involved in public affairs.

Even the political scientists most firmly devoted to scholarship saw no impropriety in dealing with current issues. The prospectus for the discipline's first journal, the *Political Science*

---

[1] Herbst, *op. cit.,* p. 22.

[2] *European Schools of History and Politics,* Johns Hopkins Series 5, #12, pp. 19–20.

[3] Herbert B. Adams devoted considerable time to the Chautauqua movement. Burgess was immersed in the town politics of Montpelier, Vermont. Baldwin became Chief Justice and later Governor of Connecticut. J. A. Fairlie served as the secretary to the New York State Canal Commission, Ernst Freund as a member of the Illinois Commission for Unifying State Laws, and Harry A. Garfield as President of the Municipal Association of Cleveland and a member of the Executive Committee of the National Municipal League. Isidor Loeb held membership on Missouri's State Tax Commission, John Bassett Moore the position of Third Assistant Secretary of State, and Bernard Moses membership on the United States Philippine Commission. Paul Reinsch was a delegate to two Pan American Conferences and later Minister to China, Leo S. Rowe a member of the Commission on Laws for Puerto Rico and subsequently an Assistant Secretary of the Treasury. Andrew D. White was chosen member of the New York State Senate and a delegate to state and national Republican conventions before moving up to more prestigious diplomatic posts. There is hardly need to mention the political career of Woodrow Wilson.

Quarterly, announced that particular attention would be given to "contemporaneous events" at home and abroad. The treatment of these events, potential subscribers were assured, would of course be "scientific." The first of these pledges was amply honored. Some 135 articles were run in the five volumes published, respectively, in the sample years 1888, 1892, 1896, 1900, and 1904. Of these, at least 83 dealt directly, and another dozen or so, indirectly, with "contemporaneous events."

The editors were less successful in living up to their second promise. Not all the items were characterized by the objectivity of outlook normally associated with the term "scientific." In fact, the authors' political biases are often unmistakable. For instance: Burgess, describing events prior to the Spanish-American War, proudly recalled that "we began at once publishing articles in the *Political Science Quarterly* against any steps being taken by our government which would lead to war with Spain."[4] (Actually, his memory was a bit faulty in this instance. Maybe because events moved too quickly for even the *Quarterly*'s alert editors, no articles were run along the lines he indicated.) Nevertheless, the journal did serve the purpose suggested by Burgess' reminiscence. In the years following the war he and his associates published a number of papers severely critical of American foreign policy. Even earlier, an 1896 issue of the *Quarterly* carried three articles on the Monroe Doctrine in what was apparently an effort to persuade Washington policy makers that the nation's hemispheric commitments did not warrant a war with Great Britain over the Venezuelan border dispute. And, when free silver became a key issue in the presidential election of 1896, the *Quarterly* hastened into print with another trio of essays expounding the virtues of a "sound currency."

Objection might be made that the *Quarterly* reflected little more than the special orientation of Columbia's political scientists. Admittedly, the journal was primarily a "house organ" for School of Political Science faculty and graduate students for the first several years of its existence. But after 1896 or so, it became increasingly representative of the profession at large. By 1900 about a third of the contributors held appointments at other

[4] *Reminiscences,* p. 314.

schools; by 1904 almost half of the articles were written by scholars at Johns Hopkins, Pennsylvania, Harvard, Chicago, Michigan, Bryn Mawr, New York University, Texas, and Illinois —and their pieces were no less heavily current events directed than those of the Columbia staff. These statistics do not preclude, of course, a selective editorial bias.[5]

As noted above, many American social scientists of the era, including some of the most prominent, were intensely concerned with public affairs. This concern afforded political scientists a spur and a sanction for a type of interest and activity which has carried down to the present day. Not until the post-1945 period did a sizable segment of the profession begin seriously to reflect on the possible incompatibility between the scientific pursuit of knowledge and participation in programmatic and applied policy undertakings.

EDUCATION FOR CITIZENSHIP AND PUBLIC AFFAIRS

While all academic disciplines tend to have common characteristics, in one respect American political science is unique—it has assumed responsibility for transmitting to the nation's youth the knowledge and the patriotic sentiments deemed essential for the successful functioning of our democratic system. Almost from the beginning, the obligation to prepare college students for their future roles as citizens and leaders was urged upon the profession. An 1885 University of Iowa Commencement Address is typical. "Our University," the speaker impassionately declared, "owes its existence to the government. Let her pay the debt by teaching its principles, its history, its purposes, its duties, its privileges, and its powers."[6]

But the task of educating for citizenship and public affairs

[5] The editors during this period were Munroe Smith (1886–1894) and then William A. Dunning. Although one might argue that Dunning, in later years, became increasingly a historian, at this stage in his career he definitely regarded himself as a political scientist. See American Historical Association, *Report,* vol. I (1896), p. 219.

[6] Crick, *op. cit.,* 23, n.

PART 1: A DISCIPLINE IS BORN

was not thrust upon the discipline by outsiders alone. Many political scientists were quite willing, if not eager, to shoulder these burdens. Andrew D. White, a member of the first Executive Council of the American Political Science Association, as well as a distinguished scholar and University president, had been profoundly impressed by the attention given at European universities to preparing young people for participation in public affairs.[7] American institutions of higher education, White subsequently lamented, were not providing "suitable instruction for the natural leaders arising from the mass."[8] It was far better, he proclaimed, "to send out one well-trained young man, sturdy in the town meeting, patriotic in the caucus, vigorous in the legislature, than a hundred of the gorgeous and gifted young cynics who lounge about city clubs, talk about 'art' and 'culture' and wonder why the country persists in going to the bad."[9] White's main objective in establishing an undergraduate department of political science at Cornell was to provide an instrument for preparing future government officials, as well as leaders in other walks of life. Training in political science and history, he argued, would correct a situation wherein "State and Nation are constantly injured by their chosen servants, who lack the simplest rudiments of knowledge which such a department could supply."[10]

Burgess was also committed to educating persons for public life. When seeking the support of Columbia's trustees for the proposed School of Political Science, Burgess acknowledged that while his "prime aim" was "the development of all branches of political science," there was a "secondary aim" as well—the preparation of young men for all branches of the public service."[11] The curriculum of the School, he subsequently declared,

[7] *European Schools of History and Politics, op. cit.* This short study was a revision and expansion of an address originally given at Johns Hopkins in 1879. Also, see Herbst, *op. cit.*, pp. 161 ff., for a contemporary analysis of public service training at the German universities.

[8] *Ibid.*, p. 27.

[9] *Ibid.*, p. 32. If some recent descriptions of our college youth are accepted at face value, we have apparently come full circle.

[10] Herbert B. Adams, *Study of History, op. cit.*, p. 133.

[11] *Reminiscences*, p. 199 (Burgess was staunchly opposed to graduate education for women—and less than enthusiastic about their fitness for

46

was directly influenced by his conviction that it was a university's "duty to do something for democracy, even in letters and science." As H. B. Adams was quick to note, Columbia's *Political Science Quarterly* regularly devoted considerable space to subjects of "semi-popular" interest.

Nor were White and Burgess exceptional in their views. In his inaugural lecture at Michigan's short-lived (1881–87) School of Politics, Dean Charles Kendall Adams made a "vigorous plea for the encouragement of political science in the interest of good government and the general welfare of the people."[12] Edmund J. James, who helped organize the College of Commerce and Politics at the University of Chicago, had similar interests.[13] Herbert Baxter Adams, to take another example, also devoted a good share of his prodigious energies to carrying citizenship education outside the classroom via Hopkins' extension program and the Chautauqua movement.

From its very inception, then, the profession was committed to the pursuit of truth and to the propagation of democratic values and practices. What if the pursuit of truth led to the conclusion that other political forms were superior to, or at least no worse than, the American democratic system? How freely and how effectively could the political scientist, in one capacity, study and criticize the political order whose virtues he was obligated, in his second role, to praise, defend and maintain? So long as it was obvious to all right-thinking men that democracy was the best and highest form of government, the inherent contradiction between

---

higher education in general.) On this point, we would say that Herbst (*op. cit.,* p. 176) is clearly mistaken in suggesting that Burgess' original intent was to train persons for the public service and that he turned to the training of "teachers of political science" largely in an effort to increase the School's enrollment.

[12] Quoted by H. B. Adams, *Study of History, op. cit.,* p. 115. Charles Kendall Adams was actually more concerned with preparing young persons for public service and journalism than for academic careers.

[13] Edmund J. James, "The Place of the Political and Social Sciences in Modern Education, and their Bearing on the Training for Citizenship in a Free State," *Annals,* vol. 10, (1897), pp. 359–388; see also Lepawsky, "The University and the Public Service," *Journal of Legal Education,* vol. 2 (1950), pp. 253–71.

these two obligations could escape notice. But either of two developments, a questioning of democratic dogma or a movement toward "scientific" objectivity, would disclose the latent conflict. Both would occur in later years. The resulting dilemma is one which the profession has yet to resolve.[14]

[14] Dag Hammarskjold recently wrote of the "most dangerous of all dilemmas," that which arises from the desire "to conceal truth in order to help the truth to be victorious."

part 2
the
emergent
period,
1903–1921

*L*ate in the afternoon of December 30, 1903, twenty-five persons gathered in the Tilton Memorial Library at Tulane University and voted the American Political Science Association into existence. With this action, American political science may be said to have shed the chrysalid garb of its formative years and to have donned the full vestments of a learned discipline.

Yet, to suggest that any single date divides two eras is to imply too much, for many aspects of the discipline's history stubbornly and inconveniently defy such neat compartmentalization. There were strong and unmistakable continuities in thought and action between the formative and the emergent periods. During these years the substance of political science changed relatively little. Even what seem to be patent discontinuities and innovations often prove, on closer examination, to have roots solidly embedded in the past.

Nevertheless, the establishment of the Association—in the words of a founding father, "the most important event which has occurred in the history of the scientific study of matters political in this country"—marked the beginning of a new period. This is true for two quite different reasons. First, and most obvious, was the Association's external role. Its existence was tangible proof that political science was now an independent discipline; it also served as an active and often effective instrument in promoting that independence. American political science could hardly have grown as it did without a visible national organization to represent it in dealings with other disciplines, foundations, institutions of higher learning, the press and related media, and governmental officials.

Second, the Association had a far-reaching impact within the profession. Learned disciplines have certain common structural features and a couple of these had already become visible in American political science prior to 1903. Thus, Columbia and Hopkins had established graduate departments offering advanced training in political science.[1] In addition, there existed a scholarly journal, the *Political Science Quarterly,* whose pages were generously, if not exclusively, devoted to articles in political science. With the Association, there came the remaining—and hitherto absent—formal characteristics of a learned discipline: an official organization, an officialdom, an official journal, and regular, officially prescribed meetings of the membership.

All of these performed important functions. They also fostered another requisite of a learned discipline—a *common state of mind.* If a discipline is to flourish, its practitioners must be in general agreement about their subject matter, their techniques, and the interests and behavior appropriate to the practice of their profession. Such a state of mind had developed, we have seen, in the formative decades. Still, the vastly expanded opportunities for contact and communication afforded by the newborn Association would do much both to strengthen and to shape the views shared by its members.

In this section we trace the evolution of American political science from 1903 to 1921. Chapter 5 describes the founding of the Association and the professional expansion which followed. Chapter 6 examines the way in which American political scientists approached their scholarly endeavors during these years. Chapter 7, lastly, deals with their extra-scientific responsibilities and activities.

[1] Strictly speaking, it is inaccurate to say that these were "departments" of political science as we know them today. During most of the formative era, as we have seen, doctoral training in political science was not clearly differentiated, even at Hopkins and Columbia, from training in history, economics, and sociology. The relatively unhardened nature of disciplinary boundaries is reflected in the by-laws of the short-lived Political Science Association of the Central States (founded 1895) which made it clear that, the organization's title notwithstanding, the membership was to include economists, sociologists, and historians.

V
professional development 1903–1921

FOUNDING OF THE AMERICAN POLITICAL SCIENCE ASSOCIATION

By the turn of the century, according to W. W. Willoughby, many political scientists began to feel the need for an organization "which should do for political science what the American Economic and American Historical Associations are doing for economics and history."[1] Impelled by this desire, a group of leading practitioners met in Washington, D.C., on December 30, 1902, to consider founding an "American Society for Comparative Legislation." Deciding that the projected "Society" would be too narrow in scope, the Washington conferees appointed a committee, headed by Cornell's Jeremiah Jenks, to study the "necessity for a national association that should have for its sphere of interests the entire field of political science."

Professor Jenks' committee deliberated through the spring of the following year. Finally, in late fall, it issued a call for a general meeting to be held in conjunction with the forthcoming December conventions of the American Historical Association and the American Economic Association at New Orleans. There, in short order, the assembled political scientists chose Professor Frank Goodnow

[1] *Political Science Quarterly,* vol. 19 (1905), p. 109.

51

to chair their deliberations, proposed and accepted a constitution, and nominated and elected officers. So the American Political Science Association came into being.[2]

Annual "conventions" followed regularly thereafter. For a decade the learned papers (other than presidential addresses) delivered at these conventions, plus summaries of panel and business discussions, were published in the *Proceedings of the American Political Science Association*. Then, in 1914, the Executive Council voted to discontinue the *Proceedings,* to enlarge the *Review,* and to print in the latter "such of the papers read at the annual meetings of the Association as may seem desirable in the opinion of the Editorial Board of the *Review.*"

That these annual gatherings afforded a convenient forum for the exchange of scholarly knowledge and ideas is readily apparent. They served, however, other useful purposes. For one thing, they provided a welcome alternative to publication as a means of attaining professional "visibility." An invitation to read a paper, or to participate in a panel discussion, testified to the recipient's scholarly acceptability. Repeated invitations demonstrated that he was in good standing with, if not actually a member of, the Association's inner circle, adding measurably to his academic desirability. Regular attendance at the meetings enabled political scientists, particularly the younger ones, to enlarge their circle of acquaintances and to build a network of personal contacts which would keep them informed of promising job openings and opportunities for research support. Once well established, these lines of communication greatly strengthened the professor's bargaining position in negotiations with his "home" institution, since they multiplied

[2] And so, too, there passed from the scene the second of the two giants of the previous era, John W. Burgess (H. B. Adams had died in 1901). Burgess had been involved in the planning meeting for the Society on Comparative Legislation but apparently took no part in the newly created Association. He continued on occasion to publish in the *Quarterly* (though not in the *Review*) but, for all practical purposes, seems otherwise to have dropped out of the discipline. His erstwhile colleagues occasionally referred to his major opus but, for the most part, he simply receded into the midnight of neglect—an unhappy fate, indeed, for the man who more than anyone else was responsible for the creation of political science as a learned discipline, who had put his stamp upon it for a generation, and whose basic ideas and objectives, though almost never associated with his name, are today enthusiastically accepted by a sizable segment of the profession.

his chances of moving elsewhere should local conditions of employment prove less than satisfactory. And, of course, the meetings served as a "slave market" where prospective employers and aspiring employees could be brought into fruitful juxtaposition. All of these developments, it should be noted, tended to shift the locus of power, and individual loyalties and ties, from the several departments to the discipline itself.

The Association's official journal, the *American Political Science Review,* began publication in November, 1906. The *Review* played a multi-faceted role. Its many pages devoted to personal and personnel items (appointments, promotions, departmental events, awards, honors, deaths) kept political scientists, and especially those unable to attend the annual meetings, informed of what was going on elsewhere. In this capacity the *Review,* as did the Association itself, nurtured a sense of communal interest and professional fraternity among its readers. At the same time, it inevitably infringed the previous near-monopoly of the graduate departments as centers of disciplinary intelligence.

Beyond this, the journal was a primary outlet for articles and related writings. Of course, publication in the *Review* did not then carry with it the kudos it does today.[3] Neither the solidly established *Political Science Quarterly* nor the *Annals of the American Academy of Political and Social Science* were immediately eclipsed by their johnny-come-lately competitor. During a great deal of the formative period, in fact, the *Review* was as much a newsletter as a learned journal, with the bulk of its issues devoted to "notes" on legislation, court decisions, governmental trends, Association and personal reportage, and similar matters. For a good deal of the period, most of the really scholarly articles in political science continued to appear in the *Quarterly* or the *Annals,* rather than the *Review.*

Still, publication in the *Review* carried the Association's implicit imprimatur,[4] and its pages are an invaluable guide to the "approved" interests of American political scientists. But the journal did more than merely reflect what was being done and thought. Where its editors had strong doctrinal convictions, as

[3] Albert Somit and Joseph Tanenhaus, *American Political Science: A Profile of a Discipline,* New York, 1964, pp. 86–98.

[4] And until its demise, in the *Proceedings.*

was sometimes the case, the official understanding of what was "sound" political science could be ignored only by the most illustrious or the most foolhardy and stubborn practitioners.[5] In this sense, the *Review* molded no less than it mirrored.

Whatever the founding fathers expected the Association "to do for political science" it seems to have done quite satisfactorily. Between 1903 and 1921, the profession enjoyed a steady if not spectacular growth. Undoubtedly, the Association contributed materially to this expansion by strengthening and promoting the discipline's claim to independent academic status.

With the Association, to be sure, came new strains and problems. After 1903, the hitherto predominant position of the graduate departments was challenged by the national organization. Political scientists were increasingly torn by divided loyalties, for the interests of the Association, representing the discipline, and those of the departments, as agents of the colleges and universities, were not always identical.[6] As membership grew, there arose the danger that an official organization would "bureaucratize" the discipline, and that a small minority would be able to exercise a disproportionate influence over the life of the profession.

These problems, needless to say, were not unique to political science. From the turn of the century to the present day, they have been among the most troublesome issues in American higher education. If political science has not been overly successful in coping with them, neither have the other academic disciplines.

[5] Since political scientists were expected to be "productive scholars," with advancement often turning on the length of one's bibliography, editorial favor or disfavor had grave personal, as well as intellectual, consequences.

[6] Both the Association and the departments had a commitment to scholarship, to high standards, and a general concern with the welfare of political science. On the other hand, each had its special interests. The Association sought a greater voice in the affairs of the discipline, the development among the members of a loyalty to the profession itself, and was research, rather than teaching, oriented. The departments, as working units of the colleges and universities, sought to foster institutional rather than professional loyalties and to involve their faculty members in institutional, rather than disciplinary concerns. And, at least for public consumption, the departments and the institutions placed inspiring pedagogy high on their list of honored skills.

GROWTH, 1903–1921

Growth of the profession after 1903 can be traced in the rising number of (a) political scientists, (b) political science departments, and (c) doctoral degrees earned.

POLITICAL SCIENTISTS

The determination of just who was, and who was not, a political scientist is not easy for an era when academic titles were uncertain guides to duties and interests. The simplest and most defensible standard is membership in the Association. In its first year of existence (1904), the Association attracted 214 individual and institutional members. By 1910, the figure was 1,350. A half-decade later, it was 1,462, a slight fall-off from the previous year when it became necessary to drop "more than one hundred members . . . because of non-payment of dues." American participation in World War I is reflected in the 1920 decline to 1,300.

Although we are accustomed to thinking of the Association as largely composed of academicians, these actually constituted a minority of the membership throughout this period.[7] In 1912, one of the few years for which detailed statistics are available, 20 per cent were "professors and teachers," 31 per cent were "lawyers and businessmen," 37 per cent could not be classified, and the remaining 12 per cent represented library and institutional affiliations.[8] Although outnumbered, the professors and teachers were apparently a well-organized and effective minority, regularly domi-

[7] William Anderson has estimated that, of the Association's original (i.e., 1904) membership, perhaps 50 to 100 were instructors and professors "giving all or most of their time and attention to what we now call political science." Haddow, *op. cit.*, p. 258.

[8] "The Teaching Personnel in American Political Science Departments. A Report of the Sub-committee on Personnel of the Committee on Policy to the American Political Science Association, 1934." *APSR*, vol. 28 (1934), pp. 726–65. This report will hereafter be cited simply as "Teaching Personnel."

nating the offices of the Association and the Editorial Board of the *Review*.[9]

POLITICAL SCIENCE DEPARTMENTS

The emergence of political science as a full-fledged discipline was also evidenced by increasingly frequent departmental recognition in the colleges and universities.[10] As might be expected, the first step tended to be representation in a joint department; autonomy followed later. The best sources for information on this subject are the interim and final reports of the Haines Committee.[11]

According to the Committee, there were 38 institutions with separate political science departments in 1914.[12] At the majority of schools, political science was combined with some other discipline. Here, practices varied widely. At 89 colleges, political

[9] This was least true of the presidency. Of the first seven presidents, only Frank Goodnow, the initial incumbent, was actually a professor at the time of his election. The next three (Albert Shaw, Fredric Judson, and James Bryce) were really not academicians; Lowell and Wilson, who followed, were university presidents at the time of their elevation; and the seventh, Simeon E. Baldwin, though a sometime law professor, had spent the previous decade and a half as a member of Connecticut's Supreme Court. As the years passed, however, the presidency was increasingly reserved for de facto professors, with non-academicians rarely advancing beyond the rank of 2nd vice president.

[10] Practically every learned discipline has some form of departmental representation. But this is a necessary, rather than a sufficient, sign of disciplinary status. There are also such non-disciplinary departments as "radio and television," "speech," "drama," etc.

[11] Since there were four different "Haines Reports" a word of clarification may be useful. The first was "Is Sufficient Time Devoted to the Study of Government in our Colleges?" *Proceedings* (1910), vol. 7, pp. 202–09. This study, conducted by Charles Grove Haines alone, was prompted by the 1908 Report of the Committee on Instruction cited on p. 64 below. Next came the Haines Committee's (also referred to occasionally as the Committee of Seven) preliminary report, the "Report on Instruction in Political Science in Colleges and Universities" (1913), *Proceedings,* vol. 10, pp. 249–66. Then followed the so-called final report entitled "Report of Committee of Seven on Instruction in Colleges and Universities," *APSR,* vol. 9 (1915), pp. 353–74. This final report, considerably expanded, was published in book form as *The Teaching of Government,* Report by the Committee on Instruction, of the American Political Science Association, Charles Grove Haines, Chairman, New York, 1916. To reduce confusion to a manageable level, we will identify the report cited by the appropriate date.

[12] The number rose to forty by the time of the Committee's 1915 report.

science was joined with history; with history and economics at 48; with economics and sociology at 45; with economics alone at 22; and with history, economics, and sociology at 21.[13] Separation came slowly even at some of the larger universities[14] and the number of independent departments had yet to hit the 50 mark by 1920.

Though gradual, this development had a pervasive impact upon the discipline. As departments proliferated, they gave political science an element of formal organization which, aside from Hopkins and Columbia, had been largely lacking in the previous period. The stronger of the newcomers, too, were soon challenging the hegemony of Hopkins and Columbia, a competition from which the profession in general, and a handful of hotly sought-after political scientists in particular, undoubtedly profited. And, their rivalry notwithstanding, the common interests of these departments provided a salutary counter-weight to the growing influence of the Association.

DOCTORAL OUTPUT

Annual doctoral production can only be estimated for the years before 1927.[15] Interestingly enough, the problems entailed in making this estimate change drastically as we move from the formative to the emergent era.

During the former, there were only two institutions with meaningful doctoral programs in political science. However, Johns Hopkins did not begin to identify its political science Ph.D.'s as such until 1901 and, until a much later date, Columbia lumped together all degrees granted by its Faculty of Political Science (which also gave doctoral work in history, economics, and sociol-

[13] Acting, no doubt, on the principle *mens sana in corpore sano,* one college brought together history, political science, and the "director of athletics."

[14] Departmental independence was not attained, for example, at Harvard until 1911; Minnesota, 1913; Northwestern, 1915; University of Southern California, 1916; Kansas, 1917; and Stanford, 1918.

[15] In 1927, Donald B. Gilchrist, acting at the behest of the National Research Council and the American Council of Learned Societies, sought to reconstruct reasonably complete and accurate data for the total number of Ph.D.'s granted in each field for the years 1926–1927 to 1932–1933. However, a breakdown by university was not given for these years.

ogy). For these early years, then, the difficulty is that of determining which doctorates were taken in political science and which were taken in other fields.

When we come to the emergent period, the lengthening roster of departments offering advanced training poses a problem of far greater magnitude—that of recovering fugitive records from a substantial number of universities. To be sure, in the 1930's an Association committee published a tabulation of political science doctorates by year and school for the two decades under discussion.[16] Unfortunately, the committee's figures are less than reliable.[17]

Our own investigation, based on university records of degrees granted,[18] suggests the following estimates of *annual* Ph.D. output: From 1885 to 1900, three or four; from 1900 to 1910, six to ten; from 1911 to 1915, ten to fifteen; and from then to 1921 about eighteen to twenty. To repeat, these are estimates.

Columbia and Johns Hopkins continued to be the major doctoral sources. Columbia granted a total of some 20 Ph.D.'s from 1901 to 1910, and perhaps twice that many in the succeeding decade. Hopkins, which went into a decline with the death of Herbert B. Adams (awarding only six doctorates between 1901 and 1910), came back strongly with 18 Ph.D.'s in the next ten

[16] "Teaching Personnel," *op. cit.*, p. 750.

[17] For instance, no data are provided for Johns Hopkins which, according to the Johns Hopkins *Half-Century Directory, 1876–1926,* bestowed Ph.D.'s on some two dozen political scientists between 1901 and 1920. And, while the information for some departments seems fairly accurate, there are wide discrepancies in the data for others. Chicago is recorded as having granted 42 Ph.D.'s in political science between 1902 and 1920—but Chicago's *Register of Doctors of Philosophy, June 1893–April 1938,* lists only nine. Minnesota is credited with a single doctorate prior to 1921—yet Minnesota's *Register of Ph.D. Degrees, 1888–1938,* indicates that one degree was granted annually in 1901, 1908, and 1913, and none in the year (1916) shown in the committee's report. The committee, to take another discrepancy, found no evidence that Harvard had produced learned doctors in government in 1905, 1908, 1911, and 1915—the years, respectively, in which Edmond D. Fite, Frederic A. Ogg, Charles H. McIlwain, and Kenneth W. Colegrove received their degrees there.

[18] The annual *Review* compilations of "dissertations in progress" are of little help here. They do not square with more reliable sources; they report (at this time) more dissertations in history than in political science; they are notoriously repetitive; and they suggest an almost incredibly high attrition rate.

years. The only other departments of consequence were at Wisconsin, Harvard, Pennsylvania, and Chicago, but their combined production did not vastly exceed that of Columbia alone. Not until the mid-twenties did Illinois, Iowa, Harvard, and Wisconsin become prolific sources of advanced degrees.

DEPARTMENTAL STANDING

Unless the academic world has changed, there were substantial differences in prestige among the aforementioned departments. Since the first formal rating study was not made until 1925,[19] we can reconstruct the prevailing "pecking order" in only approximate fashion.

Conceivably, Ph.D. output was indicative of departmental stature. If so, Columbia was first, Johns Hopkins a distant second, and Harvard, Wisconsin, Pennsylvania, and Chicago made up a third category. On the other hand, a recent survey suggests that the correlation between output and prestige is occasionally far from perfect.[20]

Another possible measure is the composition of the profession's Establishment, i.e., those serving as Association officers, Council members, *Review* editors, and members of Association committees. If we take 1914 as a sample year, there were 58 such positions. What, then, were the institutional connections of this 1914 Establishment?

No useful metric emerges when we classify the colleges and universities at which members of the Establishment were employed. Manifestly, the Association deliberately tried to distribute these posts, not only among the several geographic regions but between large and small schools, and public and private institutions, as well. Chicago, Harvard and Illinois led with three representatives each; four departments (Columbia, Wisconsin, Pennsylvania, and Iowa) had two apiece. Some of the schools with one man were Nebraska, New York State Normal College, Louisiana

[19] Raymond M. Hughes, *The Graduate Schools of America,* Oxford, Ohio, pp. 22–23. Also see below, pp. 105–06.

[20] Albert Somit and Joseph Tanenhaus, "Trends in American Political Science: Some Analytical Notes," *APSR,* vol. 57 (1963), pp. 933–38.

State, Oberlin, Northwestern, Worcester Polytechnic Institute, Bowdoin, Virginia, Texas, Dartmouth, and Princeton.

The doctoral origins of those comprising the 1914 Establishment may be a more reliable gauge of departmental status. Of the 31 American Ph.D.'s involved,[21] ten had been earned at Columbia and five at Johns Hopkins. Pennsylvania was next with four, Brown and Wisconsin followed with three each, Chicago and Harvard had a couple apiece; and the remaining brace had been awarded at Yale and Michigan.

This indicator may be distorted in two ways. The selective process which sought "proportional representation" for geographic areas and the like may have affected, in some manner that cannot be discounted, the choice of persons for Association office. Moreover, quite a few members of the 1914 Establishment took their Ph.D.'s at a time (i.e., prior to 1900) when doctoral training was largely monopolized by Hopkins and Columbia. This second source of bias, unlike the first, can be controlled by excluding from consideration those who received their degrees before the end of the century. When this is done, there remain sixteen Establishmentarians who earned American Ph.D.'s after 1900. Seven of them did their work at Columbia; two each at Pennsylvania, Wisconsin, and Chicago; and one each at Harvard, Brown, and Johns Hopkins. Again, Columbia comes out in front, and by a margin considerably greater than its strictly arithmetic share of doctorates for the post–1900 decades.

The results obtained by this last measure are corroborated if we examine the individuals elevated for the first time to Association position after 1914 (i.e., from 1915 to 1920). Fifteen members of this group took post-1900 American doctorates. Five were trained at Columbia, two each at Hopkins, Pennsylvania, Harvard, and Wisconsin, and one each at Chicago and Cornell.

To the extent that these data on the sources of Establishment Ph.D.'s constitute a valid index of prestige, and they should not be totally disparaged, Columbia stood impressively ahead of its nearest competitor. There is no clear claim to second place, for any differentiation among the other institutions with substantial doc-

---

[21] One person on the list did not receive his doctorate until 1921 and was excluded from the tabulation.

toral production (Johns Hopkins, Pennsylvania, Harvard, Chicago, and Wisconsin) seems unwarranted by the evidence at hand.

THE "AMERICANIZATION" OF POLITICAL SCIENCE

One of the most striking discontinuities between the emergent and the formative periods was the rapid "Americanization" of the discipline. Whereas nearly half of those making up the 1904 Establishment had pursued formal graduate study on the Continent, less than a third of those holding Association posts in 1914 took any training abroad.[22] Even this statistic conceals the magnitude of the change, since ten of the 1904 elite also belonged to the 1914 inner circle. When these long-tenured dignitaries are excluded, only eleven of the remaining forty-seven political scientists had gone to Europe as part of their academic preparation. The speed with which the profession was being Americanized is further underscored when we look at the 18 persons newly added to the Association's Executive Council between 1915 and 1920. Only three had followed the earlier pattern of a student hegira to the Continent.

This change in the nature of graduate education was soon reflected in the scholarly journals and in the classroom. In 1886, the *Political Science Quarterly* gave full-length signed reviews to fifty-five books. Twenty of these (36 per cent) were published in languages other than English. Ten years later (1896), the figure was just over 40 per cent. After the turn of the century, though, a noticeable decline can be traced in both the *Quarterly* and the *Review* (see Table 1 on p. 62).

A second and more exotic measure gives additional evidence of diminishing attention to European scholarship. In 1886, about half of the *Quarterly*'s articles carried references to foreign language sources. By 1906, the incidence of such references had dropped to 22 per cent for the *Quarterly* and was just a bit higher (28 per cent) for the newly founded *Review*. The figure for the

[22] Work taken at English universities has been excluded from this analysis.

TABLE 1: *NON-ENGLISH PUBLICATIONS REVIEWED IN THE* QUARTERLY *AND IN THE* REVIEW, *1906, 1910, 1915, 1920**

Journal	Percentage of Foreign Language Publications Among Books Reviewed			
	1906	1910	1915	1920*
PSQ	25	18	14	4
APSR	25	36	11	3

* The 1920 figures are probably biased by the impact on European publication of World War I.

Quarterly held at the 1906 level for the balance of the emergent period, perhaps because the journal ran a number of articles in the field of European history. In the *Review,* though, it fell to about 15 per cent by 1920.[23]

As might be expected, there occurred a concomitant decline in classroom attention to European politics and government. The most frequently encountered undergraduate course in 1910 seems to have been a combined "comparative government/general political science offering," with "American government" holding second place.[24] Barely five years later, the Haines Committee found that American government had moved into the lead, comparative government was a poor second, and "general political science" was third in popularity.[25] Significantly, the Committee recommended that the basic course be a two-semester survey of American government and politics. It is only fair to add that the Committee did recommend that "whenever practicable some illustrative materials and suggestive comparisons with foreign governments be presented."[26]

[23] Another index that will undoubtedly occur to quantitatively oriented readers is the number of foreign language citations per article/page. We made the necessary investigation (there were approximately 1.17 foreign language citations per article/page in 1906, 1.12 in 1910, and 1.06 in 1915) but the staggering differences in this respect between one article and another makes these averages of dubious value.

[24] Haines Report, 1910, *op. cit.,* p. 204. Actually, the shift of emphasis from comparative to American government may have begun at a somewhat earlier date and may have been concealed by the bias in Haines' sample, which consisted largely of small colleges.

[25] Haines Report, 1916, *op. cit.,* pp. 358–59.

[26] *Ibid.,* p. 203.

VI
scholarly responsibilities, 1903–1921

*T*he founding of the American Political Science Association in 1903 was an event of major significance. Still, neither that date nor any other from 1880 to 1921 marked dramatic changes in thinking about the nature of political science or about the responsibilities of its practitioners. Though there were frequent outbursts of dissatisfaction, usually aimed at contemporary methodological practices, similar expressions of discontent had been voiced in the preceding era. These continuing criticisms were only a prologue to the full-scale debate on this and related issues which took place in the post–1921 decade.

POLITICAL SCIENCE AS A LEARNED DISCIPLINE

THE SCOPE OF POLITICAL SCIENCE

From time to time during the formative period (i.e., 1880-1903), spokesmen for the new discipline sought to define its domain and to articulate its claim to territorial sovereignty. Once the American Political Science Association had been launched and formal organizational independence achieved, there was little point in pressing an argument designed to convince academicians interested in political phenomena that they should consider themselves *political scientists* rather than historians, sociologists, economists, or even

academic lawyers. What the discipline now sought was departmental recognition and, even better, departmental autonomy. In
that task, learned commentary on the scope of political science
was not apt to be of much assistance; in some situations it could be
manifestly counter-productive.

It is not surprising, therefore, that the professional journals presented very few systematic analyses of the proper division of labor
between political science and the other social sciences. To be sure,
the leading undergraduate political science textbooks[1] did touch
on the differences between that discipline and history, economics,
sociology, jurisprudence, and the like. Two features, though, characterized these discussions: first, their brevity; second, the literature cited was almost entirely from the pens of European scholars.
The inference seems clear—this was not a topic in which American political scientists were greatly interested.

The only extended treatment of the relationship between
political science and another discipline (in this case, history)
appeared in an Association committee's report "Instruction in
American Government in Secondary Schools."[2] According to the
committee, the subject was improperly taught in the high schools
because it was too often incorporated into what were fundamentally history courses. The "close relationship" between political
science and history, the committee warned, "should not blind us
to the great differences in subject matter, method, and aim, which
distinguishes these two sciences." The differences between the two
disciplines sprang in large measure from their diverse "materials of
study." Politics was not confined to "printed accounts of documents of past history," but extended to the "political facts them-

[1] Four such texts, the Haines Committee reported, were most widely
used in teaching the basic political science course: Garner's *Introduction to
Political Science* (1910), Gettell's *Introduction to Political Science* (1910),
Leacock's *Elements of Political Science* (1906), and Dealey's *The State*
(1909). Of the four, only Garner dealt with the relationships between
political science and the other social sciences at any length: Leacock gave
the subject about six pages; and Dealey and Gettell disposed of it in three.
Curiously enough, all four authors agreed that political science's closest ties
were with sociology rather than, as had previously been the prevailing view,
with history.

[2] "Report of the Committee of Five of the American Political Science
Association on Instruction in Secondary Schools," *Proceedings,* vol. 5
(1908), pp. 219–57.

selves—the fact of voting, of courts, of juries, of police, of various municipal services, of official action, etc."[3] All this led the Committee, reasonably enough, to recommend state legislation which would require that every person licensed to teach in the public schools be proficient in political science.

No more attention was given to delineating the central core of the discipline than to drawing suitable boundaries. Perhaps the Association's first presidential address set the example. The special nature of the occasion, declared President Goodnow, tempted him to explore the question "What is political science?" Nevertheless, he resolutely continued,

To this temptation I have determined not to yield. For it seems to me that such an attempt at definition is dangerous, particularly if it should result in the endeavor to formulate a definition of Political Science which is at the same time inclusive and exclusive. Such an attempt is not only dangerous, but, even if successfully made, it is not in my opinion sufficiently fruitful of practical results to justify the expenditure of thought and time necessary to secure the desired end.[4]

This disavowal did not prevent Goodnow from claiming "as the field of the American Political Science Association" the entire area relating to the "realization of State will" not "systematically treated by the other societies [history and economics] already in existence." Nor did it prevent him from advancing one of the few really penetrating analyses of what the discipline was all about.[5]

At the next Association meeting (1905), Henry Jones Ford, a specialist on American politics, read a paper entitled "The Scope of Political Science."[6] Ford chided his colleagues for limiting their investigations to "the national, popular state of Western civilization." They were ignoring, he pointed out, "the very states whose activities are the chief centers of disturbance in world politics . . . China, Russia, and Turkey." Worse, they risked mistaking as "objective reality" what might eventually prove to be transitory political forms.

[3] *Ibid.,* p. 233.

[4] Frank J. Goodnow, "The Work of the American Political Science Association," *Proceedings,* vol. 1 (1904), p. 35.

[5] Goodnow identified three central concerns: the formulation, the substance, and the administration of public policy. (*Ibid.,* p. 37.)

[6] Henry Jones Ford, "The Scope of Political Science," *Proceedings,* vol. 2 (1905), pp. 198–206, at 200.

Several other persons also took exception to the kind of work political scientists were turning out. Their remarks, though, were directed less at what the profession was doing than how it was being done.

Arthur Bentley's now-classic *The Process of Government* (1908) was the only thoroughgoing attempt to reconsider both the boundaries and the core of political science. Bentley was not a professional political scientist. He was not even a member of the Association, and he was almost completely ignored by those who were. Nevertheless, his ideas deserve particular mention. For one thing, Bentley belonged to that small group of "realists" who spoke out against the formalistic literature of the period, although he diagnosed the problem as one of improper focus and the others (Lowell, Bryce, and Wilson, for example), as one of faulty methodology. Secondly, Bentley's thesis, as restated by David Truman, was to have a resounding impact in the early 1950's.

The purpose of his book, Bentley announced, was "to fashion a tool." Regrettably, the opening sections, devoted to a caustic survey of the social science of his day, far more resemble a demolitions project. The concepts espoused by von Jhering, Small, Ward, Dicey, et. al., are summarily dismissed as "nothing at all except verbiage." A mordant chapter, two and a quarter pages long, disposes of political science—pretentious, formalistic, "dead". Literally dead, said Bentley, because it evaded "the very central structure of its proper study—*the activities which are politics*."

Thus, some 175 pages into his exposition, Bentley arrived at his "tool." The raw material with which the student of politics must concern himself is "activity"—activity, "first, last, and always." But this raw material "is never found in one man by himself, it cannot even be stated by adding man to man." It is found only "in many men together," i.e., *groups*.

The "great task" of political science, then, is the study of "political groups" for "there are no political phenomena except group phenomena."[7] What is a political group? The question is

---

[7] Bentley conceded that other groups (economic, for example) may well be "more fundamental in society," but the unique characteristics of political groups—they are "highly differentiated," the political process occurs "well up toward the surface of a society," they have a closer "con-

not altogether welcome.[8] Still, splitting the phrase into its component words, Bentley essayed an answer. "Political" groups are "groups that appear in politics" and which engage in "political action." Half of the problem neatly resolved, he took even greater pains with "group" because, he explained, he intended to use the word "in a technical sense." Above all the group is an "interest." There is no group without an interest, and interest is the "equivalent of a group."[9] Group, interest, interest group, and group interest are all the same.

As every interest group exerts "pressure" in behalf of its interest(s), every interest group is actively or latently[10] a pressure group. All political behavior arises from the actions and interactions of interest (pressure) groups inside and outside the formal structure of government and parties. Only by dealing with interest groups can the discipline come to grips with the real stuff of political life. Only the study of groups will lend itself to that which alone makes possible the development of a true science—quantification. In short, when the group is "adequately stated, everything is stated." And, he added grandly, "when I say everything I mean everything."

Bentley's proposal for what would have been a radical reconstruction of political science elicited widely varying reactions. Charles A. Beard, then a young adjunct professor at Columbia, hailed the *Process of Government* as a "thought-provoking book that will help to put politics on a basis of realism, where it belongs."[11] The volume was equally well received in the *Annals,*

---

nection" with ideas and emotions, and they represent group activity in its "most manifest, most palpable, most measurable form"—warranted dealing with them first.

[8] "Who likes may snip verbal definitions in his old age when his world has gone crackly and dry."

[9] Is the interest responsible for the existence of the group or the group responsible for the creation of the interest? "I do not know or care," Bentley says. It is sufficient to know that the interest group is our "raw material and it is our business to keep our eyes fastened to it."

[10] Some persons have been unkind enough to suggest that the idea of a "latent" group is not greatly dissimilar to the "spook"-like notions which Bentley accused other political scientists of fostering.

[11] *Political Science Quarterly,* vol. 23 (1909), pp. 739–41. Beard rebuked Bentley for his rudeness but endorsed Bentley's claim that his (Bentley's) ideas were really not very original.

where it was reviewed by the sociologist Carl Kelsey. Though Bentley's method was "too new, the evidence too complex to be mastered at once," Kelsey felt that Bentley was clearly on the "right track" and had produced a book "which will command respect and provoke thought."[12]

On the other hand, most political scientists were notably less enthusiastic. The general reaction was perhaps typified by James W. Garner who, writing in the *Review,* commented that a "hasty reading of some of these chapters fails to impress the reviewer with their value as a contribution to the literature of political science."[13] Garner had nothing much kinder to say in the rest of his one paragraph analysis. So far as his contemporaries were concerned, Bentley might never have existed and we can only speculate as to what might have happened had his ideas been given the reception they were to get forty years later. By then, as events demonstrated, it was too late to re-orient the profession in the direction he had proposed.

If, Bentley aside, published discussions of "scope" were infrequent and meager, the textbooks, monographs, and articles of the period still tell a good deal about the interests of political scientists during these years. Formal governmental structures and processes were described in meticulous detail. Scholars relied heavily on statutes, ordinances, charters, and written constitutions for their materials, with the contents of these documents usually accepted at face value. There is an occasional acknowledgment of the disorderly reality beneath the world of form but the references are illustrative and unsystematic. When, in 1909, Paul Reinsch published a book of readings intended to show how the American federal government actually functioned, less than a half-dozen items by academic political scientists were included in his more than 100 selections.

Another striking feature was the lack of interest in political theory. Though the textbooks in political science devoted substantial space to some aspects of the subject (i.e., the origin, nature, evolution, province, and ends of the State), little of the literature cited was written by Americans. Even this modicum was

[12] *Annals,* vol. 33 (1909), pp. 467–69.
[13] *APSR,* vol. 2 (1907), p. 457.

principally the work of Burgess and Willoughby, dating from the formative era. The contents of the professional journals also testify to the neglect of theory. Consider, for example, the 1906, 1910, and 1915 volumes of the *Review* and the *Quarterly*. For the latter, only 2 of 27 articles in 1906, 2 of 28 in 1910, and 1 of 25 in 1915 can, by any stretch of the imagination, be classified under this heading. Comparable statistics for the *Review* are 1 of 14 items in 1906, nothing at all in 1910, and 1 of 29 in 1915. A similar analysis of doctoral dissertations "in progress" shows that graduate students apparently shared their mentors' disinterest. The few articles and dissertations which do deal with theory, moreover, are almost invariably normative or descriptive, rather than analytic.

To summarize: with a few exceptions shortly to be examined, the political science of this period tended to be legalistic, descriptive, formalistic, conceptually barren, and largely devoid of what would today be called empirical data. It bore faint resemblance, we can safely say, either to the discipline originally envisaged by Burgess when he founded the School of Political Science at Columbia or to the kind of political science soon to be advocated by the proponents of a "science of politics."

METHOD

Early in the formative period, Burgess and Adams spearheaded a campaign to replace the prevailing "deductive" method with the "historical-comparative" approach of the German publicists.[14] Hardly had historical-comparativism carried the field when it, in turn, came under fire from the "realists." According to these critics, formal documents, no matter how original, were not enough. Political scientists must also attend to what really transpired in political life. To be sure, some of the realists were content merely to talk about the necessity of getting out of the libraries and archives and into the places where "political actors" performed. Less easily satisfied, others, such as Bryce and Lowell, took to the field.

But these men were the exceptions. The typical study by an

14 Above, pp. 30–31.

American political scientist in the last decade of the nineteenth century, and for long thereafter, made small use of either the historical-comparative method or the mode of inquiry advocated by the realists. It consisted, instead, of a routine description and pedestrian analysis of formal political structures and processes, based on the more readily accessible official sources and records. Genuflections to realism were common enough; efforts to develop hard data about actual behavior all too rare.

Only when we keep in mind the character and quality of this "typical" study can we begin to appreciate why a common theme runs through the three major methodological discussions of the period. Fittingly enough, these were presidential addresses by the profession's senior realists—Bryce, Lowell, and Wilson. All three were troubled by the prevailing standard of contemporary scholarship.

In electing James Bryce to be its fourth president, the Association honored itself no less than the Briton generally regarded as one of the world's foremost political scientists. Bryce's speech has since become famous (or notorious) for its alleged emphasis on "facts."[15] Some commentators, misconstruing his remarks, have placed at his door much of the blame for the discipline's subsequent empiricist tendency.[16]

This was not at all what Bryce intended, as a careful reading of his address makes evident. He was primarily concerned with the need for greater realism in the study of politics and the "facts" which he seemingly eulogized were the literal facts of political life. To examine the formal, legal character of a given political institution, Bryce argued, was only to start. Three additional aspects

[15] The two most quoted passages are his precept "Keep close to the facts. Never lose yourself in abstractions"; and the admonition "The Fact is the first thing. Make sure of it. Get it perfectly clear. Polish it till it shines and sparkles like a gem." "The Relations of Political Science to History and to Practice," *APSR,* vol. 3 (1909), pp. 1–19, at pp. 4, 10.

[16] This is essentially the argument of both Easton, *op. cit.,* and Crick, *op. cit.* Their thesis is open to three objections. First, as both concede, there was already evident in the profession a strong "anti-theoretical, pro-empiricist tendency." Second, Bryce himself warned *against* just that over-emphasis upon discrete fact which he is supposed to have encouraged, if not actually induced. Third, the case assumes precisely what it must demonstrate —that Bryce's speech, however misconstrued, did have the influence attributed to it.

should be probed: 1) " the needs it [the political institution] was meant to meet and the purposes it actually serves"; 2) "the character of the men who work it"; and 3) "the ideas entertained respecting it by the people among whom it lives, the associations they have for it." In other words, "every political organism, every political force, must be studied in and cannot be understood apart from the environment out of which it has grown and in which it plays."

Bryce went out of his way to deny that his concern with facts implied "any disparagement of historical generalizations or political theory" or any denigration of systematic and analytic inquiry. The study of facts, he warned his audience, "is meant to lead up to the establishment of conclusions and the mastery of principles, and unless it does this it has no scientific value." Unfortunately, this caveat was largely ignored by his own and succeeding generations.

Looking back, it seems clear that Bryce was objecting to two types of formalism regularly encountered in the political science of his day. One was purely abstract analysis—the other, uncritical descriptions of formal political structures and/or processes.[17] Both, in his opinion, lost contact with reality. Although Bryce was too modest to say so, his monumental *American Commonwealth,* with its detailed analysis (based on observation and interviews) of the actual functioning of political institutions, narrow-range theoretical generalizations, and suggestive cross-national comparisons, was precisely the sort of study he considered a worthy model.

Bryce's successor as the Association's ranking officer was his good friend, A. Lawrence Lowell, previously Eaton Professor of the Science of Politics at Harvard, chairman of its Department of Government and, after 1909, president of that august institution. Though being a Lowell of Massachusetts was not exactly a handicap, he had fairly earned his eminence. An inspiring teacher and a forceful administrator, Lowell was also one of America's

---

[17] This was essentially the verdict of the Haines Committee in its 1916 Report. "There are indications," the Committee wrote, "that political science, in some quarters at least, has been too strictly confined to theories about civil society and too little concerned with political affairs as they are. Students of politics . . . have been inclined to philosophize and work out abstract principles rather than to search laboriously the records and activities of society in its myriad and complex operations." *Op. cit.,* p. 188.

71

great political scientists. If his first "big" work, *Governments and Parties in Continental Europe* (1897), did not quite match the *American Commonwealth* in scope or brilliance, his *Government of England* (1908) compared well even with Bryce's masterpiece.[18] In between had come the elegant "Oscillations in Politics,"[19] the first rigorous application of statistics to political data for analytical purposes. Finally there was the classic *Public Opinion and Popular Government* (1913), a work which laid the foundations, as Merriam saw it, for the "application of psychology to the new politics"[20] and which makes Lowell, in Crick's phrase, "the father of public opinion analysis."

These massive accomplishments notwithstanding, Lowell vies with Burgess for the melancholy distinction of being the discipline's "forgotten man."[21] This near total eclipse of Lowell's reputation is not without irony, as we shall soon see.

Lowell's 1909 presidential address, "The Physiology of Politics,"[22] is an essay on methodology impressive for that time and ours. He dealt with the same problem to which Bryce had alluded the year before—the need to study the purposes political institutions do in reality serve. By "physiology" Lowell meant what is today called "functionalism," since physiology, as he understood it, was the science concerned with the functioning of organs. Applied to political science, the physiological approach would fix

[18] There were many similarities between Bryce and Lowell. Both men treated their subjects by much the same methods, for both were concerned less with describing formal governmental structures than with explaining the way political institutions actually functioned. In two respects, though, Lowell outshone even the famous Englishman. For one thing, he made more imaginative use of quantitative data, as demonstrated in his "Oscillations" study. More noteworthy was Lowell's superiority in analytic theory. Where Bryce rarely ventured beyond propositions of a fairly narrow gauge (even Woodrow Wilson was critical of him here), Lowell demonstrated an impressive capacity for middle-level generalizations—a talent as rare then as it is today.

[19] *Annals,* vol. 12 (1898), pp. 69–97.

[20] UNESCO, *Contemporary Political Science,* Paris, 1950, p. 240.

[21] When American political scientists were recently asked to name the persons who had made the most significant contributions to the discipline prior to 1945, Bentley and Wilson were each nominated by about 10 per cent of the respondents, Lowell and Burgess by fewer than 1 per cent. Somit and Tanenhaus, *op. cit.,* p. 66.

[22] *APSR,* vol. 4 (1910), pp. 1–15.

on the functions that political organs "actually do perform" rather than those which they are "intended, or supposed to perform."[23]

To urge a more realistic approach to politics, Lowell conceded, "may seem like watering a garden in the midst of rain." Yet nothing could be further from the truth. Anyone "familiar with the current political literature" was aware that studies by political scientists were "for the most part conducted in the air." Too many political scientists were too much engrossed with "what ought to happen, rather than what actually occurs; and even when they condescend to deal with facts it is usually on a limited scale with very superficial attention to the conditions under which the facts took place."[24] Too often, the formal structures being described were "shams" and the resulting descriptions obscured, rather than revealed, the true manner in which the institutions worked.[25] It was imperative, in examining a political institution, to treat its functioning as well as its formal structure, although the former "can be found in no book, and is in its nature intangible." However agonizing the prospect, political scientists would simply have to get out into the field and conduct first-hand investigations of the phenomena with which they were concerned.

Lowell also advanced two other methodological recommendations which deserve mention. He called for a wider use of statistics, "proverbially deceptive, but ever more needed in political research." Statistics were an invaluable tool "both for discovering new facts and for verifying facts obtained by other means. . . . We ought to collect them much more freely than we do, and the results obtained from them, and from observation, ought to be used constantly to check one another." Second, the study of politics should not be limited to purely public agencies, for "a great deal may be learned from a candid observation of clubs, associations, organizations, and institutions, of all kinds, their mode of operation and the forces that control them." Politics, he wryly

[23] "The Physiology of Politics," *op. cit.*, p. 2. "[U]nfortunately for the patient inquirer," he added, "this is by no means the same thing."

[24] It was hardly surprising, he told his probably uncomfortable audience, that "men in active public life tend to disregard suggestions from academic sources" or that "students of politics do not lead public thought as much as they ought to do."

[25] As examples of such "shams" he pointed to the American electoral college and the British "literary theory of the constitution."

added, are sometimes "not as active or heated in a state central committee as in a sewing circle."

There may be some danger of reading too much back into Lowell and of portraying him as a turn-of-the-century behavioralist. Nonetheless, many of his ideas are unmistakably modern in substance, if not always in language—the distinction between structure and function, the concern with terminology, the stress on prediction and quantification, the injunction to study political behavior, the thesis that "politics" is not limited to the strictly governmental or overtly political, the preference for "pure" as against "applied" research,[26] and the quest for greater objectivity.[27] Of all his generation, Lowell would have been least uncomfortable in the company of today's quantitatively minded, methodologically self-conscious, empirically oriented practitioners.[28] The decline in his reputation is thus both unwarranted and untimely. By any standard, Lowell is entitled to rank with Merriam as a progenitor of the "new science of politics" of the 1920's and as intellectual godfather of the current behavioral movement.

Woodrow Wilson, the third member of this distinguished triumvirate, headed the Association in 1910, the same year in which he was elected Governor of New Jersey. Wilson had increasingly withdrawn from political science after assuming the presidency of Princeton University in 1902. The ensuing abstention from matters intellectual is apparent in his address, "The Law

[26] "Let no man grieve because the truth he reveals may not seem of direct utility. . . . Still less let him fret that he cannot himself give effect to his ideas; that it is not his lot to wield the sickle in the ripened field." It was the "province" of the political scientist, Lowell counselled, "to discover the principles that govern the political relations of mankind, and to teach those principles to the men who will be in a position to give effect to them hereafter."

[27] The student "must not set out with a prejudice for or against particular institutions . . . for if he does he will almost inevitably be subject to a bias likely to vitiate his observation." Science, he noted, "made little progress . . . so long as natural phenomena were studied for the purpose of showing their beneficence to man." Lowell denied, however, that a completely "objective" political science was either possible or desirable.

[28] Of course, he would not be altogether comfortable, either. But, then, who is?

and the Facts."[29] Still, lurking in the interstices of Wilson's orundities are traces of his long-felt commitment to a realistic political science.

By "law," as used in the title of his remarks, Wilson meant enacted law. The responsibility of political science, to savor his language, was the "accurate and detailed observation of those processes by which the lessons of experience are brought into the field of consciousness, transmuted into active purpose, put under the scrutiny of discussion, sifted, and at last given determinate form in law." More prosaically stated, the proper concern of political science was the development of public policy.

This "imperative" assignment was admittedly "difficult, elusive, complex." To accomplish the task, students of politics would have to break with their comfortable, established formulae. They would have to dig behind lawbooks, statutes, and court decisions. It was not enough "to look at men congregated in bodies politic through the medium of the constitutions and traditions of the states they live in, as if that were the glass of interpretation. Constitutions are vehicles of life, but not sources of it."

Other passages testify that the intervening years of administrative and political experience had considerably mellowed Wilson's outlook. Political scientists, he pleaded, should put themselves into the places of those whom they studied and seek to understand why they acted as they did. Realism should be tempered and leavened by "insight, and sympathy, and spiritual comprehension." Literature and art could teach political scientists a good deal about political behavior.

Regrettably, these flashes of wisdom and insight were all too rare. Wilson's career as a political scientist was now far behind him. He was already preoccupied with weightier matters. For the most part, what he had to say did not rise above such pronouncements as "organic processes of thought will bring you organic processes of law."

There were, of course, a few more practicing realists—Ford, Macy, Goodnow, Beard, and Bentley. Of these, the last-named alone wrote at any length about the methods of political inquiry. "Scope" and "method" are so intricately intertwined in the Bentlian system that the essence of his position has already been

[29] *APSR,* vol. 5 (1911), pp. 1–11.

sketched. We need mention only his insistence that "first, last and all," investigation should be empirical. Conceding that "there is no way to get hold of one interest group except in terms of others," he recommended that the student of politics isolate an interest group and observe its "progress." Then, when he [i.e., the student] has "made sure" of one group, he can move on to another "with less painstaking." After comparing many sets of groups, Bentley added reassuringly, if cryptically, "we shall know better what to expect."

There is little evidence that the realist position was openly disputed within the profession. Instead, discussions of methodology seem to have been shunned by those sympathetic to the more traditional approach. When the Association set up a committee in 1911 to explore the subject of laboratory and field training for graduate students, the committee hastily recast its mandate and moved in a different direction.[30] Even the textbook treatments of methodology are embarrassingly thin. Of the four most popular volumes, only Garner's devoted any space to the topic.[31] But if these ideas were not disputed, neither were they acted upon. Realism and the realists, in fine, achieved passive acceptance in principle and were assiduously ignored in practice. The issue was left smoldering, to flare up again in the years immediately ahead.

POLITICAL SCIENCE AS "SCIENCE"

Of the handful of political scientists who wrote on the nature of the discipline between 1880 and 1903, most held a scientistic point of view. That is to say, they believed that the methodology they associated with the natural sciences was appropriate for investigating problems of fundamental concern to political science, and that proper application of this methodology would lead to the development of "laws" with explanatory and predictive power.

Even before the close of the nineteenth century, there began a

---

[30] Below, p. 82, fn. 9.

[31] Garner listed six recognized methods of inquiry: (1) experimentation (not possible); (2) the sociological and biological method; (3) the psychological method ("which in recent years has been overexploited by a certain class of writers, mostly French"); (4) the juridical method ("too narrow"); (5) the comparative method; and (6) the historical method. The latter two, he declared, were regarded as most appropriate to political science.

shift from analytic conceptualization to what became essentially institutional description; there was a concomitant decline in the use of comparative data for other than illustrative purposes. This trend was accompanied by a diminished interest (or belief) in "laws of politics" similar to those operative in the natural sciences. So little concern was there with the scientific potentialities of the discipline that only one of the four leading political science textbooks even broached the idea.[32]

Although the word "science" continued to be generously employed in professional discourse, it normally connoted no more than serious inquiry and dispassionate scholarship. For example, when Albert Shaw, the Association's second President, exhorted his colleagues to carry out their "scientific work" in a "scientific spirit,"[33] he meant "absolute calmness and impartiality," "complaisance and serenity," and an atmosphere of "reasonable discussion." Horace Flack's paper entitled "Scientific Assistance in Law Making" advocated the creation of legislative reference bureaus to assist in drafting statutes.[34] And, to take a last illustration, Goodnow's presidential speech employed the terms "scientific study," the "science of states," and studies of "scientific values" as synonymous with traditional scholarly inquiry.[35]

While the realists touched, from time to time, on the possibility of a scientific political science, their several positions ranged

[32] Here, after both finding and identifying himself with a consensus for mutually exclusive viewpoints, the author ended his analysis with the forthright declaration that: "We must conclude, therefore, that both reason and the weight of authority justify the claim of politics to the rank of a true science. It renders practical service by deducing sound principles as a basis for wise political action and by exposing the teachings of a false political philosophy. As a science it falls short, of course, of the degree of perfection attained by the physical sciences, for the reason that the facts with which it deals are more complex and the causes which influence social phenomena are more difficult of control and are perpetually undergoing change. On account of the impossibility of forecasting results with the same exactness and precision possible in the physical sciences, a fully developed science of the state must of necessity remain always an ideal. As yet it is still probably the most incomplete and underdeveloped of all the social sciences." Garner, *op. cit.,* p. 19.

[33] Shaw, "Presidential Address," *APSR,* vol. 1 (1906), pp. 177–86.

[34] Flack, "Scientific Assistance in Law Making," *Proceedings,* vol. 10 (1914), pp. 215–21.

[35] See above, p. 65.

from the distinctly anti- to the strongly pro-scientistic. Wilson and Bryce were the most skeptical. For Wilson, political relations were "intensely human" and "intimately personal." These relationships, "whether in the family or in the state, in the counting house or in the factory, are not in any proper sense the subject matter of science. They are the stuff of insight and sympathy and spiritual comprehension." Wilson objected, accordingly, to the term "political science," preferring the usage "politics."[36]

Bryce was equally cool to scientism. He denied that political science could ever approximate mechanics or, for that matter, even meteorology. Political science could never achieve greater "certainty" than history—and history could never become a science because "human phenomena may be described, but cannot be counted or weighed as you count and weigh natural phenomena."

Lowell fell somewhere between the two polar positions. Though priding himself on the predictive utility of his work,[37] he was aware of the profound gulf between the "observational" and the "experimental" sciences. This difference notwithstanding, Lowell insisted that the political scientist study politics "as a series of phenomena of which he is seeking to discover the causes and effects," a rule he sought to apply in his own research. On the other hand, Lowell firmly believed that the "ultimate object of political science is moral, that is the improvement of government among men," a conviction which strengthened as he grew older. He therefore denied the desirability, let alone the feasibility, of a discipline which eschewed moral questions.

At the scientistic end of the scale were Ford, Macy, and Bentley. Ford had argued, in 1905, that political scientists could develop principles "universal in application" if they would enlarge their horizons to include all types of political communities and all forms of political authority. Once such principles were discovered, he promised, statesmen would come "imploring" for counsel.[38] Ford reiterated this idea in his presidential speech a decade later. Political science, he conceded, was still essentially "historical and descriptive" but he was unshaken in his conviction that it would

[36] "The Law and the Facts" *op. cit.,* pp. 10–11.

[37] See, for instance, his letter to Frank W. Taussig in Henry Aaron Yeomans, *Abbott Lawrence Lowell, 1856–1943,* Cambridge, 1948, p. 505.

[38] Ford, "The Scope of Political Science," *op. cit.*

78

ultimately become a "genuine science" capable of providing "plain interpretation, clear foresight, and practical guidance to those who consult it."[39] Another Association President, Jesse Macy, also clung firmly to the scientistic views he had voiced before. In fact, his 1916 presidential paper suggests that Macy's was the most extreme position of all. He seems to have believed that political actors themselves, as well as political scientists, would some day be able to carry out their duties in a manner as thoroughly scientific as that employed by biologists.[40]

Finally, there was Arthur F. Bentley. As we have seen, Bentley was persuaded that politics, properly studied, could eventually become nearly as quantitative and predictive as the natural sciences. Not satisfied merely to proclaim this goal, he actually sought to develop a theoretical framework that would make it possible. By so doing, Bentley became the first American student of politics since Burgess seriously to undertake the task. He was not the last.

[39] Henry Jones Ford, "Present Tendencies in American Politics," *APSR*, vol. 14 (1920), pp. 1–13.

[40] "The Scientific Spirit in Politics," *APSR*, vol. 11 (1917), pp. 1–11.

VII

*extra-scientific
responsibilities,
1903–1921*

From the very outset, American political scientists were committed to two activities not ordinarily associated with the practice of a learned discipline—education for citizenship and public service and, second, personal participation in public affairs. The commitment was reaffirmed early in the emergent period by President Albert Shaw who urged his colleagues to "lose no chance to influence the statesman on the one hand, and to supply intellectual pabulum to the people on the other hand."[1] The exhortation, everything considered, was hardly necessary.

EDUCATION FOR CITIZENSHIP AND PUBLIC SERVICE

President Goodnow had barely donned the mantle of his newly created office when he appointed a "Committee[2] on Instruction," chaired by W. A. Schaper of Minnesota, to survey what was being done to prepare American youth for democratic citizenship. Pro-

---

[1] *APSR, op. cit.,* p. 182. James Bryce put the idea more delicately when he urged the Association's members to place their "facts and conclusions at the service of statesmen and citizens." *Ibid.,* vol. 3 (1909), p. 4. But the following year, it will be recalled, Lowell dwelt at painful length on the distressing lack of interest shown by "statesmen and citizens" in these same "facts and conclusions."

[2] Then called "section."

fessor Schaper's report, provocatively entitled "What Do Students Know About American Government Before Taking College Courses in Political Science?" was delivered at the Association's second annual meeting. The answer, it seems, was "very little," but Schaper's specific findings[3] are of less significance than (a) his matter-of-fact assumption that schools supported by public funds should educate for democratic citizenship and (b) his recommendation that courses in American government be made compulsory at both the pre-college and college levels.

In what was soon to become a time-honored tradition, the Association promptly set up a second committee, again with Schaper as chairman, to study the teaching of government in the secondary schools.[4] The new committee resorted to a mail questionnaire, prefacing the instrument with a "statement of purpose" which took it for granted that both the secondary schools and the colleges had an obligation to prepare the young for citizenship and possible public service.[5] The most tangible result of the second

[3] Among these were (1) that the elective system made it possible for a student to go from grammar school through college without ever taking work in American history or government; (2) that college students who had taken no college course in the subject were abysmally ignorant about American government; that the college students who had taken work (a few of these were included by mistake in his sample) were reasonably well informed; and (4) that few public officials had any college training in the social sciences. *Proceedings,* vol. 2 (1905), pp. 207–28.

[4] See "Report of the Committee of Five of the American Political Science Association in Instruction in American Government in Secondary Schools." *Proceedings,* vol. 5 (1908), pp. 219–57.

[5] "Is it not a curious fact," the Committee declared, "that though our schools are largely instituted, supported and operated by the government, yet the study of American Government in the schools and colleges is the last subject to receive adequate attention? The results of the neglect of this important branch of study in our educational institutions can easily be seen in the general unfitness of men who have entered a political career, so that now the name of statesman is often used as a term of reproach, and the public service is weak, except in a few conspicuous instances. Are the schools perhaps to blame for the lack of interest in politics shown by our educated men until the recent exposures arrested the attention of the entire nation?

We think the best place to begin the work of regeneration and reform is in the American secondary schools and colleges. Here we find the judges, legislators, diplomats, politicians and office-seekers of the future in the making. Here are the future citizens, too, in their most impressionable years, in the years when the teacher has their attention." (*Ibid.,* pp. 221–22.)

Schaper report[6] was that it inspired another inquiry, this by Charles Grove Haines.[7]

Haines' first study, undertaken without benefit of committee, was limited to a curiously chosen group of colleges and universities. His findings were quite alarming. "80 or 90 per cent of the students graduating from our institutions," he announced, "leave college without any special training for citizenship or for the assumption of leadership in matters relating to law, government and politics." Better instruction "along these lines" was an "absolute necessity."[8]

Although Haines' sample of schools, as he subsequently realized, was hardly representative of the larger population it was supposed to mirror, his colleagues were moved to decisive action. They set up a new study group, originally known as the Committee of Seven[9] and then, after a curious chain of circumstances led to Haines' appointment as chairman, as the Haines Committee.[10] The philosophical premises of this Committee differed from its predecessor's only in the specificity with which they were articulated. Witness the Committee's declaration, in its preliminary report, "that departments of political science are called upon to perform services of three distinct types: (1) to train for citizenship; (2) to prepare for professions such as law, journalism, teaching, and public service; (3) to train experts and to prepare specialists for government positions." The Committee remarked,

[6] It recommended, among other things, that more American government be taught in both primary and secondary schools, and that high school teachers ought to be especially trained for this work.

[7] See fn. 11, p. 56 above, for the family tree of "Haines reports."

[8] Haines, "Is Sufficient Time Devoted to the Study of Government in Our Colleges?" *Proceedings,* vol. 7 (1910), pp. 202–09, at 206–07.

[9] Still another committee was established at the same Association meeting which set up the committee Haines was eventually to chair. This second committee was asked to evaluate the methods of laboratory training provided graduate students in political science. But the members of the committee quickly changed its name to the "Committee on Practical Training for Public Service" and then proceeded to prepare a report which almost totally ignored their original mandate. See, "Preliminary Report of the Committee on Practical Training for Public Service," *Proceedings,* vol. 10 (1913), pp. 301–56.

[10] Haines was not even a member of the Committee of Seven at first. He was appointed to it as chairman only after Professor George H. Haynes of Worcester Polytechnic Institute resigned his post in 1913.

almost as an afterthought, that "for the universities a fourth group might be added including courses primarily intended to train for research work."[11]

This ordering was apparently unchallenged during the Committee's subsequent deliberations. Few persons were surprised, it is safe to say, by its eventual recommendation that, to further education for citizenship and public service, "a full year's course in American government be given as the basic course for undergraduates" and that, where independence had not already been attained, political science be established as a separate department to ensure political scientists a freer hand in pursuing this urgent objective.[12]

Beyond doubt, the members of the Committee were motivated by a sincere belief in the virtues of democracy and a genuine desire to preserve and strengthen the American way of life. Beyond doubt, too, neither they nor their fellow political scientists were totally oblivious to the practical benefits which would accrue from the adoption of these recommendations. Here, as in other instances, there was a happy conjunction between the profession's philosophic and patriotic convictions and what, from another vantage point, might be regarded as its worldly interests.

PUBLIC AFFAIRS

Personal participation in public affairs, common during the formative decades,[13] continued unabated into the emergent period. Biographies of the First (i.e., 1904) Establishment show that three out of five of its members took part in the nation's political life in more than a casual manner. The same pattern recurs in the Second (i.e., 1914) Establishment. At least thirty-four of the fifty-seven persons for whom we have data were so engaged at one time or another. So widespread was the profession's involvement that a 1911 Association committee attempting a survey of these activities

[11] "Report on Instruction in Political Science in Colleges and Universities," *Proceedings,* vol. 10 (1913), pp. 249–70 at 264.

[12] "Report of the Committee of Seven on Instruction in Colleges and Universities," *APSR,* vol. 9 (1915), pp. 353–74 at 358.

[13] See above, pp. 42–45.

found itself literally swamped by responses.[14] "Information began to pile up," its members complained, "until it was clearly impossible to include such lists in the final draft of [our] report."[15]

The *Political Science Quarterly* continued, too, its practice of publishing a large proportion of articles devoted to current events.[16] From 1889 on, the *Quarterly* also provided its readers with a semi-annual "Record of Public Events" running about twenty-five pages in length. The editors of the newly founded *American Political Science Review* evidently thought the feature worth copying. From the outset, each issue of the *Review* contained a 20–25 page section devoted to "Notes on Current Legislation." The title of the section was changed to "Legislative Notes and Review" in 1915 and, though the number of items was reduced, the individual notes became longer than before. The net amount of space devoted to this material thus remained about the same, e.g., perhaps one-third that alloted to "scholarly" articles.

But this was only the start, for the articles themselves were heavily "current-events" oriented. At least half the items in the first volume of the *Review* dealt with contemporary subjects; rarely did the proportion in subsequent issues drop below this level. In some years, and 1920 is a case in point, almost every piece bore on some current question or recent political development. The treatment of these topics, it is essential to repeat, was far more often descriptive than analytical. Those accustomed to the austere contents of professional periodicals today may find it hard to realize, in going through these early volumes, that they are reading a scholarly journal rather than a somewhat badly written version of *Harpers* or the *Atlantic Monthly*.

The papers presented at the annual meetings paint the same picture. About a dozen papers delivered at the 1904 convention were published in the *Proceedings* and practically every one had a contemporary events focus. Ten years later, to take the last issue of the *Proceedings,* the number of papers (and panel topics) had doubled, but there was no significant change in the percentage dealing with current affairs. The level of analysis, as might be expected, was on a par with that in the *Review*.

[14] This was the Committee on Practical Training for Public Service.
[15] *Proceedings,* vol. 10 (1914), p. 319.
[16] Above, pp. 43–45.

Doctoral dissertations show the same topical orientation. At least half of the dissertations listed as "in progress" during 1910, 1913, and 1920 (to take three years at random) dealt with ongoing problems in public policy or some recent governmental development. Subjects of this sort, furthermore, were as common toward the end of the period as at its beginning. Needless to say, these choices could hardly have been made in the face of faculty disapproval. The regularity of the pattern points to precisely the opposite conclusion. So does the other available evidence. During these two decades, most certainly, the profession's attention to public affairs continued unabated.

part 3
the
middle
years,
1921–1945

*B*oth the opening and close of this period, which we shall term the "middle years," are marked by historic events within and outside the discipline. 1921 signals the "return to normalcy" after World War I; it was also the first year of Merriam's momentous effort to move the profession toward a "science of politics." The termination of the era is fixed in a similar fashion. 1945 dates the end of World War II and the beginning of the Nuclear Age; about then, too, the apostles of a scientific political science again girded their loins for battle and sallied forth, now under the banner of "behavioralism."

During this quarter-century, not one, but *two,* attempts were made to recast the nature of American political science. Of these, the campaign for a "scientific" political science is the better known and the more significant. Launched by Merriam in 1921, and given tremendous impetus by the three National Conferences on the Science of Politics (1923–5), the movement reached high tide shortly before the end of the decade, receded almost overnight, and then began to gather renewed strength as the middle period drew to a close. Between its proponents and opponents, almost all the major arguments for and against a science of politics were voiced during the 1920's and 1930's. But, like the pieces of an unassembled jigsaw puzzle, they lay scattered, almost unrelated to one another. By 1945, they were ready to be sorted out and fitted together into coherent, reasonably systematic doctrines—the one behavioral, the other antibehavioral. This post–1921 dispute over the scope and methods of the discipline thus represented a confrontation between ideas and aspirations which had previously clashed, early in the profession's history, and which are today again locked in conflict.

Less well known is the second attempt to reorient the discipline, an enterprise led by Thomas Reed under the aegis of the Association's Committee on Policy. Beginning in the late 1920's, as the science of politics movement ebbed, Reed and his associates pressed hard for a political science primarily concerned with immediate questions of public policy, with training for the public service, with the preparation of youth for democratic citizenship, and with adult political education. By 1935 this thrust, too, had spent its force.

Though neither Merriam nor Reed captured the Holy Land, or came very close to it, both crusades left their mark on the discipline. With the passing of time, even those hostile to scientism came gradually to utilize some of the movement's concepts and techniques. And, in the years immediately following World War II, Reed and his fellow activists—this time with considerably greater foundation backing than before—were able to enlist a large number of their colleagues in much the same sort of venture which had been attempted some twenty years earlier.

These intellectual currents will command the lion's share of our attention. But there were many other important developments during the middle years. The American Political Science Association more than doubled in membership. Doctoral output rose steadily, as did complaints about the nature of doctoral training and the quality of the end product. Political science became increasingly academicized and began to experience a problem common to most academic disciplines—the centrifugal pull of field specialization and the appearance of potentially competitive organizations and journals. The Americanization of the profession was near-complete, although this parochial tendency was partially offset by the arrival of an impressive group of refugee scholars in the 1930's and, subsequently, by the generous opportunities for foreign travel provided by the armed services between 1941 and 1945. During this quarter of a century, too, service in the New Deal and defense agencies gave political scientists a large-scale opportunity to test their expertise, an experience which led them to take a second and highly critical look at many of their accepted notions about the nature of the governmental process. For the first time since the heyday of Burgess and Adams, research came to be widely acknowledged as the guild's primary function, though practice and principle did not always coincide. And, for the first time, too, there emerged a painful awareness of the inherent incompatibility of the several roles which the profession had traditionally sought to play.

VIII

professional
growth
and
development,
1921–1945

THE AMERICAN POLITICAL SCIENCE
ASSOCIATION

MEMBERSHIP AND STRUCTURE

*T*he Association's roster provides the best single measure of growth during this era. Except for the worst depression years, membership expanded steadily—1300 in 1920, 1800 by 1930, 2800 a decade later, and 3300 by 1945. These figures actually understate the number of practicing political scientists for, as a 1929 study revealed,[1] many of those teaching the subject at institutions of higher learning were not members of the Association. The list of political science departments also lengthened, with "News and Notes" reporting the establishment of new departments well into the early 1940's.

---

[1] *Report of the Committee on Policy, APSR,* vol. 24 (1930), Supplement, Appendix VII, p. 144. William B. Munro, who conducted the survey, which included some two hundred institutions (among them "virtually all the more important ones"), found that political science departments had a larger percentage of part-time instructors than did other departments. The reasons advanced were the sharing of personnel with history and with law schools, and the use of practicing lawyers and public officials to give courses in political science (pp. 131–32).

91

By 1932, another study found, the trend toward academization had taken giant strides.[2] In 1912, less than two-fifths (38.9 per cent) of the classifiable non-institutional members of the Association held faculty appointments. Two decades later, this group constituted a majority. If anything, academization reinforced the long-standing emphasis on publication as the hallmark of the "good" political scientist. Harold Laski, a sympathetic as well as a knowledgeable observer, remarked on the American "tendency to judge men by their volume of published output . . . a facile test of promotion naturally welcome to busy administrators."[3] Ten years later, a native political scientist repeated the charge that, at large universities, "quantity of writing" was the "usual test by which men are promoted."[4] Needless to say, where quantity was the measure, quality did not always triumph.[5]

As the Association grew, attendance at the annual conventions multiplied. Meetings rarely attracted more than 150 registrants in the early 1920's; the figure doubled by 1930, and passed 1000 by 1940. The growing impersonality of the national meetings undoubtedly contributed to the establishment of smaller and more intimate regional, state, and local organizations. One, the Southern Political Science Association, was of particular importance because its *Journal of Politics* (founded in 1939) soon became a highly respected publication outlet.

The national Association itself did not change structurally during the middle years. It continued to function without a national headquarters or permanent professional staff. Presidential and vice-presidential candidates were proposed by a nominating committee, with acceptance of the committee's slate almost a fore-

[2] "The Teaching Personnel in American Political Science Departments, A Report of the Sub-Committee on Personnel of the Committee on Policy to the American Political Science Association, 1934," *APSR*, vol. 28 (1934), pp. 726–65 at 729.

[3] *The Dangers of Disobedience and Other Essays*, New York, 1930, p. 113.

[4] Benjamin E. Lippincott, "The Bias of American Political Science," *Journal of Politics*, vol. 2 (1940), pp. 124–39 at 138.

[5] Lippincott, *loc. cit.*, characterized much of what had been published in recent years as "sterile empirical" studies which resembled the "compilation of a telephone directory."

gone conclusion. Since these offices carried one-year terms, the consequences of the system were predictable: the President, who presumably attended to broad policy matters, had little advance warning of his selection, practically no bureaucracy to assist him, and was on the way out of office before he had mastered his job.

Organizational decisions required the approval of a fifteen member Executive Council, whose members were elected for over-lapping three-year terms. Though the Council, which met annually, could and occasionally did give advice, criticism, and direction, its usual role was to rubber stamp the actions taken by the Association's ample covey of committees. Under these circumstances, policy-making was apt to be haphazard. Indeed, before the middle period was well under way, concern about the Association's lack of purpose led—most unwisely, as events were to prove—to the creation of a Committee on Policy.[6] To this Committee we shall, in due course, return.

The Assocation's housekeeping chores were handled by the Secretary-Treasurer who, like the Managing Editor of the *Review,* held office for an extended period of time. When the Secretary-Treasurer's duties became intolerably burdensome, the position of Assistant Secretary-Treasurer was created.

So organized, the Association limped along until its normal operations were disrupted by World War II. Though the loss of membership and income during the war years was only moderate, rising costs forced the curtailment of various activities and threatened to close down the *Review.* Travel restrictions made it difficult for committees to function, and compelled the cancellation of the regular Association conventions between 1942 and 1944.

However, wartime Washington had attracted many political scientists. To fill the void resulting from the partial incapacitation of the Association, some of these formed the so-called "Washington Committee." This group took upon itself the task of recruiting new members, of arranging a program for an annual APSA Washington meeting, and, as matters progressed, of preparing an

---

[6] After assessing the situation, the Committee uncharitably declared that, with a few exceptions, "the Association has not, up to the present time, contributed directly to the improvement of either research or instruction in political science." *Report of the Committee on Policy, op. cit.,* p. 17.

indictment of the manner in which the *Review* was being run.[7] Superfluous, even dysfunctional, as the Washington Committee may have become by the end of the war, it served an important need from 1942 to 1945.

THE AMERICAN POLITICAL SCIENCE REVIEW

Like the Association, the *American Political Science Review* was not dramatically different in the middle years from what it had been during the emergent period. A succession of managing editors believed that the *Review* should perform an intelligence function for its readers. It fulfilled this task by a steady stream of items dealing, often in surprising detail, with decisions made at Executive Council and Association business meetings, the panel and round table discussions at the national convention (and at a variety of conferences and institutes held in the United States and abroad), the deliberations of the Association's numerous committees and sub-committees, and the activities of individual political scientists and departments. This news was of inestimable value to those who were unable to participate directly in the Association's affairs or did not maintain effective contact with their fellow practitioners. These items also have a utility of quite another sort: they make it possible to trace developments that would otherwise be difficult, if not impossible, to reconstruct.

Until 1939, the *Review* was the profession's only general journal. It was, therefore, an extraordinarily important outlet for articles, especially in those subject areas where alternatives were meager or virtually non-existent. In some fields, such as international law, state and local government, and public law, specialized periodicals already existed and access to the *Review* was less vital. But to the extent that the *Review* constituted the principal scholarly journal, it shaped as well as reflected the research interests of the discipline. Then, as now, the decision to undertake a given project had to take into consideration whether the results could be published. The *Review*'s editorial policy during this span is therefore a matter of particular concern.

[7] For the activities of the Washington Committee, see *APSR,* vol. 37 (1943), p. 123; vol. 38 (1944), pp. 124, 131–32, 139–40; and vol. 39 (1945), pp. 141–42.

For almost the entire quarter-century, the journal's Managing Editor was Frederic A. Ogg.[8] Several years after assuming office, Ogg produced a lengthy statement expounding his editorial objectives and guidelines.[9] As under his predecessors, the substantive contents of the *Review* were divided between articles and a variety of "notes" dealing with special fields or topics. The latter, Ogg explained, were normally written "by request," though a few were submitted by writers "on their own initiative." On the other hand, only about a third of the articles published had been solicited. The remainder were selected from papers delivered at the annual meetings and from those sent in by hopeful authors. There were 30 to 40 such submissions annually and half of these were "worthwhile." On the basis of Ogg's figures, he was able to publish about half of these "worthwhile" items.[10]

"From the outset," Ogg declared, his intention "was to supply, not only fuller discussions appropriate to main articles of a philosophical or descriptive character, but also succinct reviews or surveys of current governmental activities, and likewise critical and bibliographic apparatus for use both in research and in administration." As he saw it, the primary function of the *Review* was "to keep its readers abreast of the latest advances in the discipline with which it has to do." Because there were quite a few laymen in the Association whose dues permitted activities that would otherwise have to be curtailed or abandoned, he also sought to ensure that the *Review*'s contents "must not be so technical, in manner and substance, as to repel the intelligent but non-specialist reader."

Ogg reported regularly on the space allotted to "main articles"

[8] The first Managing Editor, W. W. Willoughby, served from 1906 to 1917; his successor, John A. Fairlie, from 1917 to 1925; and Ogg, from 1925 to 1949. There was also considerable continuity in the Editorial Board, selected then, as now, by the Council on the nomination of the Managing Editor. During this period, few members served for less than three to five years, and 17 held their posts for between five and ten years. Management of the various departments (substantive "notes" in the several specialized areas, news and notes, and book reviews) reflected the same stability. In 1930, we might add, Ogg was receiving a munificent $600 per year for what was at least a half-time job.

[9] "Report of the Committee on Policy," *APSR* Supplement, *op. cit.,* Appendix 11, pp. 187–97.

[10] See below, pp. 96–97.

and that used for "succinct reviews or surveys of current government activities." In 1926, according to one of his early tabulations, 297 of some 900 pages were given over to articles, 222 to assorted "notes," and the remainder went for professional news (73 pages), book reviews (165 pages), and an index of "Recent Publications of Political Interest" (148 pages).[11] Ten years later, two changes can be discerned. The proportion of space devoted to articles had decreased and additional "departments" dealing with current developments (notes on Public Administration and on Rural and Local Government) were added. By 1944, articles consumed only about a fifth of the journal, and over half of these dealt with contemporary state, national, and international developments.[12]

Every profession has its malcontents and political science proved no exception. From time to time, those who were not convinced that Ogg was doing the best of all possible jobs were sufficiently numerous or sufficiently persistent to force an inquiry of the manner in which the *Review* was edited. For example, the Sub-Committee on Publications of the Committee on Policy reported, in 1934, an inconclusive discussion of the "apportionment of space between interpretative articles and the periodic summaries of constitutional, political, and administrative changes." A year later, carefully noting that it was the "Managing Editor, who handles almost alone the reading and evaluation of manuscripts," the Sub-Committee acknowledged that it had "heard some criticisms concerning the quality of the leading articles and the apportionment of space between the general articles on the one hand and descriptive articles and digests on the other hand." The Sub-Committee hinted that it might be "desirable and practicable to obtain a larger number of high-grade articles of a general interpretative and polemical character."[13] The Managing Editor, obviously, thought otherwise.

When rumblings of dissatisfaction became ominously loud in the early 1940's, Ogg rose to his own defense.[14] There simply was not enough space, he maintained, "for any one interest or field as is likely to be expected." Although the pressure had been some-

11 *APSR*, vol. 21 (1927), p. 155.
12 *APSR*, vol. 39 (1945), p. 133.
13 *APSR*, vol. 29 (1935), p. 128.
14 *APSR*, vol. 36 (1942), pp. 126–27.

what relieved by the "continuing multiplication" of specialized journals, these latter had "a very marked tendency . . . to draw away from the *Review* the best manuscripts" in their fields. Moreover, he complained, "in most recent years, the number of manuscripts offered by young and inexperienced writers (often graduate students) has increased steadily in proportion to the number offered by established scholars. . . . In fact, the number in the latter category is extremely small." At Ogg's suggestion, a Committee on the *Review* was appointed to look into these problems.

The Committee largely confined its preliminary report to lamenting the war-time conditions which hindered the execution of its assignment. Perhaps fearing that the matter would be permitted to end there, the aforementioned Washington Committee[15] proceeded to draft a severely critical appraisal of Ogg's stewardship. A copy of this statement fell into the Managing Editor's hands before its authors had intended and Ogg promptly struck back.[16] This time, though, he did not stand alone. The Committee on the *Review* belatedly produced its final report, a fascinating exercise in logic and diplomacy. After discussing numerous criticisms that had been leveled at the journal, the Committee blandly concluded that "the *Review* has been maintained as an exceptionally well-balanced publication throughout the years, something amply demonstrated by the annual reports of the Managing Editor as well as the most cursory examination of the *Review*'s contents over a period of years, and this no doubt explains the general satisfaction of the membership."[17]

The Committee's reassuring words notwithstanding, of discontent there was plenty. The full fury of the storm did not break, though, until shortly after the end of the middle period.[18]

THE COMMITTEE ON POLICY, 1927–1935

There was some feeling, mentioned above, that the Association was not adequately promoting the scholarly and teaching interests

[15] See above, pp. 93–94.

[16] *APSR*, vol. 38 (1944), pp. 135–36.

[17] *APSR*, vol. 38 (1944), pp. 141–50, at 144. This comfortable sense of well-being, it should be added, was not shared by one member of the Committee. His sharp comments, in the form of a letter to the Committee chairman, were appended to the Committee's report.

[18] See below, pp. 155–57.

of the discipline. Reflecting this sentiment, President Charles A. Beard suggested, in 1926, that "Committee on Policy" might serve a useful purpose. His successor, William B. Munro, promptly appointed such a committee and, naturally enough, designated Beard as its chairman. Beard resigned in May, 1927, and was replaced by Thomas H. Reed. That same year the Committee on Policy received a grant of $7,500 from the Carnegie Corporation to study how the Association might be made "more mobile, more articulate, and more effective."

The Committee's basic statement, published as a separate volume in 1930,[19] makes it clear that Reed, presumably with the tacit concurrence of his fellow members, hoped to transform the Association into an instrument which would deliberately shape and direct the discipline. Among the major activities contemplated

[19] *Report of the Committee on Policy, APSR,* vol. 24 (1930), Supplement. This 199 page volume consisted of three parts: (1) a letter of transmittal signed by Reed; (2) a 22-page Committee statement, which is the report proper; and (3) 12 Appendices, each by a different member of the Committee. These Appendices, and their respective authors, were

  I. Conditions Favorable to Creative Work in Political Science: Charles A. Beard.
  II. Research Problems in the Field of Parties, Elections, and Leadership: Charles E. Merriam.
  III. A General Survey of Research in Public Administration: W. F. Willoughby.
  IV. Research in International Relations: Pitman B. Potter.
  V. Support for Research by Mature Scholars in Colleges and Universities: Russell M. Story.
  VI. Facilities for Publication in the Field of Political Science: John A. Fairlie.
  VII. Instruction in Political Science in Colleges and Universities: William B. Munro.
  VIII. Political Science Instruction in Teacher-Training Institutions, Colleges of Engineering, and Colleges of Commerce: Earl W. Crecraft.
  IX. Training for the Public Service: Thomas H. Reed.
  X. Problems of Personnel in Political Science: William Anderson. This report led to the later report on Personnel that we have already used extensively.
  XI. The American Political Science Review: Frederic A. Ogg.

The twelfth appendix is simply a financial report by J. R. Hayden. The Committee on Policy subsequently published five *Annual Reports* running from the *First Annual Report* in 1931 to the *Fifth Annual Report* in 1935. It is safe to assume that the 1930 report proper was written by Reed, though it was probably worked over by other members of the Committee. The *Fifth Annual Report* was a highly personal statement by Chairman Reed himself.

were the sponsorship and coordination of research, a broad program of adult and public school education, the publication of research findings, digests of legislation and other public documents, and the supervision of training for, and placement in, the public service.[20] Largely on the basis of these proposals, Reed obtained from the Carnegie Corporation an additional $67,500 for the Committee's use, the money to be expended at the rate of $15,000 annually the first four years and $7,500 in the fifth and final year.

For those days, this was a princely sum—and it enabled Reed to pry from the Association a truly extraordinary set of powers. In effect, they made a reconstituted Committee on Policy a law unto itself within the Association, and the chairman a law unto himself within the Committee. Reed, needless to add, accepted the chairmanship.[21]

Then, as well as later, Reed was an avid proponent of what might be called political activism. A goodly portion of the Carnegie money was used to underwrite some forty conferences between politicians and political scientists. Concurrently, he sought to open the Association to the "public-at-large." With the Pittsburgh area as a test case, 500 selected prospects were each sent three letters (one from the Association's president, another from Reed himself, and a third from a well-known Pittsburgh civic figure) plus a copy of the *Review*—manifestly a fatal blunder. The net gain was twelve new members. Undaunted, Reed projected a recruitment drive aimed at civics instructors in the high schools and teachers colleges. This, too, quickly aborted.

Reed's aspirations began to disturb a growing number of his colleagues. Many had grave doubts about the whole "better minds for better politics" notion. Some, especially among the science-oriented, regarded much of what he sought as irrelevant to the discipline's main purpose. Others, believing that the Association should be composed of persons having a common professional interest, were alienated by his scheme for bringing in lay members. By 1935, Reed's efforts to develop a broad, Association-directed program of activities had proved fruitless. The Carnegie grant had been almost completely exhausted. Most disastrous of all, he was

[20] *Report of the Committee on Policy, 1930, op. cit.,* pp. 18–24.
[21] *APSR,* vol. 25 (1931), pp. 178–80.

unable to secure additional financing for his ideas. Reed without funds was a far more vulnerable figure than Reed commanding $67,500, and his assorted opponents, apparently with Charles Merriam as prime mover, were able to secure his resignation from the Committee.

So ended the second attempt during this period to re-orient the discipline. Had Reed been successful, the course of American political science would have been drastically altered. The Committee's fifth and final annual report (in effect, Reed's apologia), gives a fascinating picture of what "might have been." That he failed is perhaps less significant than the fact that, for several years, he was able to bend the Association to his purpose. Reed's ability to go as far as he did is prima facie evidence that there was still no consensus among American political scientists as to the role of the Association nor real agreement about the function and tasks of the discipline itself.

THE GRADUATE DEPARTMENTS—DOCTORAL OUTPUT, TRAINING, AND PRESTIGE

DOCTORAL OUTPUT

In political science, as in other disciplines, possession of the doctorate was regarded as the "most important evidence that an applicant for a teaching or research position can present as proof of his training and ability."[22] A few might complain, as did an Association sub-committee in the early 1930's, that the Ph.D. "has become a fetish, and the degree a sort of union card in a closed shop industry."[23] Yet most were plainly of another mind. The "closed shop" principle was carried to its logical conclusion in 1941 when the Association decided to list in its teacher placement service "only those persons who either have received the Ph.D. or

[22] William Anderson, "Requirements for the Doctorate in Political Science," *APSR,* vol. 24 (1930), pp. 711–36 at 711.

[23] "The Teaching Personnel in American Political Science Departments," *APSR,* vol. 28 (1934), pp. 727–65 at 740. This study was prepared for the sub-committee by William Anderson.

will receive it by August of the current year."[24] The edict was not enforced and was soon quietly dropped.

If initial appointment did not require the doctorate, promotion and tenure increasingly did. More and more political scientists hastened to add the "cabalistic" Ph.D. after their names. Estimated[25] annual output went from 35 Ph.D.'s in 1925 to 45 by

[24] *APSR*, vol. 35 (1941), p. 138.

[25] It is impossible to arrive at more than an estimate. First of all, the data come from a variety of sources. For the years before 1933–34, the best single reference is the 1936 edition of the American Council on Education's *American Universities and Colleges*. For the years after 1933–34 we relied upon information gathered by the Association of Research Libraries for the National Research Council and the American Council of Learned Societies, published annually in the volumes entitled *Doctoral Dissertations Accepted by American Universities*. These statistics, grouped by seven-year periods, are also given in *Doctorate Production in United States Universities 1936–56*, compiled by the Office of Scientific Personnel, Publication 582, National Academy of Sciences—National Research Council, Washington, D.C., 1958.
A second and more serious problem is analagous to that previously encountered in attempting to determine which degrees fell into political science and which belonged in other fields. Three separate categories are employed in the National Research Council tabulations mentioned above— political science, international relations, and law. Most, but definitely not all, of the "international relations" dissertations belong in political science. Apart from the obvious impact upon total degree count, the inclusion or exclusion of "international relations" dissertations changes the percentage of doctoral output contributed by certain schools, particularly Harvard and Chicago. It would not, however, affect departmental *rank order* in Table 1.
The "law" category is much more troublesome, especially in dealing with Columbia, where many persons who must be considered political scientists took degrees reported under this heading. A decision one way or the other here affects both Columbia's relative position as well as its total production count. If "law" degrees are combined with those in political science and international relations, Columbia emerges as a major doctoral source. If "law" degrees are not counted, Columbia drops to secondary importance (and a number of persons who unquestionably are political scientists must be excluded from the tabulation). Given the central role that Columbia played in the discipline's history, the question involves more than merely ensuring a correct tally for a particular institution.
The rule followed in handling the international relations and law degrees was as follows: All of the former were counted as belonging to political science. All law degrees were excluded with the exception of those granted at Columbia between 1934 and 1945 to persons listed, in one or another of the Association's directories, as practicing political scientists. The figures for Columbia for the years 1926–33 are those given in "The Teaching Personnel in American Political Science Departments," *op. cit.,* at 750.

1930, 60 in 1935, and 80 in 1940.[26] There was, of course, a sharp fall-off during the war years.[27]

With increasing enrollments came substantial changes in the roles of the various graduate departments. The major doctoral sources between 1925–26[28] and 1944–45 were:

TABLE 1: TEN LARGEST INSTITUTIONAL SOURCES OF POLITICAL SCIENCE DOCTORATES, 1926–1945, BY DECADE

	1926–1935			1936–1945	
School	Number of Doctorates	% of Total Output	School	Number of Doctorates	Output % of Total
1. Columbia	62	11.7	#1. Harvard	80	12.2
#2. Harvard	52	9.8	2. Chicago	78	11.9
3. Hopkins	44	8.3	3. Columbia	52	8.0
4. Chicago	43	8.1	*4. California	35	5.4
5. Wisconsin	35	6.6	5. Wisconsin	32	4.9
6. Iowa	33	6.2	6. Iowa	30	4.6
7. Illinois	27	5.1	7. Princeton	28	4.3
*8. California	24	4.5	8. Yale	22	3.4
9. Pennsylvania	20	3.8	9.5. Illinois	19	2.9
10. Brookings	19	3.6	9.5. Stanford	19	2.9
Sub Total Ten Largest	359	67.7		395	60.4
All Others	171	32.3		259	39.6
Grand Total	530	100.0		654	100.0

Includes Radcliffe.
* Includes U.C.L.A.

The old order had given way to the new. In the preceding era, Columbia had been by far the largest producer, awarding well over 20 per cent of all American doctorates in political science. Although the number of Columbia Ph.D.'s granted between 1926–

[26] The number of doctoral dissertations reported "in progress" by the *Review* rose from nearly 180 in 1925–26, to 340 a decade later, and almost 400 when the U.S. entered the war in 1941. The ratio of dissertations reported "in progress" to degrees granted annually remains fairly constant at about five to one.

[27] Output dropped to 25 by 1945.

[28] Technical problems of the sort discussed in notes and text, pp. 57–58 made it impractical to push our inquiry any further back than 1925–26.

1945 was almost double that for 1901–1920 (114 as against about 60), the school had lost its over-riding dominance. Not only did its share of Ph.D. output decline precipitously but, by the end of the era, Columbia was no longer even in first place.

Johns Hopkins, the next largest producer in the first two decades of the twentieth century (its 24 doctorates constituted some 10 to 15 percent of the total), continued strong in the early years of the middle period, then faded altogether. Pennsylvania followed Hopkins into the shadows. The other three previously significant sources of political science doctorates, Wisconsin, Harvard, and Chicago, continued to play leading roles. In fact, Harvard and Chicago experienced a spectacular rise in productivity, accounting for nearly one doctorate in four by the last decade of the middle period. Other developments included the steady rise of California, the belated blossoming of Yale and Princeton, and the remarkable performance of the Brookings Institution's short-lived graduate school.

Table 1 also reveals the beginnings of what was eventually to be a major change in American graduate education, a decrease in the proportion of doctorates awarded by the largest producers. In the 1926–1935 decade there were seven institutions whose output constituted five per cent or more of all political science Ph.D.'s. In the decade which immediately followed, the number of "five per centers" dropped to four. Similarly, the ten largest sources, collectively responsible for nearly 68 per cent of the 1926–1935 crop, accounted for only 60 per cent of the 1936–45 total.

PROBLEMS OF GRADUATE TRAINING

Reservations about the quality and nature of doctoral training had been voiced in previous periods. During the middle years, booming business notwithstanding, almost every aspect of doctoral work came under attack, often for conflicting reasons.

The purpose of the Ph.D. program, most political scientists agreed, was to turn out "original, creative researchers."[29] But many who held this view felt, a sub-committee reported in the early 1930's, that students were not being adequately trained and that the doctorate "was being conferred as a routine matter upon

[29] *APSR*, vol. 39 (1945), p. 158.

increasing numbers of men not of the first order of ability and not interested in research.[30] At the same time, another contingent objected to the "over-emphasis" on research and deplored the alleged failure to provide a solid foundation in "history and philosophy."[31]

From other quarters came other complaints. President Jesse S. Reeves lashed out at the dissertation, describing it as "a form of exercise . . . which . . . may at times be depressing to the reader and even deadening to the imagination of the author.[32] He was equally displeased with course and credit-hour requirements which left graduate students little time to read and reflect upon the classic writings. Reeves also warned that the profession, by its generosity to graduate students, was in "great danger" of emulating the theological seminaries which gave "financial aid to every applicant—a policy which is far from one attracting the best minds."[33] William Anderson discussed several other concerns of the early 1930's:[34] inadequate instruction in "pedagogics," the feeling (which he did not share) that graduate training was too "theoretical and impractical," and lax standards which permitted candidates to earn Ph.D.'s without ever really mastering French and German, languages that the "leading teachers, writers, and research scholars in political science are almost constantly, and necessarily, using."[35]

These strictures were not novel, then or now. Nor were they any more effective than those voiced before or afterward. The doctoral program in political science, like those in other disciplines, mirrored the prevailing values of the profession. To the degree that the profession was divided in its objectives, these divisions were reflected in competing notions of sound graduate education. If there were serious defects in doctoral training, these

[30] "The Teaching Personnel in American Political Science Departments," *op. cit.,* p. 746.

[31] Crick, *op. cit.,* p. 157.

[32] "Perspectives in Political Science, 1903–1928," *APSR,* vol. 23 (1929), pp. 1–16 at 13.

[33] *Ibid.,* p. 14.

[34] In "Requirements for the Doctorate in Political Science," *op. cit.,* passim.

[35] *Ibid.,* p. 716.

104

shortcomings were inherent in the nature of the discipline itself. Any far-reaching reform of the one would have to wait on a transformation of the other.

DEPARTMENTAL STANDING

Prior to World War I or thereabout, Columbia was undoubtedly the most prestigious American political science department. Hopkins, Chicago, Wisconsin, Pennsylvania, Harvard, and perhaps one or two others occupied a distinctly second-level status. Profound shifts in this order took place over the course of the middle years. These shifts are reflected in a variety of data, almost all of it pointing to the same conclusions.

The changes in doctoral output discussed above are one indication of what occurred. By this measure, Harvard and Chicago moved to the position of pre-eminence previously enjoyed by Columbia and Hopkins. Columbia fell to third place—and Hopkins dropped out of the social register altogether.

Two formal studies, one published in 1925,[36] the other in 1934,[37] afford more direct evidence of departmental reputation. Though the methodology utilized in the 1925 inquiry was hardly impeccable,[38] the findings were probably close to the mark. According to Raymond M. Hughes, who undertook this first, unsponsored investigation, the leading political science departments, in rank order, were Harvard, Chicago, Columbia, Wisconsin, Illinois, Michigan, Princeton, Hopkins, Iowa, Pennsylvania, and California. An examination of Hughes' scoring system

[36] Raymond M. Hughes, *A Study, The Graduate Schools of America,* Oxford, Ohio, 1925.

[37] American Council on Education, *Report of Committee on Graduate Instruction,* Washington, D.C., 1934.

[38] Hughes asked one person in each of 20 departments at Miami University to put together a list of schools "which conceivably might be doing high grade work leading to a doctor's degree in one or more subjects." Each person was also asked to name from 40 to 60 individuals in his own field, at least half of whom were to be "professors in colleges rather than universities." These individuals, in turn, were asked to rate the departments in his specialization at the 38 schools which appeared on the final list. The number of political scientists invited to submit ratings is unknown but it is clear that the final ratings were based upon 19 responses, although, as indicated below, not all respondents actually rated each of the 38 listed institutions.

reveals that Harvard ran well ahead of Chicago[39] and that there was also a substantial gap between Chicago and Columbia.[40] For the first time in the profession's history, Columbia no longer set the pace. In fact, a different and equally defensible scoring plan would have put Wisconsin, instead, in third place.[41] By 1925, too, Hopkins and Pennsylvania were already in decline and Berkeley was just beginning its meteoric climb.

About a decade later, Hughes undertook a second study, now under the aegis of the American Council on Education. This time, those asked to serve as evaluators were chosen in somewhat more systematic fashion[42] and Hughes abandoned his earlier four-place rating scale. Instead, respondents were sent a list of all institutions offering work in their field, together with a list of the staff at each of the departments. They were asked (a) to check the schools they considered adequate for Ph.D. work, and (b) to star the best 20 per cent. No attempt was made to rank the most frequently starred schools and the final listing was in strictly alphabetical order. Whether this change represented Hughes' sober second thoughts or the diplomatic instincts of the sponsoring agency is unknown. In any event, the "starred" departments were California, Chicago, Columbia, Harvard, Illinois, Michigan, Princeton, and Wisconsin. All eight had been on the 1925 honor-roll. On the one hand, given the difference in time and technique between the two surveys and, on the other, the similarity of their results, it seems reasonable to conclude that they provide a reasonably accurate range of prevailing opinion about the quality of the discipline's graduate departments.

Hughes' findings are generally corroborated by another indicator used in earlier parts of this study—the doctoral origins of those in the then contemporary Establishment. Between 1927 and 1940 a total of 111 persons were elected to positions as Associa-

[39] Respondents were asked to rank the schools (i.e., departments) according to a four-place scale.

[40] Columbia received only six first-level votes, seven second-level, one for third, and two for fourth.

[41] Wisconsin actually received seven first-level ratings, as contrasted with Columbia's six, but earned a smaller number of total points because it was rated by fewer respondents.

[42] The secretary of the national learned society in each field was asked to provide a list of 100 well-known scholars in that field.

tion officers or members of the organization's Executive Council. Following our earlier practice, we treated these officials as the "Middle-period Establishment" and were able to secure the necessary biographical information for 108 of them. Of this number, 89 held American Ph.D.'s, taken as follows:

TABLE 2: DOCTORAL ORIGINS OF
THE MIDDLE-PERIOD ESTABLISHMENT, 1927–1940

School	Number of Ph.D.'s	% of Total
Columbia	23	25.8
Harvard	15	16.9
Chicago	11	12.4
Illinois	9	10.1
Pennsylvania	7	7.9
Wisconsin	6	6.7
Hopkins	4	4.5
Princeton	3	3.4
Cornell	2	2.2
Michigan	2	2.2
Stanford	2	2.2
Brookings	1	1.1
Bryn Mawr	1	1.1
California	1	1.1
Iowa	1	1.1
Minnesota	1	1.1
Total	89	99.8

There is an obvious similarity between the rank order in Table 2 and that in Table 1. Even more instructive are the results obtained when we distinguish, as in the next table on p. 108, between those who took their doctorates before 1921 and those who earned their degrees after that date.

Little comment is necessary other than to note that whereas the top three schools in Panel A trained almost 63 per cent of the older members of this Establishment, the leading three departments in Panel B accounted for a bit less than 55 per cent of its younger persons.

All the evidence—doctoral production, surveys of expert opinion, and doctoral origins—indicates that the leading departments during the middle years were Harvard, Chicago, and Columbia. Not only were these three most prestigious, they also

TABLE 3: DOCTORAL ORIGINS OF
MIDDLE-PERIOD ESTABLISHMENT BY DATES OF DEGREES

	Panel A Degrees Prior to 1921			Panel B Degrees 1921 or Later	
	No.	% of Total		No.	% of Total
Columbia	16	33.3	Chicago	8	19.5
Harvard	8	16.7	Columbia	7	17.1
Pennsylvania	6	12.5	Harvard	7	17.1
Chicago	3	6.3	Illinois	6	14.6
Hopkins	3	6.3	Wisconsin	3	7.3
Illinois	3	6.3	Princeton	2	4.9
Wisconsin	3	6.3	Stanford	2	4.9
Cornell	2	4.2	Other	6	14.6
Michigan	2	4.2			
Other	2	4.2			
	48	100.3		41	99.8

produced about one-third of the discipline's Ph.D.'s and an even
larger percentage of those who eventually became members of the
profession's Establishment. Academically and organizationally,
then, political science was dominated by a relatively small number
of departments. This domination, as in almost all the other learned
disciplines, created problems for individuals and institutions alike.
To these problems we shall subsequently return.

108

IX

*political science
as a
learned discipline
in the middle years:
the "new science
of politics"*

The most important intellectual development in American political science during the middle years was the "new science of politics" movement. Although the notion that politics could be studied scientifically had been pushed by Burgess and a handful of his colleagues in the formative era, it made relatively little headway for nearly two decades after the Association's founding. Ford, Macy, Bentley, and to a lesser degree, Lowell, were among the few eminent practitioners who took this idea at all seriously. Not until 1921 did scientism emerge as a really significant tendency.

It then developed quite unevenly, waxing, waning, and gathering renewed strength toward the end of the period. Through this quarter-century, moreover, scientism remained essentially an amorphous, almost ambiguous, intellectual tendency. Like the proverbial elephant inspected by the proverbial blind men, it signified different things to different persons. Not all of its partisans shared a common doctrine, not all of its foes were opposed for the same reasons.

In this chapter our task is threefold: first, to examine the positions of some of the leading participants in the controversy over scientism; then, to trace the movement from 1921–1945; and finally, to evaluate its accomplishments.

THE ANTAGONISTS

LEADING PROPONENTS: MERRIAM, MUNRO, AND CATLIN

The foremost advocate of a science of politics was, of course, Charles E. Merriam. His extraordinarily influential essay on "The Present State of the Study of Politics,"[1] led to the appointment of an Association Committee on Political Research, to three National Conferences on the Science of Politics, and eventually, it is only a slight exaggeration to say, to the creation of the Social Science Research Council. Merriam's ideas were restated in the progress reports of the Committee on Political Research and, considerably expanded, in his *New Aspects of Politics* (1925). Although he returned to the subject from time to time, his contributions to scientism were made before the 1920's ran their course.

The "present state" of affairs plainly left much to be desired. Merriam proposed, therefore, a "reconstruction of the methods of political study and the attainment of larger results in the theoretical and practical fields."[2] Toward this end, he projected a brave "new science" of politics.

The aspect of scientific inquiry which most impressed Merriam was its utility for problem solving. The scientist stated his problems in hypothetical terms, then developed precise evidence in an effort to establish or reject his hypotheses. Members of his own profession, Merriam observed, tended not to proceed in this way. When a political scientist wished to substantiate an insight, he more or less haphazardly weighed whatever bits of evidence, however imprecise, were conveniently at hand. Merriam's survey of the work done in other learned disciplines led him to believe that two particular "agencies of inquiry" could profitably be applied to political questions.[3] One of these was statistics, the other, psychology.

Merriam insisted that he had no desire to jettison the historical-comparative and legalistic approaches to politics—"I am not

[1] *APSR*, vol. 15 (1921), pp. 173–85.

[2] *Ibid.*, p. 174.

[3] *New Aspects of Politics*, Chicago, 1925, p. 11.

110

suggesting that we ask our older friends to go." On the contrary, the insights developed by the older approaches were to provide many of the problems that needed precise measurement and testing. Whatever their sources, these should be investigated by methods appropriate to their solution. For many questions this meant a reliance on the methods of psychologists and statisticians.

Merriam's quest for a scientific politics sprang from his concern with social policy (he used the term "political prudence" to denote what would subsequently be called "policy science"), rather than from any great desire for knowledge for its own sake. A science of politics would permit a "more intelligent control of the process of government" and facilitate "the conscious control of human evolution toward which intelligence moves in every domain of life."[4] It would make possible, he prophesied, "the elimination of waste in political action" and "the release of political possibilities in human nature"; it would "avoid or minimize" war, revolutions, and the "imperfect adjustment of individuals and classes"; it could deal with "graft, spoils, exploitation, inaction arising from inability to overcome inertia and deadlock" and with other evils leading to "lowered productivity and lowered good feeling, each of which affects the other in making up the sum of human well-being." These, he declared, "are the tasks and these are the tests of scientific politics."[5]

There is a temptation to mistake Merriam's brimming optimism for naïveté. Yet he was aware of the formidable obstacles such a science would have to overcome. "The student of government," he warned,

is confronted with difficulty in determining specific units, and with many variable factors which may make the accurate interpretation of a result very difficult and perhaps impossible. Political situations are usually complex, containing many factors which it is difficult to isolate successfully. The relations of the variables are not always readily disentangled, and their confusion may be the source of the most serious error.[6]

He was also conscious of the pitfalls of bias and the logical problems entailed in trying to establish causality. Beyond all this,

4 *Ibid.*, p. xvi.
5 *Ibid.*, pp. vii–ix.
6 *Ibid.*, pp. 124–25.

he recognized the danger that political scientists might become so wrapped up in methodological concerns that the subject matter of the discipline "may disappear in microscopic monographs, isolated, never synthesized, barren in interpretation," and political philosophy be "obscured in a maze of mathematical terminology and method."[7]

Since the new politics would prove its worth by serving society, there was little room for normative neutrality in Merriam's conception of science. In the first place, he was skeptical that any real degree of objectivity was possible; in the second, the idea ran counter to his deepest personal feelings. His devotion to democracy and "his frequent expressions of benevolence toward his fellow creatures and formulation of ideal objectives which indicate unmistakably that he is on the side of the angels,"[8] are legendary. It may be, too, that Merriam saw no potential conflict between these values and his commitment to a scientific politics because he so firmly believed that science and democracy went hand in glove. "Jungle politics and laboratory science," he insisted, "are incompatible, and they cannot live in the same world."[9]

A last characteristic of his thought should be noted. He was interested above all in better methods for solving existing, pressing social problems. His initial exposition of the case for a scientific politics was virtually devoid of any systematic treatment of analytic theory, of the concepts which might provide a useful theoretical framework for such a science, or of the desirability and likelihood of developing fundamental regularities or laws. Not until his 1934 *Political Power* did he turn his attention to these topics. The book added little to his reputation. As a kindly reviewer put it, his treatment of power had "a certain vague and elusive quality which is not altogether satisfying."[10]

---

[7] On balance, he considered these fears overdrawn and the risks rather minor. Merriam was less worried about another sort of boundary consideration: that political scientists would become so enmeshed in the study of political man, or group, or process, as to be unable to differentiate themselves from the practitioners in other disciplines investigating social processes. "The fundamental problem," he felt, "is that of human behavior, however we may separate its various phases."

[8] William A. Robson, (book review) *APSR*, vol. 29 (1935), p. 299.

[9] *New Aspects of Politics*, p. 247.

[10] Robson, *op. cit.*, p. 300.

The awkward truth is that scientism bore scant fruit in Merriam's own work. But this in no way detracts from the importance of his role during the 1920's. It was Merriam who inspired renewed attention to methodology and pointed the way toward what would eventually become behavioralism. If he himself did little more than exhort, those whom he encouraged amply redressed the balance. To an astounding degree, the leading contributors to the scientistic literature in the middle years and beyond were people who had been associated with him at Chicago. One need only consider a partial listing: Lasswell, Gosnell, Key, Quincy Wright, Leonard D. White, Wooddy, Beyle, Mott, Overacker, Almond, Pritchett, Simon, Leiserson, and Truman. It is hard to believe that the association was pure coincidence.

Another major advocate of a scientific politics, William Bennett Munro, was far more explicit than Merriam in stressing the desirability and feasibility of uncovering fundamental laws of political behavior. This constitutes, in fact, a recurring theme in his epigrammatic *Invisible Government* (1927). According to Munro, there are

. . . inexorable laws which control the general course of (a people's) progress. I use the word laws with malice aforethought. There must be laws of politics, for laws are the most universal of all phenomena. Everything in nature inclines to move in seasons, or in undulations, or in cycles.

These laws could be brought into "better visibility" if the political scientist would give up his "methodological affiliation" with philosophers and sociologists, "whose company he has habitually been keeping to the detriment of his own quest for truth," and adopt instead "the methodology and objectivity of the scientists."[11]

The kind of scientist Munro had in mind was spelled out in his presidential address, "Physics and Politics—An Old Analogy Revised."[12] According to an unenthusiastic contemporary, this statement "very aptly summed up the prevailing scientistic currents

[11] *Invisible Government, op. cit.,* pp. 35–37. His declaration that "if I thought that the voice of the people was the voice of God I should be sorely tempted to become an atheist" is a model of such objectivity.

[12] *APSR,* vol. 22 (1928), pp. 1–11.

among American Political Scientists."[13] Political science, argued Munro, "should borrow by analogy from the new physics" in ridding itself of "intellectual insincerities" about natural rights, the consent of the governed, the rule of public opinion, the equality of men, laissez-faire, and the like. The discipline should search for "concepts that will stand the test of actual operations, and upon these it should begin to rebuild itself by an intimate observation of the actualities." As had physics, political science should move from visible, large-scale phenomena to the sub-atomic, "to the invisible and hitherto much neglected forces by which the individual citizen is fundamentally actuated and controlled."[14]

Without deigning to employ the methodology he urged upon his colleagues, Munro went on to articulate some of the laws he had in mind—geographic determinism, racial determinism, economic determinism, and above all, the "law of the pendulum." This last discovery, unaccountably slighted by posterity, held that "extremes always generate their opposites" and that "all history, indeed, can be divided into periods of two general types, centrifugal and centripetal." Munro did not believe that predictions based upon such laws would ever achieve the certainty of the hard sciences because "even the 'constants' of human nature are to an extent modifiable by experience and by environmental influences." Nonetheless, the underlying consistency in human conduct left open the feasibility of building a "science of human behavior in relation to human affairs."[15]

A third leading proponent of scientism was G. E. G. Catlin. For all of their sagacity and wit, his writings abound in statements which make him an easy target for ridicule. Though he professed himself a "political experimental scientist" who believed that "there is no more inherent impossibility in experimenting with men than with pigs,"[16] his experiments were largely confined to testing the patience and credulity of his readers. This aspect of Catlin's

[13] W. Y. Elliott, "The Possibility of a Science of Politics: With Special Attention to Methods Suggested by William B. Munro and George E. G. Catlin," in Stuart A. Rice (ed.), *Methods in Social Science,* New York, 1931, p. 74.

[14] "Physics and Politics—An Old Analogy Revised," *op. cit.,* p. 10.

[15] *Invisible Government, op. cit.,* p. 37.

[16] Catlin, "The Doctrine of Power and Party Conflict," *APSR,* vol. 19 (1925), p. 1.

career aside, his *Science and Method of Politics* (1927) was the period's most fully developed discussion of the presuppositions of a scientific politics. It was also a serious, and not unimpressive, attempt to construct a general theory of politics.[17]

Catlin maintained that politics, unlike history, could be studied scientifically. A sizable portion of the book is devoted to rebutting the more serious contemporary arguments that a scientific politics was a foolhardy and unattainable goal. It was possible, he maintained, to formulate principles which could turn political science from a "conglomerate of historical excursus, of belles lettres about 'liberty' and the like, and of debating points prepared for a party platform" into a science of "prediction." By prediction, Catlin meant statements of the character "if this is done, then that will, *ceteris paribus,* happen."[18]

To date, there was "no such thing as political science in more than a barren name."[19] The discipline lacked general concepts which "threw light upon the entire field of political phenomena,"[20] a lack which stemmed partly from a failure to define properly the discipline's scope and partly from the inadequacy of its methods. Abstract analytical theories which could delimit its subject matter and meaningfully order the data provided by experience and experiment were desperately needed. Catlin set out to meet the need.

Where Merriam looked to psychology and statistics, and Munro to physics, Catlin turned to classical economics for his model. Just as economics had shifted its focus from the business enterprise to an abstract analytical construct, economic man, political science should turn from the state to the abstract construct, political man. Economic man is moved by the will to consume or possess. Consequently, economics deals with the production and exchange of goods. Political man is moved by a will to dominate, by an impulse to make his will prevail against his

---

[17] The book drew respectful notices even from some who were highly critical of what its author had to say. See the review by A. Gordon Dewey in the *Political Science Quarterly,* vol. 42 (1928), pp. 617–21, and Elliott, in Rice, *op. cit.,* pp. 82 ff. Charles Beard was somewhat less enthusiastic, *APSR,* vol. 21 (1927), p. 652.

[18] *The Science and Method of Politics,* New York, 1927, p. 112.

[19] *Ibid.,* p. 84.

[20] *Ibid.,* p. 233.

fellows. Accordingly, the proper subject matter of politics should be *power*. The "political arena," Catlin pointed out, could be regarded as a "market" for power.[21]

Catlin was well aware that the analogy between classical economics and politics, even to this point, was not without certain strains. He realized also that his greatest challenge was yet to be faced: that of finding a standard unit of measurement. Economics had less of a problem here, since the value of goods could be stated in terms of money. What could serve as a parallel yardstick of power? In nineteen tortured, if highly imaginative pages, Catlin floundered in that Serbonian bog.[22]

In primitive relationships, where heads are cracked instead of counted, measuring power did not seem hopelessly formidable. Military equipment, trained manpower, and armament statistics were all more or less useful indices of relative physical strength. But in more civilized social relations a metric was harder to discover. Although social status and money could occasionally be employed as indirect measures of political power, something more directly relevant was needed, some sophisticated standard for weighing the support or backing which constituted the effective political power which a man or party possessed.

Eventually, Catlin decided upon the "vote" because, as he put it, the vote is "very near to the heart of the political relationship." While less than pellucid on this point, Catlin apparently thought of voting as any balancing of support and opposition, not merely a formal rendering of ayes and nays. He knew that votes per se were hardly a satisfactory unit and that it was thoroughly unrealistic to assume that votes are "coins of equal purity, that the electorate is actively interested and of approximately equal intelligence, intensity, or persistence of conviction, and military strength." Besides, some men speak not only for themselves but for "groups, and

[21] "What men seek in their political negotiations is power, whether as a 'right,' which is assured by co-operative labour and a general social convention, or as 'control' by the acquisition of a personal superiority over their neighbors by direct dominance, or as the 'influence' which comes with great support, or as the 'prestige' which declares it." *Ibid.*, p. 244.

Catlin recognized that there are numerous "markets" for power, and a person who does exceedingly well in one, say his own village, may carry no weight in a "metropolitan or international society."

[22] *Ibid.*, pp. 251 ff.

count as such." Catlin was hopeful, however, that ultimately it might be possible to develop more sensitive and precise measures of support.

Although optimistic about the potential of his theoretical structure, Catlin admitted that its utility had yet to be demonstrated. Only painstaking inquiry would establish whether it could "reveal causes and connections bringing hitherto disjointed facts into place, and exhibit the existence of a process which subsequent observations confirm and which we can therefore tentatively affirm."[23] If this could be done, at last there would be a science of politics.

Catlin, more strongly even than Munro, insisted that a true political science was necessarily value free. A scientific politics should be concerned with means, not ends. It is not the political scientist's task "to instruct men about political values" any more than it is the "task of the teacher of sculpture to instruct his pupils in themes and ideals for artistic expression. His business is to teach well the principles of technique, and to tell them what can and what cannot be done with the material."[24]

Despite its glaring weaknesses, this was a bold effort to provide the discipline with a full-blown general theory. Not since Bentley, twenty years earlier, had anyone tried to restructure so sweepingly the scope and method of American political science. Catlin was no more successful than Bentley had been—and another two decades would elapse before someone else would again attempt the task.

LEADING OPPONENTS: ELLIOTT, CORWIN, AND BEARD

Probably the most comprehensive indictment of scientism was provided by William Yandell Elliott. No admirer of traditional political science (he found much of value, for example, in Bentley's group approach), Elliott severely criticized the scientistic creed in his *The Pragmatic Revolt in Politics* (1928) and in a later essay entitled "The Possibility of a Science of Politics: With Special Attention to Methods Suggested by William B. Munro and

[23] *Ibid.*, p. 278.

[24] *Ibid.*, pp. 298–9. By the mid-1930's, however, his ideas changed considerably.

PART 3: THE MIDDLE YEARS, 1921-1945

George E. G. Catlin." The proponents of scientism, he charged, "have, through a natural envy, wished to steal some of the prestige that experimental science enjoys in the modern world."[25] No matter how they tried, the study of politics could never be made into such a science. Political science, Elliott argued, has no "constant unit which lends itself to measurable variables," cannot be treated in universalized abstractions, is concerned with phenomena which are in essential ways unique, does not permit of experimentation, deals with processes that are hopelessly complex, and must account for human beings capable of enough "self-direction and . . . novelty in social adjustment" to confound "rigid deterministic laws."[26]

Elliott had no quarrel in principle with the quest for objectivity, the use of quantitative techniques, or the search for regularities and laws. What aroused his ire was the actual performance of those who professed these commitments. A yawning chasm separated precept from practice. "One is continually struck," was the gentle way he put it, "by the amount of half-baked philosophy current in so-called 'scientific' studies in politics—values dragged in without criticism, and, what is worse, without consciousness that they are *values* and not the purest 'facts.' "[27] The desire to discover "laws" fostered a tendency to pull political phenomena out of cultural context;[28] still worse, many political scientists did not have a sufficiently sophisticated understanding of what psychologists, sociologists, economists, and statisticians were doing "to prevent the foisting-off of pseudo-scientific 'results' on us."[29]

There was, however, one aspiration of scientism, particularly that variety advocated by Munro and Catlin, which Elliott regarded as thoroughly wrong-headed. Political science, whatever else it need do, should not abandon its traditional concern with policy and the ideal ends of government. "It is no more for political science to leave out all considerations of these values than for the philosopher to abstract *in vacuo.*" Even public administra-

---

"The Possibility of a Science of Politics. . . ." *op. cit.,* p. 72. See also *The Pragmatic Revolt in Politics,* p. 8.

[26] "The Possibility of a Science of Politics. . . ." *op. cit.,* p. 79.

[27] *Ibid.,* pp. 89–90.

[28] *Ibid.,* p. 91. "Timbuctoo cannot be governed like the island of Britain—though its government may offer some amusing parallels to that of Chicago, if one goes behind forms to political realities."

[29] *Ibid.,* p. 86.

tion, an area especially suitable for the application of scientific technique, cannot be entirely divorced from policy. Take, he drolly suggested, such a seemingly technical matter as sewage disposal. "The scientific element is exhausted when one has disposed of the engineering details. The where and how of disposal become embarrassingly political."[30] On this broad issue, Merriam and Elliott occupied common ground.

Edward S. Corwin shared Elliott's views of the obstacles to meaningful experimentation in political science. While he professed no animus to the use of the new methodology, he shared Elliott's disenchantment with the accomplishments of scientism. Among its practitioners, he remarked, "there was always an immense unlimbering of apparatus, an immense polishing of a technique already spotless; but it was all apparently for the sake of the game itself."[31]

What troubled Corwin most of all was the question of ethical and normative neutrality. Should the discipline actually turn in this direction, a possibility he did not preclude, it would abandon its worthy objectives for a "mess of pottage." Rather than ape the "infantile . . . obtuseness" about social values often encountered in the natural sciences ("brandishing sticks of dynamite with the insouciance of a four-year old"), political scientists should stay with their ancient goals. Their proper task "is criticism and education regarding the true ends of the state and how best they may be achieved." To the extent that the techniques of science can advance these goals, the more use made of them the better. But where they cannot, they should be abandoned as irrelevant to the discipline's "true destiny."[32]

There were numerous other critics of scientism, some of the more prominent being Luther Gulick, Walter J. Shepard, James Hart, H. Mark Jacobsen, and Charles A. Beard.[33] With the

---

[30] *Ibid.*, p. 77.

[31] "The Democratic Dogma and the Future of Political Science," *APSR,* vol. 23 (1929), p. 588.

[32] *Ibid.*, pp. 591–92.

[33] Walter J. Shepard, in Harry Elmer Barnes (ed.). *The History and Prospects of the Social Sciences,* New York, 1925, pp. 396–443; James Hart, "Political Science and Rural Government," *APSR,* vol. 19 (1925), pp. 615–20; J. Mark Jacobsen, "Evaluating State Administrative Structure—the Fallacy of the Statistical Approach," *APSR,* vol. 22 (1928), pp. 928–35; Luther Gulick (rapporteur), *APSR,* vol. 20 (1926), pp. 403–04.

exception of the last named, they had little to say that is not found in the writings of Elliott and Corwin. We can conclude our survey, therefore, with a brief glance at Beard's views.

His presidential address, "Time, Technology, and the Creative Spirit in Political Science,"[34] was a searing indictment of the discipline. Beard directed his fire at scientism and the more conventional approaches alike for having neglected the twin modern Western "Leviathans," time and technology. These were "relentlessly devouring" the old order and "convulsively recasting" entire social systems into "ever-new kaleidoscopic patterns." The profession should look to the future and devise ways of coping with these two forces. We must try, Beard warned, "to bring our flow of consciousness into such intimate relation with the world stream that we may, by creative effort, better help to prepare our students—and through them the nation—for its destiny."[35]

American political scientists had done almost nothing creative[36] to meet this need. Why? Four "incubi," Beard argued, were substantially at fault.[37] Two of these (the mentality of the political lawyer for whom the discipline "has too long been a household drudge," and the "baggage provided by the professional historian") had no particular relevance to scientism. Nor could any particular group among political scientists be held responsible for the third impediment, the academic environment.[38] The fourth

[34] *APSR*, vol. 21 (1927), pp. 1–11.

[35] *Ibid.*, p. 6.

[36] *APSR*, Report of the Committee on Policy, *op. cit.*, Appendix I, pp. 27–8. By "creative" Beard "meant the discovery of hitherto neglected or overlooked relations between or among the data of social life. The discovery of emergent realities in our civilization likely to give novel direction to our political destiny. The discovery of laws of political evolution—when, as, and if. A divining of the future, near or proximate, using the observation of data and intuitive insight. The discovery of more efficient and economical methods of accomplishing work in any department of government. The exploration of political mythology. The examination of current slogans and assumptions with the aid of merciless Socratic elenchus. Penetration into underlying realities beneath the surface of accepted customs and practices in politics."

[37] "Time, Technology and the Creative Spirit in Political Science," *op. cit.*, pp. 6–9. See also Beard, "Political Science," in Wilson Gee (ed.), *Research in the Social Sciences*, New York, 1929, pp. 288 ff.

[38] The academic environment has "not made for venturesome explorations, with their terrible risks of error, failure, ridicule, and futility." Since educational institutions must maintain the respect of their benefactors,

obstacle to creativity, though, lay in the values of the discipline itself. Here, scientism was partially to blame. The kind of research it "praised and patronized" led to "monoculous" studies and accumulations of data "on detailed problems with reference to specific practical ends." It also led to the neglect of "venturesome judgments," broad interests, and concern with "large matters of policy." In his opinion,

research under scientific formulas in things mathematically measurable or logically describable leaves untouched a vast array of driving social forces for which such words as conviction, faith, hope, loyalty, and destiny are pale symbols—yielding to the analysis of no systematists.

The imaginative deductive process of the poet and artist is as necessary to the creative spirit as the inductive method of "microcosmic" research.

Whatever Beard's original sympathy for certain aspects of scientism, and his initial reactions suggest a somewhat open mind,[39] the notion of a morally neutral political science struck him as preposterous. Convinced that "there can be no great creative work in political science without ethics,"[40] he was soon ridiculing "the passionless pursuit of passionless truth—the naive performance popular in certain quarters of the academic world where inquirers do not inquire into the nature of inquirers and seek to discover how they got that way."[41] He became equally hostile to the methodological innovations of the new politics, rejecting them in favor of the historicism he had earlier decried. The historical method, he wrote in 1934, "is the only approach open to the human mind." In the final analysis, man can "speculate only in

---

businessmen and politicians, a college professor who challenges the established verities is considered disloyal and "lacking in the qualities of a gentleman." Beyond this, academic practices such as heavy teaching responsibilities, and the lack of support for political research, are "detrimental to creative thinking."

[39] Beard, in Gee (ed.), *op. cit.*, indicated his belief that while "no science of politics is possible, or if possible desirable," nonetheless "the scientific method is highly useful" in dealing with certain kinds of political problems.

[40] *Committee on Policy*, Appendix I, *op. cit.*, p. 29.

[41] Beard, book review, *APSR*, vol. 27 (1933), p. 118.

terms of the things he knows—things that have come out of the past."[42]

By the early 1930's everything there was to say for and against a science of politics had been pretty well said, over and over again. By then, too, the profession had apparently had its fill of the subject. To the extent that the *Review* reflected the interests of the membership, this was definitely the case. Whereas almost every volume from 1921–1932 carried some discussion of the pros and cons of scientism, from 1933–1940 the issue almost disappeared from its pages. But the armistice, if such it was, proved only temporary.

THE COURSE OF SCIENTISM, 1921–1945

The scientistic drive in the middle years is usually dated from Merriam's aforementioned 1921 article. Its course thereafter fell roughly into three periods. The first was one of growing momentum which reached its zenith by the end of the decade and then quickly receded. An event that conveniently, if tardily, marks this change in climate was the Association's grant, in December, 1930, of sweeping authority to a reconstituted Committee on Policy headed by Thomas H. Reed. Scientism's nadir (quiescence might be a better term), the second period, continued pretty much throughout the 1930's. It is impossible to give a definite date for the beginning of the third period, but a renewed interest in a scientific politics is evident as World War II approached its end.

Merriam's critique had a predictable result: he was appointed chairman of a committee to study methods of improving political inquiry. This group, the Committee on Political Research, came up with a series of recommendations which led, immediately, to the several National Conferences on the Science of Politics (1923–25) and, ultimately, to the founding of the Social Science Research Council. All the characteristics of the scientism of the 1920's, its zeal, aspirations, strengths, and weaknesses, are epitomized by the three National Conferences. Slighted in the literature

[42] Beard, "The Historical Approach to the New Deal," *APSR,* vol. 28 (1934), p. 12.

of our day, these heavily attended meetings were a landmark in the discipline's intellectual evolution.

The central purpose of the first Conference, and of those which followed, was "to investigate the possibility of developing and employing more scientific methods for testing the theories and hypotheses of current political science." Discussions at the Conference would "therefore be devoted almost entirely to problems of technique and methodology."[43] But this was not a concern with methodology, or even with science, for its own sake. The official spokesman for all three conferences was Arnold Bennett Hall, and his remarks leave little question that the participants sought, at least initially, an instrumental "science of politics" capable of effectively coping with "pressing problems in the field of politics and administration."[44] Society was faced with issues requiring "immediate action"; officials were compelled to make "decisions of great public importance . . . without adequate knowledge of the facts and theories that are involved." Small wonder, said Hall, "that legislative and administrative action is too frequently the result of guess-work and speculation rather than of precise knowledge and scientifically determined principles."

The solution was as clear to Hall as it had been to Plato— "the whole scheme of governmental activity requires a body of scientific political principles for even reasonable efficiency and success." Patently, it was "the function of political science to provide this science of politics."[45]

To agree on "the great need of the hour" was one thing, to accomplish it another. Each of the approximately 100 persons

43 *APSR*, vol. 17 (1923), pp. 463–64. An earlier statement, along the same lines, appears in *APSR*, vol. 17 (1923), p. 268.

44 Hall wrote the introduction to each of the three Conference Reports, *APSR*, vol. 18 (1924), pp. 119 ff.; vol. 19 (1925), pp. 104–09; and vol. 20 (1926), pp. 124–26. There is the possibility that Hall's opinions were not shared by his colleagues but this seems unlikely. First, there was no published objection to his interpretation of the Conference's goals. Second, Merriam and those who followed him were themselves committed to the notion of an applied science of politics. Third, there is not much indication in the initial Conference reports of an interest in science for its own sake.

45 *APSR*, vol. 18 (1924), p. 119. A year later, after a pessimistic survey of world conditions, he declared that "the hope of the future [of mankind] seems to lie in a continuous and insistent struggle to devise a technique for the power-controlling sciences that will be adequate to the tremendous problems of modern life." *APSR*, vol. 19 (1925), pp. 109–10.

(annual Association meetings then drew perhaps 150 members) who attended the first National Conference at Madison, Wisconsin, in September 1923, was assigned to one of eight subject-matter "round tables." Some of the round tables focused on practical governmental concerns (i.e., public finance, efficiency ratings, and nominating methods); two dealt with more general aspects of a science of politics, one with psychology and politics, the other with political statistics.[46] Each panel was given two tasks. First, to formulate the outstanding problems in its area of interest; then, to indicate "the methods by which the objective evidence" bearing upon these problems "could be secured and accurately interpreted."[47]

This explicit assignment notwithstanding, progress came slowly. As Hall himself confessed, "during the first two days of the session the groups seemed unable to visualize their problems," manifesting an "impulse to get away from the question of method and to stray into the field of general prudence, opinion, and speculation." Subsequently, matters improved as the conferees came to grips with actual research problems.[48] Enough enthusiasm was generated, in any event, so that those attending the Conference voted unanimously to hold another meeting a year later.

The Second National Conference on the Science of Politics met in Chicago in 1924. It was attended by about the same number of participants, organized in much the same manner, and voiced the same confidence that "the need of placing political science upon a really scientific basis will be obvious to everyone." Though the basis for the judgment is not readily apparent, the

[46] Interestingly enough, a projected ninth panel on the formulation and testing of "political reason" failed to materialize, though listed on the original Conference agenda.

[47] "Reports of the National Conference on the Science of Politics," APSR, vol. 18 (1924), p. 120.

[48] For example, the panel on "psychology and political science" pondered the applicability to political research of various psychological tests developed by Binet, Pressy, Hart, Moore, Achilles, Cohs, and Downey, as well as the general implications of the work of Darwin, Galton, Wundt, Ebbinghaus, Jung, and Freud. As rapporteur for this panel, Charles F. Merriam declared that "it is believed that significant advances were made toward more scientific study of traits of human nature underlying political action, and the processes that in reality constitute government. From a continuation of such efforts genuine progress in the study of politics is likely to be made." Ibid., p. 125.

participants rated the Conference a "marked improvement" over its predecessor and scheduled another gathering for 1925.

New York City was the locale for the Third National Conference. Many of the same persons were again present and essentially the same organizational structure was employed. Now, however, there were ten rather than eight round tables. Political statistics disappeared as a separate problem area, perhaps in obedience to the Second Conference edict that "every round table needed the presence of both a psychologist and a statistician,"[49] and new panels were added on municipal administration, regional planning, and political parties. Now, too, some groups were able to consider empirical studies which had been prepared in the intervening two years[50] and to move beyond the preceding general discussions of problems and methods. Enough seems to have been accomplished to justify the expectation of additional conferences. Hall's introduction to the Report for the Third Conference expressed his hope for funds that would make it possible, at future meetings, to assign a psychologist and a statistician as consultants to each round table —and, where necessary, a biologist, an economist, a psychiatrist, a neurologist, etc., as well. The money was not forthcoming and the Third Conference turned out to be the last.

What did the three National Conferences on the Science of Politics accomplish? Hall's own assessment had a bittersweet tone. The meetings were productive and helpful but "concrete results" could not be "definitely stated." However, a "new impetus" was given to the "drive toward objectivity" which "in the minds of many, constitutes the chief hope for the future of the science."[51]

[49] *APSR,* vol. 19 (1925), p. 107.

[50] At the public law round table, Isidor Loeb presented a statistical analysis of Supreme Court decisions from 1914 to 1924. Loeb found "that there were twenty-eight cases involving due process of law, where the results were clearly favorable or unfavorable to labor. Fifteen of these were by a unanimous court and thirteen by a divided court. Of the unanimous decisions, thirteen were regarded as favorable to labor, two unfavorable to labor. In the thirteen divided decisions, three justices voted every time they participated on the side favored by labor, and one voted every time for the side opposed by labor." Rinehart Swenson also reported on a quantitative analysis of anti-trust cases. All present agreed that the results of these inquiries were significant and that more elaborate studies should be encouraged. *APSR,* vol. 20 (1926), pp. 127–34.

[51] *APSR,* vol. 20 (1926), p. 125.

This may seem a strange conclusion when one remembers that the Conferences had as their original goal a political science able to cope with the problems of a democratic society. Yet it reflects, inadvertently or otherwise, the rapidly shifting emphasis from applied to pure science.

Perhaps the Conferences served their greatest purpose in affording the opportunity for mutual encouragement, exhortation, and rededication needed for the survival, let alone the success, of any crusade. Attended by many of the discipline's leading figures, the Conferences also gave the stamp of professional respectability to scientism.[52] They undoubtedly provided a better springboard for the science of politics movement than the more traditionally organized APSA meetings.[53] It may well be that one reason for abandoning the Conferences was the feeling that their work could be carried on reasonably well at the profession's regular annual gatherings. In fact, some of the subjects considered at the Conferences had begun to appear as topics for discussion at Association conventions before the National Conferences had run their course.

The next several years witnessed the high tide of optimism. In 1926, the members of an Association round table on electoral problems agreed that "there are few limitations to the application of the scientific method in the field of the social sciences . . . even if the experimental method cannot be applied (and this may be possible in the future)."[54] 1927 brought both the publication of Catlin's *Science and Method of Politics* and the assurance from a leading political scientist-social psychologist that soon "it will be possible for political scientists to cease considering their field as one of formal description and legalistic philosophy, and regard it as a *natural science.*"[55] And, in February of 1928, the *Review*

[52] The *Review* gave the Conference Reports full coverage, each being allotted about 50 pages. *APSR,* vol. 18 (1924), pp. 119–66; *APSR,* vol. 19 (1925), pp. 104–62; and *APSR,* vol. 20 (1926), pp. 124–70.

[53] Apparently there was some concern that the National Conferences would adversely affect the annual Association meetings. One of the "notes" announcing the First Conference carried the reassurance that "it is not expected that the conference will in any way supersede the annual meetings of the American Political Science Association, but that it will supplement these meetings by furnishing an opportunity for a more leisurely and intensive discussion of political topics." *APSR,* vol. 17 (1923), p. 639.

[54] *APSR,* vol. 21 (1927), p. 394, Louise Overacker, rapporteur.

[55] Floyd Allport, "Political Science and Psychology," in W. F. Ogburn (ed.), *The Social Sciences and Their Interrelations,* Boston, 1927, p. 277.

carried Munro's sanguine presidential address, mentioned above.

Not all the energy of those with scientist leanings went into dialectics. Substantive studies in the "new" style began to appear by 1924. Three noteworthy books bear that date. Holcombe's *Political Parties of Today* classified congressional districts by region, economic characteristics, and degree of urbanization, and then applied these categorizations to the analysis of American party politics. Stuart A. Rice, a political sociologist who played an active part in the science of politics movement, brought out his *Farmers and Workers in American Politics,* a volume widely cited in the political science literature of the day. He employed both Pearson's "grades" and product moment correlations in relating aggregate voting patterns to demographic and ecological data. More important, Rice developed indices of cohesion and likeness, the first advances in legislative roll-call analysis since Lowell's pioneering work some two decades earlier.

Also published in 1924 was the Merriam and Gosnell *Non-Voting, Causes and Methods of Control.* The significance of this book would be hard to overestimate. The problem itself was one about which little of a systematic character was known and the study provided a means of introducing a bevy of young graduate students to field research. More to the immediate point, though, it was based upon survey rather than aggregate data. Although the sampling methods utilized would not pass muster today, they were quite sophisticated for their time. Interviewers were trained for their assignments, the schedules were carefully structured, and Hollerith cards and counter-sorters were used in data processing. With *Non-Voting,* the Chicago department took a giant step toward establishing itself as the national center for the scientific study of politics, a position it was to hold during much of the middle period.

In the half dozen succeeding years, several other major scientistic studies reached fruition. Outstanding among them were: Gosnell's classic "experiment" in stimulating voting, reported in *Getting Out the Vote* (1927); Lasswell's *Propaganda Technique in the World War* (1927); Rice's *Quantitative Methods in Politics* (1928); and Leonard D. White's pioneering survey of community attitudes toward governmental employees, *The Prestige Value of Public Employment in Chicago* (1929). Finally, in 1930, came Lasswell's *Psychopathology and Politics,* the first in a brilliant trilogy (the others were *World Politics and Personal Insecurity* (1935) and *Politics: Who Gets What, When, How* (1936) which did so much to establish their author's reputation as the discipline's most creative figure.

The *American Political Science Review* also reflected, to some degree, the science of politics movement. Notes and articles which can broadly be classified as "science oriented"[56] constituted 7.3 per cent of the 190 items published in the *Review* from 1921–25. For the next five years, the percentage was 13.7 per cent of 241 articles and notes. Despite this increase, enough such articles were run in other journals[57] to warrant the suspicion that the *Review* was not overly hospitable to contributions in the scientific mode.

By the end of the 1920's, a sharp change in intellectual climate was under way. We have already suggested that the Association's grant of power to Thomas H. Reed and his Committee on Policy in December of 1930 can be regarded as symbolizing this shift. There is considerable other evidence of an altered outlook. The programs for the annual meetings testify that interest in science and methodology gave way to emphasis on citizenship training, political education, and related matters. In the mid- and late-1920's, the *Review* frequently noted books by non-political scientists dealing with methodology, statistics, and psychology. By the early 1930's, any mention of this kind was a rarity. Scientistic[58] items in the journal fell from 13.7 per cent in 1926–30 to 9.5 per cent for 1931–5 (26 of 273). As the early

[56] An item was considered scientistic if it fell into one of five categories: general discussion of scientism; discussion of particular quantitative techniques; discussion of analytic theory considered by its author to be appropriate for guiding empirical investigation; report of substantive research employing quantitative methods more elaborate than percentages and raw counting; report of substantive research which employed raw counting or simple percentages in an analytic rather than in a merely descriptive fashion. One of the authors and a graduate assistant independently classified all articles and notes in the above manner. In the few cases where there was a difference of opinion about the propriety of including an item in one of the above categories, the benefit of the doubt was given to scientism and the item included in the scientistic count.

[57] Some rough impression of the substantial number of such items that appeared in other journals can be gained from Harold F. Gosnell's, "Statisticians and Political Scientists," *APSR*, vol. 27 (1933), pp. 392–403.

[58] For basis of classification see above, fn. 56.

128

1930's unfolded, American political scientists were increasingly absorbed by a myriad of pressing economic and political problems. Intellectually and emotionally, the dominant impulse was toward action and commitment, rather than objectivity and scientific research.

By 1940, though, there could be heard the first rumblings of a renewed discontent in the profession. Complaining that political scientists had not expanded the scope of their studies "beyond what it was at the end of the nineteenth century," Benjamin Lippincott attributed the shortcomings of the profession to two factors.[59] First, there was a political bias. "As members of the middle class," he charged, "especially as important members, political scientists have been content to think almost entirely in terms of its framework. They have accepted as all but final the assumptions of capitalist democracy."[60] Second, there was the general commitment to empiricism and the consequent minimization of "logic, reflection, and imagination." Too many political scientists believed that the "facts will speak for themselves" and that "preconceived theories or ideas about facts are not only unnecessary but positively dangerous."[61] Political science would have to become aware of and break away from its ideological attachments; it would have to develop the *systematic theory* which it had so far eschewed.

Three years later, the cannonading began in earnest. In an article entitled "A Challenge to Political Scientists,"[62] William F. Whyte charged that because of "middle-class prejudice" and "unquestioning acceptance of the democratic ideology," few in the profession had truly attempted "to probe into the processes of politics." If political scientists hoped to advance—and his language as well as his ideas were prophetic—"they should leave ethics to the philosopher and concern themselves directly with the description and analysis of political behavior."[63]

This attack was soon broadened. In 1944 Robert D. Leigh

[59] "The Bias of American Political Science," *Journal of Politics,* vol. 2 (1940), pp. 125–39.

[60] *Ibid.,* p. 135.

[61] *Ibid.,* p. 130.

[62] *APSR,* vol. 37 (1943), pp. 692–97.

[63] *Ibid.,* p. 697.

warned that the meager "quantity of scientific content accumulated in our field" left political scientists open to the "danger of being exposed as quacks."[64] Political science was deficient as a discipline; it had serious shortcomings as a profession. Without naming those whom he had in mind, Leigh wrote that

I should like to look forward to the day when the social science professions would have a code of intellectual conduct and would visit discipline, disapproval, or ostracism on those who would bring the integrity of the guild into disrepute by prostitution of their talents for quick gain, notoriety, or unscientific reformism.[65]

The same issue of the *Review* carried a statement from the Research Panel on Comparative Government describing its dissatisfaction with the existing structure of the field and its search for more rewarding concepts and techniques.[66]

Whyte's proposal for a normatively neutral political science was immediately attacked by John H. Hallowell.[67] Tracing the notion of a positivistic discipline back to Catlin and Munro, Hallowell argued that political science could not avoid making value judgments. A "neutral" political science, he declared, was neither feasible nor desirable. A report of the Panel on Political Theory reveals that battle lines, all too familiar, were again beginning to form. The panel was divided, its chairman confessed, between those who supported, and those who rejected, the possibility of "value-free" inquiry. Accompanying the report was a statement by Ernest S. Griffith expressing the conviction that greater attention should be given to concepts and to "conceptual *systems*."

The situation within American political science as the middle years ended was described best of all by the Association's Committee on Research. The Committee's troubled report spoke of "the uneasiness, sharpening at times into profound dissatisfaction, which pervades our profession in its more introspective moods."[68]

[64] "The Educational Function of Social Scientists," *APSR*, vol. 38 (1944), pp. 531–39.

[65] *Ibid.*, p. 534.

[66] Karl Loewenstein, "Report of the Research Panel on Comparative Government," *ibid.*, pp. 540–48.

[67] "Politics and Ethics," *ibid.*, 1944, pp. 639–55.

[68] *APSR*, vol. 39 (1945), pp. 148–64.

While it was not possible to guess the direction in which the discipline would move, the Committee felt that one prediction could be safely ventured—"The end of the present war seems likely to be [a] turning point for the American Political Science Association, and especially for the research activities of its membership." The Committee's expectations, or forebodings, were to be amply fulfilled.

THE ACHIEVEMENTS OF SCIENTISM

Now the inevitable question: What did the scientism of the middle years accomplish?

To begin, the post-1921 years witnessed the publication of quite a few first-rate substantive research reports by the scienticists. We have already considered some of the more important books and monographs. Others include: Quincy Wright's, *The Causes of War and the Conditions of Peace* (1935) and his monumental *A Study of War* (1942); Carroll Hill Wooddy's, *The Case of Frank L. Smith* (1931); Harold F. Gosnell's *Negro Politicians* (1935), and his sadly neglected magnum opus, *Machine Politics: Chicago Model* (1937); and the Lasswell and Dorothy Blumenstock, *World Revolutionary Propaganda* (1939).

Another consequence of the new politics movement was the growing competence developed in the newer social science research methods by a small group of younger scholars, largely, but not exclusively, Chicago trained. While use of time series, partial correlations, factor analysis, and tests of significance was hardly common, by the late 1930's it was no longer a rare phenomenon. From 1921–1930, four articles and notes employing fairly sophisticated statistical techniques had appeared in the *Review*. During the next decade the journal ran 16 such items. Quite a few others by political scientists appeared elsewhere. Although political scientists in the middle years tended to borrow their techniques from other disciplines, there were instances in which they themselves made contributions. One may cite here Herman Beyle's work with cluster blocs (*The Identification of Attribute-Cluster-Blocs* [1931]) and the advances in content analysis attributable to Lasswell.

In the third place, there is a close temporal relationship between the drive toward scientism and what appears to be a major reordering of the discipline's hierarchy of values. In 1914 an Association committee ranked research training as the fourth of the "services" to be performed by departments of political science.[69] Fifteen years later, even the action-oriented Committee on Policy saw things differently, ranking research as the most important function of the discipline, publication second, and "instruction, including training for citizenship and for the public service," last.[70] Of course, this change in outlook might have transpired even if there had been no science of politics movement. Still, an emphasis on research was one of the scientism's most driving commitments and the sequence of events makes it reasonable to infer that scientism accelerated, if it did not actually inspire, a changed outlook in the discipline's hierarchy of values.

Fourth, a significant change was discernible in the character of much non-scientistic research. After 1925 or so, the kind of realism previously advocated by Lowell, Bryce, and Wilson won fairly wide acceptance. Prior to the National Conferences on the Science of Politics, *Review* pieces dealing with foreign elections did not differ greatly from those found in newspapers; subsequently, the authors had usually observed first-hand the campaigns they reported, interviewed some of the key figures, treated the issues in more discerning fashion, and sought to account for the results in terms of the economic, social, and political interests of the electorate. Similar changes can be noted in discussions of administrative and legislative behavior, and of American elections at all levels. Little by little attention turned to the inner workings of the political system, to the forces which shaped the end result, and to the manner in which those influences were brought to bear.

The newer emphasis was reflected in a sizable collection of books and monographs. Representative of the better literature of this genre would be: Peter H. Odegard, *Pressure Politics, the Story of the Anti-saloon League* (1928); E. Pendleton Herring, *Group Representation Before Congress* (1929); Frederick L. Schuman, *International Politics* (1933); Roy V. Peel, *The Political Clubs of*

[69] See above fn. 69, pp. 82–83.
[70] Committee on Policy, *op. cit.,* p. 3.

132

New York City (1935); Elmer E. Schattschneider, *Politics, Pressures, and the Tariff* (1935); Walter R. Sharp, *The Government of the French Republic* (1936); Dayton D. McKean, *Pressures on the Legislature of New Jersey* (1938); and Avery Leiserson, *Administrative Regulation* (1942). There was, in fine, a gradual shift in interest from structure and policy to process.

Here again, we cannot demonstrate that the new politics brought about this more analytic, more process oriented, more realistic political science. But these were the kinds of changes advocated, if in piecemeal fashion, by the leading proponents of scientism. The chronology of events makes it plausible to credit the science of politics effort for some part of the speed with which these changes took place.

Finally, the scienticists of the middle years prepared the way for the behavioralism of the 1950's and 1960's. The close kinship between the two in spirit and objectives is a central reason for dealing with the post-1921 movement at such length. As later chapters will suggest, the discipline might have been spared a good deal of its recent trauma had the history of earlier decades been better remembered.

X
the
extra-scientific
responsibilities
of
political
scientists,
1921-1945

CHANGING IDEAS AND VALUES

*T*raining for democratic citizenship and public affairs, as well as personal participation in the shaping and execution of governmental policy, continued to be key areas of concern during the middle years. Two significant changes took place, though. In principle, this type of activity was downgraded in importance, compared to research. Concurrently, the rise of scientism, and especially that version which stressed objectivity and knowledge for knowledge's sake, compelled political scientists to ponder the latent incompatibility of their several undertakings. For the first time there emerged a school of thought which argued that the discipline should abandon its extra-scientific activities and concentrate on building the systematic body of knowledge implicit in the term "science."

The line here was not necessarily drawn between the friends and the foes of the new politics. Merriam himself was greatly concerned with civic education, urged more rather than less involvement in matters of "political prudence," and sought a political science frankly dedicated to serving the needs of a democratic society. Few of his colleagues were prepared to wash their hands completely of practical matters.

Whatever the original differences on this score, historical events rather than philosophic doctrine determined the foci of attention. How could political scientists remain aloof when the Great Depression and the New Deal were, respectively, threatening and reconstructing the political, social, and economic framework of the American system? Who could seriously advocate normative neutrality in the face of communism, fascism, and national socialism? And who, in good conscience, could preach objectivity or detachment after Pearl Harbor?

EDUCATION FOR CITIZENSHIP AND PUBLIC AFFAIRS

During this period political scientists voiced an increased devotion to the scholarly aspects of their enterprise. In all likelihood, however, the profession devoted no less of its energies to education for democracy and training for public affairs. Still, this was no longer the blithe, untroubled commitment of earlier decades. Scientism may have had relatively little impact upon what most political scientists did but, the literature testifies, it inevitably fostered an uncomfortable awareness of the conflicts among their several roles. The literature also testifies to the manner in which the profession, doubts notwithstanding, pursued these two traditional tasks.

EDUCATION FOR DEMOCRATIC CITIZENSHIP

The corrosive consequences of the scientistic mood can be seen as early as 1922 in an Association committee's almost heretical declaration that "it is not the function of a [high school] course in Civics to carry on any form of social, economic or political propaganda."[1] The chairman of this committee, we should add, was William B. Munro, a champion of the "purist" position.

[1] *APSR*, vol. 16 (1922), p. 117.

Similar expressions followed. In 1926, a *Review* article proposed that the introductory political science course be designed to challenge the "validity of the thought process and opinions of the student with respect to all social phenomena and . . . indicate how much of the political *credo* of the average man has no rational quality so far as his relation to it is concerned."[2] A year later, a panel on the teaching of democracy questioned the previously sacrosanct proposition that the purpose of such a course was the "development of a better citizenship."[3]

Shortly thereafter, another discussion elicited the opinion that "it can scarcely be [the function of the political scientist] to teach any brand of 'citizenship' or 'Americanization' or any other -ization or -ism."[4] Munro sounded the same theme in his 1928 presidential speech. "All around us," he declared,

gigantic campaigns of civic education are being carried on, by organizations of every kind, every bit of it inspired by the hope of improving the attitude of the citizen toward his government, and especially his sense of civic duty. A large part of this effort is based upon the naive assumption that you only exhort people with sufficient earnestness they can be induced to accept irrational ideas embalmed in the rhetoric of patriotism.[5]

Brave new opinions, but surely those of a minority. A more orthodox viewpoint was expressed by the Committee on Policy:

In a democratic state, the results of research in matters of government, politics, and administration must be widely disseminated if they are to eventuate in action. Unless men and women are trained to comprehend and receive the results of research in these fields, such results can never be practically applied. Adequate instruction in school, colleges, and universities can alone prepare for the formation of sound public opinion, and only trained public servants can properly employ the results of research in the service of the community.[6]

A Committee survey disclosed that at only one American college in four was "any . . . course in political science" a prerequisite

[2] *APSR,* vol. 20 (1926), p. 425.

[3] *APSR,* vol. 21 (1927), p. 403.

[4] *APSR,* vol. 22 (1928), p. 962.

[5] "Physics and Politics," *APSR,* vol. 22 (1928), pp. 1–11, at p. 7.

[6] *Report,* 1930, p. 3.

for graduation,[7] an omission compounded by the failure of most institutions to offer political science instruction geared to the needs of prospective teachers. The Committee urged prompt measures to correct a condition wherein "the influence of political science on the education of youth for citizenship is at a minimum."[8]

Reed, a lifelong partisan of better minds for better government, used the Committee's *First Annual Report* to argue the urgency of "genuine progress" toward "effective citizenship training." Before another year had passed, Reed and his supporters managed to get the Association involved in what he called "the greatest movement for adult civic education that our country has yet seen,"[9] *i.e.,* a national radio program entitled "You and Your Government." The program, which lasted four years, eventually spanned some two hundred broadcasts.[10] The Association's dedication to civic education was demonstrated by recurrent statements from its sub-Committee on Civic Education and, more convincingly, by the profession's willingness to serve sans honorarium when the "greatest movement" eventually ran out of funds.

As the international outlook worsened, political scientists found themselves in an increasingly awkward situation. A 1940 Round Table on Teaching Problems confessed to "some little disagreement" among its members "concerning the desirability of deliberately basing our teaching on democratic philosophy." Acknowledging that "in time of great danger *some* modicum of agreement is necessary," the panelists reluctantly agreed that "outer

[7] *Ibid.,* Appendix VII, p. 127.

[8] *Ibid.,* p. 12.

[9] *APSR,* vol. 26 (1932), p. 147.

[10] The broadcasts, which began on April 5, 1932, were organized in the form of "series," each dealing with a general problem area. Some of the series titles were "Government in a Depression," "Constructive Economy in State and Local Government," "Trends in Government," "The Forty-four Legislatures of 1935," and "A New Deal in Local Government." The program, at first a half-hour long, was aired, fittingly enough, between Amos and Andy at 8:00 P.M., Eastern Standard Time, and the Goldbergs at 9:00 P.M. In February, 1934, it was reduced to fifteen minutes, with Thomas H. Reed assuming the duties of announcer and moderator. A "Listener's Handbook," published by the University of Chicago Press in 1934, sold some 18,000 copies. We are indebted to Dr. Evron M. Kirkpatrick for this and other information contained in the unpublished "A History of the American Political Science Association's Activities in the Field of Secondary Education in Government."

limits must be established within which the open-mindedness of liberalism is allowed to operate."[11] Peter H. Odegard, soon to head the Association, came to the same uneasy conclusion. While insistent that "as teachers we political scientists are necessarily critics of the state," he recognized the duty "to instruct those who come under our tutelage, not only in the structure and mechanics of politics and administration but also in the fundamental principles upon which modern democracy rests."[12] Remaining doubts were resolved by the events of December 7, 1941. Not long thereafter, the Committee on War Time Changes in the Political Science Curriculum frankly accepted the profession's obligation to assist in the war effort.[13]

TRAINING FOR THE PUBLIC SERVICE

Another activity which the Committee on Policy wanted the Association to supervise was the education (and placement) of persons for the public service.[14] After surveying current "training for the Public Service," the Committee, with characteristic wit, wrote that "this report has been brief, chiefly because it approximates the zoölogists famous chapter on the snakes in Ireland." Fewer than ten institutions were making "any real contribution to training young men and women for the service of the government— national, state or local—except as ordinary professional training helps to fit them for governmental posts."[15]

One reason so little was being done (the Committee's remarks were prescient) was that there seemed to be a "lack of connection between taking the training and getting the job."[16] A second reason, we might add, was the relative immaturity of public

[11] *APSR*, vol. 35 (1941), pp. 327–29.

[12] "The Political Scientist in the Democratic Service State," *Journal of Politics*, vol. 2 (1940), pp. 157–158.

[13] The Committee warned, though, that political scientists should guard against becoming "mere channels for the dissemination of war propaganda." *APSR*, vol. 36 (1942), p. 1142.

[14] Above, pp. 98–99.

[15] *Appendix IX*, pp. 174, 179.

[16] Below, p. 141.

administration as a formal area of academic specialization.[17] Leonard D. White's classic text,[18] which did so much to structure the field, was just beginning to make an impact. As public administration gained professional respectability over the next decade, more and more institutions launched formal training programs.

PERSONAL INTEREST IN PUBLIC AFFAIRS

From the beginning, Merriam envisaged the "science of politics" as a "policy science." Political scientists, he felt, should be concerned with, and involved in, public issues. By the early 1930's practically every leading exponent of the new politics had come around to the same position. Among the traditionally oriented practitioners, of course, there had rarely been any question about the propriety of such an interest.

We have already mentioned the attention devoted to these matters by the *Review*. As indicated above, the Committee on Policy sought to encourage still greater involvement in public affairs. Charles A. Beard proudly reported that political scientists had played a central role in the reorganization of many state and municipal governments, and that Association members had been involved in every important study of state and federal administration undertaken the previous two decades.[19] Other professional journals, convention round tables, committee reports, and presidential speeches sounded the same theme. Peter Odegard called on his colleagues to exercise "leadership of the highest order" in the "engineering of consent" for the expansion of the "promotional, conservation, and direct service activities of the state"[20]; President William Anderson, listing the "obligations" of political science, gave first place to the preservation of democracy and second

[17] The Committee remarked that most research in public administration was still being conducted by public and private organizations outside the academic community. *Report*, 1930, p. 4. Academicians played an important role, however, in the work done by these organizations.

[18] *Introduction to the Study of Public Administration*, New York, Macmillan, 1926.

[19] *Appendix I*, "Conditions Favorable to Creative Work in Political Science," p. 25.

[20] *Journal of Politics*, vol. 2, *loc. cit.*

to "direct service to the government"[21]; and an Association Committee proposed that "in making new appointments, political science departments should give consideration not only to the scholarship and teaching qualifications of candidates under consideration, but also to their interest and aptitude for contacts with government officials."[22]

This absorption with civic education and public affairs continued undiminished as the era closed. In 1945, after consulting 121 "leading political scientists," the Social Science Research Council's Committee on Government reported that most of them identified some aspect of public policy when asked which aspect of the discipline needed further research. That same year there was an article by Pendleton Herring limning the future of political science. The "pressure of events and the spirit of the times," Herring predicted, would combine to "foster the tendency of students of government to preach democratic values and to promote specific policies." He hoped, however, that the profession would not altogether ignore "a third objective"—"the need for a better understanding of political behavior."[23]

NON-ACADEMIC EMPLOYMENT

Naturally enough, most new Ph.D.'s looked forward to college and university posts. Unfortunately, the need for new instructors lagged behind doctoral output. Even before the depression struck, the "forty to fifty new Ph.D.'s each year were more than the market could absorb."[24] After 1929 the situation worsened rapidly. Not only was it difficult to place new men but the Association received an "extraordinary number of calls for help from older teachers who have been laid off for more or less obscure reasons on the plea of lack of funds."[25]

The New Deal did much to redress the balance between supply and demand. Hundreds of older political scientists served with one governmental unit or another; hundreds of younger

21 *APSR*, vol. 37 (1943), p. 9.
22 *APSR*, vol. 35 (1941), p. 340.
23 *APSR*, vol. 39 (1945), p. 764.
24 *APSR*, vol. 28 (1934), p. 752.
25 *APSR*, vol. 25 (1931), pp. 914–15.

political scientists went into the public service either permanently or until a suitable academic post became available. A fairly exhaustive catalog of New Deal agencies could be compiled from the *Review*'s "News and Notes" items reporting the occupational comings and goings of members.

Recovery gave way to rearmament. Between the manpower demands of the wartime agencies and the requirements of the armed forces, political science, as did the rest of the nation, enjoyed full employment. Accepting the view that the political scientist had a patriotic obligation "to demonstrate that his training was a profitable investment,"[26] the profession marshalled its energies in the national effort. A 17-page *Review* tabulation, admittedly incomplete, gives some idea of the diverse activities in which its members were engaged.[27]

Political scientists learned two chastening, if in the long run salutary, lessons during the war. They discovered that there was a profound difference between their ideas of government, politics, and administration and the actuality thereof, especially under emergency conditions. This discovery, recounted at some length in the literature, undoubtedly contributed to the post-war emphasis upon describing "real" behavior. Equally disconcerting was the realization that political science expertise was not a very marketable commodity, not even in the public service itself. Personnel officers manifested a deplorable lack of interest in applicants identified as "political scientists." One reason, a charitable commentator suggested, was that the officers "do not know what political science is." Another reason, most students later agreed, was that political scientists were generally not trained in statistics or accounting, that they usually had no substantive field competence (*e.g.* labor, finance, transportation, production, etc.), and that they ordinarily had little prior experience in, or with, governmental agencies. In short, they simply "did not get around enough." An attempt to correct these shortcomings would be made in post-1945 graduate programs.[28]

[26] *APSR*, vol. 38 (1944), p. 124.
[27] *APSR*, vol. 39 (1945), pp. 555–74.
[28] *APSR*, vol. 36 (1942), pp. 932–33.

*T*he two decades since the end of the Second World War have been years of great change for American political science. There was a tremendous increase in the number of practitioners, graduate departments, annual doctoral output, and scholarly journals. Political science became increasingly professionalized and academized. There were even signs that the discipline's intellectual parochialism had finally begun to give way.

Nor does the list of major developments stop here. One cannot overlook the near-complete restructuring of the American Political Science Association, a redistribution of doctoral output between the more and less prestigious departments, the rise and fall of a major attempt to engage the profession in training for democratic politics, the creation of the Inter-University Consortium for Political Research, and the decision by the National Science Foundation to admit political science to the elect family of "behavioral" sciences. Most important of all, these twenty-some years witnessed a bitter battle over the issue of behavioralism itself, a controversy which rocked the discipline as has no other in its past.

Perhaps a decade or so hence some of the developments mentioned above, or others also to be discussed in the pages that follow, will emerge as historic turning points. What we treat here as a single period may then be viewed as falling into two or more stages in the discipline's evolution. It is possible, too, that political scientists a quarter-century from now may see the 1945–66 span as simply the continuation of a drive for scientism which began in the early 1920's and continued, after faltering in the 1930's, through the post-1945 years. Such possibilities notwithstanding, our perspective for the events of the recent past is so foreshortened that, for present purposes, we deem it safest to treat them collectively under the rubric of "contemporary period."

In discussing this era, we employ the schema used in treating previous periods. Chapter 11 deals with professional growth and development, Chapter 12 with political science as a learned discipline, and Chapter 13 with the profession's extra-scientific responsibilities and activities.

144

XI
recent
growth
and
development

EXPANSION

A few statistics graphically illustrate the phenomenal growth of American political science since 1945. The American Political Science Association had 4,000 members in 1946; in two decades membership soared to 14,000. The number of political science departments has risen commensurately. There were about 466 independent departments in 1960;[1] today, the total is close to 500. At the rate colleges are being founded, and hitherto combined departments split asunder, another fifty will probably be added within the next five years.

Equally important has been the transformation of under-graduate into graduate departments. Between 1953 and 1962, according to an American Council on Education study, there were 64 institutions which granted one or more doctorates in political science. In the last five years, a half dozen universities have awarded their first Ph.D.'s and perhaps another half dozen are now grooming their maiden batch of candidates. At a conservative estimate, there are probably now some 75 political science departments with doctoral programs.

[1] There were an additional 320 departments in which political science was combined with some other discipline, "Political Science as a Discipline. A Statement by the Committee on Standards of Instruction of the American Political Science Association," *APSR,* vol. 56 (1962), pp. 417–21 at 418.

As the national Association has grown, so have its regional offspring proliferated. Prior to World War II, there had been founded the Midwest Conference of Political Scientists, the Northeastern Political Science Association, and the Southern Political Science Association. After 1945, the *Review* reports the creation of numerous state associations and of such larger organizations as the Western Political Science Association, the New England Political Science Association, the Pacific Northwest Political Science Association and, to the unconcealed delight of junketing APSA presidents, a Puerto Rican Political Science Association. Some of these offspring have proved quite feeble, if not moribund; others have demonstrated an impressive vitality and esprit de corps. Two of the new regional Associations founded journals—the *Western Political Quarterly* (1948) and the *Midwest Journal of Political Science* (1957)—which soon won places as respected outlets for scholarly writing. As the number of learned periodicals has increased, professional output, perhaps obeying a variant of Parkinson's Law, has kept pace. Editors report a ratio running as high as four or five to one between manuscripts submitted and those accepted.[2] Some of the latter, it must be confessed, suggest the operation of still another "law"—Gresham's.

The torrent of books produced by American political scientists affords another measure of growth. Although not all the items published come to the attention of the *Review,* given promotional slippage, its pages make possible a reasonably accurate estimate. In 1954, one of the first years for which data were readily available, some 500 new volumes were either formally reviewed or noted as "received." The annual total currently runs over the 1,000 mark. This formidable outpouring of literature, monographic and periodical alike, has undoubtedly encouraged, if it has not compelled, many political scientists to narrow their interests and to "specialize" in one or two sub-areas of the discipline.

With expansion, there has also occurred a quickening academization and professionalization of the discipline. At one time it will be recalled, college teachers constituted only a fraction of the Association's membership.[3] By 1920, the academics were in the majority; by the early 1960's they made up about 70 per cent of

[2] See below, pp. 155–56, fns. 22 and 24.

[3] Above, p. 55.

the profession. The recent demand for teaching staff, improved salaries, and comparatively modest opportunities for governmental employment have, if anything, accelerated this trend.

Academization has been acccompanied by a progressive professionalization of the discipline. The desirability of having a Ph.D. was widely recognized by the turn of the century. Since then, the dividing line between desirability and necessity has practically disappeared. Today the non-Ph.D. is almost automatically precluded from permanent appointment at a graduate department and as effectively barred from tenure at first or even second-rate colleges. In the public service, too, the doctorate has more and more become a requisite for advancement beyond a certain level.

Given this situation, it is hardly surprising that the incidence of Ph.D.'s among American political scientists has climbed steadily upward. For the entire Association (student members excluded), it went from slightly less than 50 per cent in 1953 to 55 per cent in 1964; for academics alone, from 70 per cent to 80 per cent; and for those of professorial rank the figure is now close to 90 per cent. By 1975, it would seem, all of us will be able to say, with becoming modesty, "just call me Mister."

THE AMERICAN POLITICAL SCIENCE ASSOCIATION

The present prosperous and flourishing state of the Association is of quite recent vintage. Anyone familiar with its state of health barely twenty years ago must then have viewed its condition with dismay and its future with foreboding. During and after the war years the Association experienced a prolonged budgetary crisis. The *Review* came under sharp attack. The organization was faced with a series of quasi-secessionist movements. There were recurrent and widespread complaints about control by an Establishment, about slack and inefficient management, and about the failure to provide meaningful services to the membership. Association committees sometimes functioned as semi-independent entities, if not actually divisive forces, and their performance did not always add to the discipline's reputation. On top of all this, the

147

profession was badly shaken by the discovery that its talents, skills, and knowledge commanded relatively scant regard among governmental personnel officers charged with staffing the war-time agencies.[4] With so lengthy a catalogue of tribulations to be covered, we can touch on each only briefly.

FINANCES

Many of the Association's troubles in the first post-1945 decade sprang from or were aggravated by precarious finances. Though membership held fairly constant during the war years, dues came in tardily or not at all, so that rising costs coincided neatly with declining revenues. Budgetary stringency led to a hand-to-mouth existence. It also produced—or worsened—severe organizational problems.

For one thing, it perpetuated the practice, already established by Reed's Committee on Policy,[5] of funding committee activities independently of the Association. Command of their own resources encouraged the free-wheeling inclinations of Association committees. At the same time, an empty treasury made it difficult for the President and the Executive Council to exercise effective control. In 1947, when President Gaus proposed a special session[6] of the Council "in order to promote better coordination and more adequate leadership in the work of the Association's numerous committees," he discovered that no money was available for such a meeting.[7] By default, administrative matters fell into the hands of the Managing Editor of the *Review* and the Secretary-Treasurer who split the records between them. Whatever the merits of this arrangement, it hardly provided a vigorous central direction.

Lastly, the paucity of funds made it nigh impossible to furnish the services normally expected of a professional organization. There was no staff to serve as liaison with the government, to press the interests of the Association before Congress and execu-

[4] Above, p. 141.

[5] Above, pp. 98–100.

[6] The one day per year on which the Executive Council met, i.e., the day before the annual meeting, was largely devoted to reports from the numerous regular and special Association committees.

[7] *APSR,* vol. 40 (1946), p. 349.

tive agencies, to secure research support, to arrange for the printing and release of documents, or to urge the desirability of using political scientists as consultants and advisers. Even the placement service left a good deal to be desired. In short, the members were getting less for their money than many felt they were entitled to expect.

Fortunately, as membership rose in the early 1950's, the Association's financial condition improved. Greater revenues from dues, supplemented by foundation grants, made possible the creation of a regular secretariat. This led, in turn, to better internal management, expanded services, and a more forceful representation of the profession in Washington. These changes, which coincided with a drastic overhaul and tightening up of the Association's "governmental" structure, did much to alleviate matters. By 1955 the worst was over. A decade later, the hard times of the post-1945 years had been forgotten by, or were unknown to, an increasingly youthful membership.

THE COMMITTEE SYSTEM

The imperial course pursued by Reed's Committee on Policy (1930–1935) demonstrated what could happen when the Association was unable or unwilling to keep a close rein on its committees. This warning notwithstanding, the situation was not corrected— and the bill of reckoning, with accumulated interest, was presented for payment in the mid- and late 1940's.

As already mentioned, part of the problem was the inability of the President and Executive Council to oversee the actual workings of the committees. These latter enjoyed, too, a curious status whereby their reports were "accepted" but not "endorsed" by the Executive Council. This permitted the Committees to do and say pretty much what they wanted under cover of the protest that their actions in no way committed the Association. Conditions being what they were, Association committees had to fend for themselves in securing research support. While few were successful in this quest, those that were tended to regard themselves as quasi-sovereign and to construe their mandate in latitudinarian manner. Under these circumstances, a committee's recommendations sometimes reflected little besides the opinions of its members. This

149

point was commonly not grasped by outsiders who mistakenly thought that Association committees necessarily spoke and acted for the parent body itself.[8]

Two reports which enhanced neither the public image nor the self-respect of the profession were financed and produced in precisely this fashion. One was *Research in Political Science* (1948), a collection of subcommittee reports submitted to the Committee on Research, and funded in large part by the Social Science Research Council. As its defenders hastened to observe, this volume was only a generation or so behind the times. The second was the jejune *Goals for Political Science* (1951) turned out (no other verb seems appropriate) by the Committee on the Advancement of Teaching and underwritten by a $10,000 Carnegie grant.

FORMAL ASSOCIATION STRUCTURE

The foregoing problems were compounded by, where they did not stem from, the Association's defective structure and the unsatisfactory way in which its business was conducted. Presidential powers were few and, with tenure limited to one year, incumbents barely had time to familiarize themselves with their duties. Neither the President nor the Executive Council was able to exercise more than pro forma supervision over the committees or over Association administration. Planning for the annual meetings was haphazard, their conduct occasionally no less so. Clerical functions, we have seen, were split between the *Review*'s Managing Editor and the organization's Secretary-Treasurer.

Casual and diffuse management went hand in hand with charges that the Association was controlled by an inner clique and that the rank-and-file had little real voice in the nomination and election of officers. In the minds of many, not only was the Establishment running matters but, added indignity, it was running them badly.

[8] The fortuitous conjunction between the 1945 report of the Association's Committee on Congress (under George Galloway) and the provisions of the 1946 Legislative Reorganization Act tempted other committees to come up with recommendations of equal "consequence." The report of the Committee on Political Parties, *Toward a More Responsible Two-Party System* (1950), was an instance of a less successful and more controversial venture into practical politics.

By 1947, corrective action became imperative. At the Executive Council meeting that year, V. O. Key proposed the appointment of a Committee on the Constitutional Structure of the Association to study such "constitutional questions as may appear to the committee to offer promise of greater efficiency in the operation of the Association." The motion, supported by the Council, was approved at the next annual business meeting. From the Committee's deliberations came a number of proposals designed to improve both the organization's formal structure and its mode of operation.

No political scientist need be told that a good deal of determined infighting occurred before the Committee's recommendations were implemented at the 1949 convention. Suffice it here to indicate the major changes accomplished:

1. The office of President-Elect was established. The President-Elect is automatically a member of the Executive Committee (see next item) and can use his one-year term to familiarize himself with the matters he will be called upon to handle as President.

2. The Executive Council was abolished. In its stead, there was created (a) a Council and (b) an Executive Committee. The latter is composed of the President, the President-Elect, the professional head of the Washington office (see below), and three persons appointed by the President, of whom one is the chairman of the Program Committee. Almost all powers of the previous Executive Council were transferred to the Executive Committee.[9] The new Council, with 16 members elected for over-lapping two-year periods, replaced the previous Executive Council (which had had 15 members elected for three-year terms).

3. A Washington secretariat was established.[10] An increase

---

[9] This change went through despite fears that the Executive Director and Executive Committee would actually run the Association and the Council would merely rubber stamp their decisions. See *APSR,* vol. 46 (1952), pp. 1234–35 and vol. 42 (1948), p. 1218.

[10] As the Committee on the Constitutional Structure of the Association put it, "we are of the opinion that such an office could perform a variety of services for political scientists and for the nation. It would handle the general business affairs of the Association; an assistant to the editor of the *Review* could work out of the Washington office; such an office could be instrumental in placing political scientists in active or consultative posts in the government service; it could serve as a center for political scientists

in dues, plus a supporting Carnegie grant, made possible the appointment of a small staff, headed by an Executive Director.[11] To this staff were shifted the administrative responsibilities of the Secretary-Treasurer as well as the responsibility for developing the Association's professional and promotional services.

A fourth reform should also be mentioned, though this did not come about until a bit later. No sooner had the above reorganization taken place than there arose a bitter controversy over whether the Association should continue to assign research functions to its committees or whether research should be conducted under individual and/or academic (i.e., university and college) auspices. Underlying this dispute was the Executive Committee's opposition to any type of Association undertaking which it could not control and, of course, a vivid recollection of the wide swath cut by previous research committees. The merits of the issue aside, the Executive Committee's position was immeasurably strengthened by a manifest foundation reluctance to support proposals submitted by Association committees. Since grants for similar projects were awarded to other applicants, it is an interesting question whether this reluctance reflected foundation antipathy to the principle of Association-sponsored research or whether the foundations were simply not impressed by the Association committees submitting the requests.

After Byzantine intrigues and maneuverings, the Executive Committee prevailed in 1951. The Council decided that the Association would undertake a "substantive research project" only "when the nature or the immediacy of the problem, or the requirement of facilities is beyond the control of individuals and institu-

---

doing research in Washington and also could route information of a specialized character to especially interested members; it could serve both the government and political scientists in arranging conferences between public officials and selected members of the Association on pressing issues of public policy; and, finally, it could serve as a center to draw under the influence of the Association presently independent organizations of political scientists and could aid in coordinating the work of the Association with other social science groups working in Washington." *APSR*, vol. 42 (1948), pp. 983a–83b.

[11] The first two Executive Directors, Edward Litchfield (1950–1953) and John Gange (1953–1954), served on a part-time basis. The first full-time incumbent was Evron M. Kirkpatrick, who has held the office from 1954 to the present.

tions . . ." Any such project, furthermore, was to be under the "broad administrative direction of the Executive Director; or, the Government Affairs Institute as an operational adjunct of the Association."[12] With the exception of the Carnegie-sponsored study of Congress, the Executive Committee has since been inhospitable to any proposal which would involve the Association itself in research. Even the recent three million dollar Ford grant, it can be fairly said, is directed toward service and public affairs activities, rather than research.[13]

Two points should be made before concluding this brief sketch. First, simply for the Association to have survived was no mean accomplishment. Besides the problems described above, it has been threatened by a series of secessionist movements which could well have torn it asunder.[14] In the middle 1940's there was an attempt to force a merger with the American Economic Association. Political scientists primarily concerned with International Relations have given serious thought to setting up an organization devoted exclusively to their particular interests,[15] a course actually followed by the specialists in International Law. The American Society for Public Administration has from time to time seemed to offer a more congenial professional affiliation to those working in that field. In the early 1950's there was a real danger that political scientists committed to traditional, historically oriented political philosophy would pull out and "go it alone." This last, of course, was one aspect of behavioralism's divisive impact on the discipline.

Second, these recent perils notwithstanding, the Association is presently enjoying the most prosperous years of its existence.

[12] The relationship of the Governmental Affairs Institute to the Association has undergone several metamorphoses. At one time, it could be argued, the former was an "affiliate" of the latter. After Litchfield's departure as Executive Director, the Association moved to sever all official ties with the Institute. These developments can be traced in *APSR,* vol. 45 (1951), p. 1138; vol. 47 (1953), p. 1216; vol. 48 (1954), p. 1224; and vol. 50 (1956), p. 1221.

[13] See below, pp. 154.

[14] See *APSR,* vol. 39 (1945), pp. 137, 144 ff.

[15] Perhaps the most recent discussion of this problem was Professor Fred A. Sonderman's Pi Sigma Alpha speech, "Political Science and International Relations: Conciliation? Or Divorce?" Claremont Colleges, March, 1966.

Internal administration improved noticeably after Evron M. Kirk-patrick assumed the post of Executive Director. An impressive variety of services are now provided for the membership. Several Ford grants have made possible the initiation, or the continuation, of large-scale programs in the area of state and national politics.[16] There is effective liaison with Congress and the Executive agencies. And perhaps the greatest triumph of all, the National Science Foundation has finally recognized political science as one of the behavioral sciences, opening the way for a substantial infusion of federal research funds.[17]

Much of this has been accomplished under truly difficult conditions and in a profession wracked by violent dissension. To be sure, there has been a steady, if muted, drumfire of criticism that the Association has become progressively less democratic, and that control of the profession has fallen into the hands of an

[16] In addition to the already established orientation program for freshmen Congressmen, these include (1) orientation programs for newly elected state legislators; (2) a Public Affairs Reporting Awards Program which provides seminars and fellowships for political journalists; (3) State and Local Government internship programs; and (4) a State Legislative Service Program.

[17] Major credit for this should be given to Dr. Kirkpatrick. Achieving recognition was a long, up-hill fight. In November, 1963, for example, he reported that

"I have had numerous conversations with and letters from officers of the National Science Foundation; so have many officers and members of our Association. Neither in letter or conversation have I been given a rational explanation or justification of the Foundation policy toward political science that would survive an objective analysis. It is sometimes said that there is no basic research—. . .; at other times, it is said that political science research is too closely related to controversial issues of public policy for the Foundation to support it; at still other times . . . it is said that political science does not meet the Foundation's standards of scientific objectivity, quantitative measurement and the like. These arguments as bases for the exclusion of political science are no more relevant to political science than to psychology, economics, anthropology, and sociology." (from letter to Director of the National Science Foundation, November 6, 1963)

The importance of NSF recognition is suggested by the following: in fiscal 1966, NSF awarded 17 research grants worth $335,650 to political scientists. "Report of the Executive Director (American Political Science Association), 1965–66," p. 53 (mimeo).

Establishment, however defined.[18] This may or may not be true; the evidence is hardly conclusive. If the allegation is correct, those charged with dominating the Association should also be credited with having played some part in the gains which have lately been achieved.

THE AMERICAN POLITICAL SCIENCE REVIEW

The *Review,* no less than the Association, had its troubles in the late 1940's. From diverse sectors of the profession came charges of editorial bias and discrimination. Characteristically sensitive to criticism, Managing Editor Ogg tendered his resignation in 1949. It was accepted with thanks for his "long and devoted" service. An Association committee recommended that Taylor Cole, "whose distinguished work as editor of the *Journal of Politics* is well known," be given a three-year term as Ogg's successor and that subsequent editors serve a two-year term only. Professor Cole held office for four years; his successor, Professor Hugh Elsbree served

---

[18] The conduct of the convention is a major target. In the 1963 survey mentioned above, forty-two per cent of the respondents "strongly agreed" or "agreed" that "there has developed an inner group in the American Political Science Association which, in large part, controls the key panel assignments at the annual Association meetings." Twelve per cent "disagreed" or "strongly disagreed." As one program chairman ruefully observed, "probably no phase of our associational behavior as political scientists receives more continued criticisms than the program arranged each year for the annual meeting. The complaints are numerous; the dissatisfaction is apparently widespread; and yet no two persons are even in agreement about what should be done." *APSR,* vol. 46 (1952), p. 628.

In an effort to avoid having a few schools dominate the programs, control over the panel participants was shifted several years ago from the panel chairmen to the subject matter representatives on the Program Committee. The effort has not been altogether successful. In the past five years (1962–1966) some 1400 academicians have served as panel chairmen, read papers, or were discussants at the annual meetings. The most frequently represented departments (and the number of panel members from each) were Harvard, 61; Yale, 56; Chicago, 54; Wisconsin, 54; Columbia, 48; Michigan, 47; Princeton, 41; Berkeley, 40; Stanford, 33; and Cornell, 31. The top ten schools, then, accounted for about a third of all panel appointments. See the "Report of the Executive Director, 1965–1966," *op. cit.,* pp. 8 ff. A parallel attempt to prevent "multiple assignments" has been only partially effective. Of some 400 panel and discussion participants at the 1966 meeting, some three dozen served on more than one panel.

for two; and Professor Harvey Mansfield was Managing Editor, from 1955 to 1965.

Any loss of status which the *Review* may have suffered in the 1940's was recaptured in the ensuing decade. Though there were at least ten scholarly journals catering to American political scientists by 1960,[19] competition seemed to enhance rather than diminish the *Review*'s position as *the* periodical in the field. A 1963 survey confirmed the general belief that publication in the *Review* carried far more prestige than publication in any other professional journal. In this respect, it was unmistakably in a class by itself.[20]

Pre-eminence carried its own penalty. Despite—or perhaps because of—its unique role, the *Review* remained the target of sporadic criticism. Some persons complained that its pages were open only to a coterie of "insiders" and that the acceptance or rejection of articles did not always turn on merit.[21] Others deplored the printing of what seemed to be personal, rather than scholarly, exchanges and remarks, especially in the "Communications to the Editor" section. Defending his policy on the latter score, the Managing Editor pointed out that *ad hominem* passages had, on occasion, been "deleted or moderated." Nevertheless, he stoutly continued, "when legitimate professional disagreement exists it had better be aired in print for all to see rather than confined to the rumors and gossip of convention corridors. And let it not be said that an Establishment exists to protect its favorites from criticism."[22]

Even the *Review*'s severest critics probably realized that the post-1945 rise of behavioralism created a nearly insoluble editorial problem. To publish only the traditional type of material would

[19] These other journals include: *Journal of Politics, World Politics, Political Science Quarterly, Administrative Science Quarterly, Western Political Quarterly,* and *Midwest Journal of Politics.*

[20] The two next ranking journals are *World Politics* and the *Journal of Politics.* The former is, of course, especially well regarded by those in International Relations.

[21] See Somit and Tanenhaus, *op. cit.,* p. 91, note 4. As the profession doubled and trebled in size, it should be remembered, the physical limitations of the *Review* effectively barred an increasing majority of political scientists from publication in their profession's most prestigious journal. The resulting frustrations would have inevitably produced some adverse reaction.

[22] Annual Report of the Managing Editor, *American Political Science Review,* 1965, p. 2 (mimeo.).

evoke the wrath of the behavioralists; to accept only the newer scholarship would alienate conventionally oriented political scientists; to present a "mix" of the two would evoke the charge, as events demonstrated, that the journal had no clear-cut or consistent position. Managing Editor Mansfield called attention to this dilemma and explained the guidelines he had adopted to deal with it:

An emerging problem of editorial policy . . . became more perplexing during the past year—the question of balance and emphasis, among the varied interests of *Review* readers, in the acceptance of articles that rest heavily on mathematical methods of analysis. The proportion of offerings of that sort is on the increase. Many, though by no means all of them, are products of governmentally sponsored projects that reflect the fascination of the sponsors as well as of the authors with the cultivation of mathematical techniques. Their political relevance is sometimes plain enough, and sometimes very difficult to see or assess, considering the heroic and unreal assumptions often necessary to the present applications of the methods. If the former, I have tried to be hospitable, however difficult most readers will find them. When they appear to represent triumphs of technique over purpose—if I may borrow a phrase from a friend—I have usually said no, on the principle that it will be time enough for the general audience of the *Review* to cope with the method when it is shown to have helped solve some substantive problem of significant professional concern that did not yield to previous approaches.[23]

After ten year's service during the discipline's most controversy-ridden period, controversies often sharply delineated in the *Review* itself, Mansfield stepped down from his difficult and often thankless job.[24] The first issue under the new editor, Professor Austin Ranney, differed strikingly in cover design and lay-out. Whether this foreshadows some marked shift of policy once previous publication commitments have been honored, or whether such a decision must await clarification of the discipline's intellectual direction, remains to be seen.

[23] *Ibid.*, p. 1. Since the *Review* at this time ran almost nothing which could be strictly called "mathematical" in nature, it would seem that Mansfield was referring to more elegant statistical treatments.

[24] A questionnaire dealing with the *Review* was sent to Association members in the fall of 1965. The 1291 responses, Managing Editor Ranney reported, "constitute an impressive endorsement of the manner in which Professor Mansfield has administered the *Review* for the past decade." *Annual Report of the Managing Editor, American Political Science Review,* 1966, p. 2 (mimeo).

DOCTORAL OUTPUT AND GRADUATE TRAINING

OUTPUT

Under the twin spurs of an insatiable demand for faculty, and the concomitant insistence that professors hold doctorates, social science graduate departments have experienced a boom of unprecedented proportions. Between 1946 and 1965, some 22,500 Ph.D.'s were awarded in history, sociology, economics, and political science. Almost 4300 of these degrees, a shade under 20 per cent, went to persons in political science and its cognate fields, public administration and international relations. From 1946 on, the discipline has regularly produced more doctorates than sociology, and fewer than history or economics. Although political science's share of the social science market has varied somewhat in the past two decades, ranging from 12.6 per cent in 1946 to 25.3 per cent in 1949, in recent years its proportion has remained amazingly constant. For example, the percentages for political science from 1961–1965 were 17.7, 18.7, 18.7, 18.9, and 18.7.

The output of political science Ph.D.'s has meantime almost trebled. Just after World War II (1946–1950), it averaged 115 per year. Over the last five years (1961–1965), average annual production soared to more than 300. Given the recent trend, the profession will soon bedoctor each year twice as many practitioners as the original total membership of the Association. How long our educational institutions can continue to absorb this flood of talent once the college-going population begins to level off, and what, if anything, should be done in anticipation of such a surfeit, is a matter to which few have yet given serious consideration.[25]

A significant shift has taken place in the distribution of Ph.D.

[25] Allan M. Cartter has recently predicted that "from about 1976" onward the number of persons earning doctoral degrees will "far outstrip the number required to keep faculty quality constant." See both his "A New Look at the Supply of College Teachers," *Educational Record,* Summer, 1965, pp. 267–77, and his "Faculty Needs and Resources" in *Improving College Teaching: Aids and Impediments,* American Council on Education, 1966, pp. 99–121.

output among the discipline's graduate departments. Historically, the most prestigious nine or ten schools turned out a majority of the political science doctorates. Indeed, the "big three" (Harvard, Chicago, and Columbia) usually accounted for over a third of the total production. As Table 1 makes clear, this pattern has altered of late. The "top" departments[26] are grooming proportionately fewer persons; some of the departments which lead in doctorates do not as yet enjoy a prestige commensurate with their size;[27] and the ten largest departments, prestigious or otherwise, are now harvesting less than half of the new Ph.D. crop.[28]

TABLE 1: LARGEST PRODUCERS OF DOCTORATES IN POLITICAL SCIENCE (PUBLIC ADMINISTRATION AND INTERNATIONAL RELATIONS INCLUDED), 1958–1965

School	N	%
Columbia	174	8.0
Chicago	160	7.3
Harvard	134	6.1
NYU	119	5.5
American	117	5.4
Yale	83	3.8
California (Berkeley)	81	3.7
Princeton	76	3.5
Syracuse	63	2.9
Michigan	62	2.8
Others	1116	51.1
TOTAL	2185	100.1

For the first time in its history, a majority of the discipline's incoming members are being trained at the less prestigious departments. Since the standing of the institution at which one takes his

[26] See below, pp. 163–64. For example, the six "distinguished" departments (see below, p. 165) produced only 33 per cent of the discipline's doctorates in the 1958–1965 period.

[27] New York University, American University, Georgetown, and Syracuse would be examples here.

[28] Between 1958 and 1965, the ten largest departments (by doctoral output) accounted for 48.9 per cent of the degrees granted. Comparable figures for earlier periods are: 1950–1956, 57 per cent; 1943–1949, 65 per cent; and 1936–1942, 60 per cent. Somit and Tanenhaus, "Trends in American Political Science," *op. cit.,* p. 935.

doctorate has a real bearing upon one's career prospects,[29] this situation, if prolonged, will either effect a modification of long-standing personnel practices or put the profession in the anomalous position of discriminating against most of its membership. What happens will depend on the future demand for faculty and the extent to which positions at the "better" schools can be filled by Ph.D.'s from the "better" departments.

PROBLEMS OF GRADUATE TRAINING

Animadversions about the quality of graduate training are as familiar to modern practitioners as they were to preceding generations.[30] "About half of the political scientists on graduate faculties in American universities," observed the Association's Committee on Standards of Instruction, "are dissatisfied with the state of graduate education in our discipline." As the Committee saw it, this "restless discontent" could be construed as reassuring evidence of a "healthy state of affairs for our profession."[31]

A well-founded criticism was that graduate instruction was sometimes offered by departments patently unequipped for the task. The Committee discovered, for instance, that one department awarding the doctorate had only two instructors, and a second only three; fifteen departments granting a master's degree had three or less persons on their staff. Nor was there much ground to quarrel with another committee's conclusion that few graduate schools "have made a real effort to provide training for the occupation that most of their graduates will enter"—teaching.[32]

On other aspects of graduate work opinions were often diametrically opposed. While many political scientists demanded more intensive specialization, an Association president argued that "we should re-think and recast our graduate training programs so as to develop generalists who are acquainted with the other social sciences."[33] Some political scientists prescribed increased dosages

[29] Somit and Tanenhaus, *American Political Science, op. cit.,* pp. 42–44.

[30] The problem is endemic in American graduate training. See, for instance, Bernard Berelson, *op. cit., passim.*

[31] "Political Science as a Discipline," *op. cit.,* p. 419.

[32] *Goals for Political Science, op. cit.,* p. 257.

[33] James K. Pollock, "The Primacy of Politics," *APSR,* vol. 45 (1951), pp. 1–17, at 17.

of classical political philosophy; their colleagues called, instead, for better preparation in methodology. Traditionalists advocated "tougher" language requirements; others saw these as pointless anachronisms best abolished.

The dissertation continued to be a large-sized bone of contention. The primary function of doctoral work, political scientists generally agreed, was to train competent research scholars. Satisfactory completion of the dissertation, the time-honored justification held, demonstrated the candidate's capacity to carry out "original research." There were those, however, who argued that this orientation was basically wrong. Political scientists, they observed, commonly function as teachers rather than researchers, and the doctoral program, and especially the dissertation, should be reconsidered in terms of this reality.[34] In contrast, another school insisted that too little attention was being paid to research training and that dissertation requirements should be made more stringent.

Faced with this issue, the Association's Committee for the Advancement of Teaching solemnly recommended that the discipline "work toward better-trained teachers . . . who, at the same time, are as creative in their research . . . as they are stimulating in the classroom."[35] A more useful contribution came from V. O. Key who analyzed, in the course of his 1958 presidential address, the publication records of political scientists awarded doctorates from 1935 to 1937. Twenty years after taking the Ph.D., one-fourth of this group had published nothing at all, one-sixth had produced an article or two, and one in ten, by "latitudinarian standards," had made a significant research contribution.[36] While these figures were susceptible to differing interpretations, Key saw them as indicating a need for "more, and far more rigorous . . . research training."

[34] Yale has recently instituted a program in which a "Master of Philosophy" degree will be offered for persons who complete all doctoral requirements other than the dissertation; a similar program leading to a "Doctor of Arts," degree is under consideration at Berkeley; and Michigan has just approved a "Candidate's Certificate" which testifies that the recipient has formally reached the status of a Ph.D. candidate—but has not completed the dissertation. We shall see.

[35] *Goals, op. cit.,* p. 261.

[36] V. O. Key, Jr., "The State of the Discipline," *APSR,* vol. 52 (1958), pp. 961–71 at 969–70.

This perennial debate about the proper nature of doctoral training springs from and mirrors the fundamental ambivalence of the professorial function. Like other faculty members at major graduate institutions, political scientists "are, in essence, paid to do one job, whereas the worth of their services is evaluated on the basis of how well they do another." The "one job," of course, is teaching; the "other," publication. For all of the lip-service paid to the former, it is the latter which "pays off" professionally.

Political scientists are well aware of this fact. When members of the Association were asked to rank ten factors which contributed to career advancement, (defined as "the ability to get offers from another school"), "quantity of publication" was ranked first, "quality of publication" fifth, and "teaching ability" a very distant last.[37] This assessment of academic reality is undoubtedly correct but it conflicts with another reality: as Key demonstrated, most political scientists publish little or nothing at all—and even those who do publish spend a good part of their working day as teachers. The controversy over what constitutes "good" graduate education is thus inherent in the Janus-like role of the academician.

DEPARTMENTAL PRESTIGE

In the past decade, graduate political science departments have been subjected to three formal assessments of their relative "quality."[38] The first was by Hayward Keniston in 1957;[39] the next by

[37] Somit and Tanenhaus, *American Political Science, op. cit.*, pp. 77–85. The pressure to publish has led to a situation, it has been observed, wherein "a great deal of foolish and unnecessary research is undertaken by men who bring to their investigations neither talent nor interest." In political science (as elsewhere), Bernard Crick has written, "too many books . . . are now addressed neither to problems nor to public . . . but only to prestige and preferment in a needlessly bureaucratized profession." *Op. cit.*, p. 232.

[38] Obviously these studies measure reputed quality, rather than quality itself, since there are no accepted metrics for directly, precisely, and unambiguously assessing the merits of either a department or a university. Needless to say, reputation and reality do not necessarily correspond.

[39] *Graduate Study and Research in the Arts and Sciences at the University of Pennsylvania,* Philadelphia, 1959, p. 142.

the authors of this volume in 1963;[40] and the most recent by Allan Cartter, under the aegis of the American Council on Education, in 1964.[41] The three studies varied considerably in technique. Keniston based his conclusions on replies from twenty-five department chairmen. Somit and Tanenhaus utilized the responses of more than four hundred political scientists drawn from a random sample of the Association's membership. Cartter relied upon a panel of 35 chairmen, 66 "senior scholars," and 64 "junior scholars." Nonetheless, the ratings, shown on p. 164, were quite similar. This is especially true of the two later studies. As Cartter remarked, "the [1963 and 1964] surveys, based on very different methods, gave almost identical results for the leading departments; thus they tend to corroborate each other's findings."[42]

The Keniston and Somit-Tanenhaus rankings listed the departments in the order of their reputed quality. Cartter did the same but, in addition, designated the top six departments as "distinguished," the next dozen as "strong," the next 10 (with only two actually ranked) as "good,"[43] and a final nine as "average plus."[44] These pejorative terms, to repeat, are Cartter's—*not* ours.

As Cartter emphasized,[45] the Somit-Tanenhaus rankings virtually coincide with his. The same six schools hold the first six positions, in almost identical order. With barely an exception, the next dozen schools listed are the same—and their standing rarely differs as much as two places. Common sense, courtesy, and caution all dictate, therefore, that we regard the latest study as the more authoritative and rely upon it rather than our own in the following discussion.

Cartter's inquiry supports the belief that departmental quality changes quite slowly or (and the two are not necessarily exclu-

[40] *Op. cit.,* pp. 28–41.

[41] Allan M. Cartter, *An Assessment of Quality in Graduate Education,* American Council on Education, Washington, D.C., 1966.

[42] *Loc. cit.,* p. 9.

[43] In addition to Duke and Syracuse, the "good" departments, in alphabetical order, were New York University, Ohio State, Pennsylvania, Texas, Vanderbilt, Washington (St. Louis), and Washington (Seattle).

[44] In alphabetical order, Brown, Claremont, Iowa, the New School, Oregon, Penn State, Pittsburgh, Rutgers, and Virginia.

[45] Cartter, *op. cit.,* p. 100.

TABLE 2: RANKING OF GRADUATE DEPARTMENTS OF
POLITICAL SCIENCE: 1925, 1957, 1963, 1964

1925 (Hughes)	1957 (Keniston)	1963 (Somit-Tanenhaus)	1964 (Cartter)
1 Harvard	1 Harvard	1 Harvard	1 Yale
2 Chicago	2 Chicago	2 Yale	2 Harvard
3 Columbia	3 Calif. (Berk.)	3 Calif. (Berk.)	3 Calif. (Berk.)
4 Wisconsin	4 Columbia	4 Chicago	4 Chicago
5 Illinois	5 Princeton	5 Princeton	5 Columbia
6 Michigan	6 Michigan	6 Columbia	6 Princeton
7 Princeton	7 Yale	7 Michigan	7.5 M.I.T.*
8 Johns Hopkins	8 Wisconsin	8.5 Stanford	7.5 Wisconsin
9.5 Iowa	9 Minnesota	8.5 Wisconsin	9 Stanford
9.5 Pennsylvania	10 Cornell	10.5 Calif. (U.C.L.A.)	10 Michigan
11 Calif. (Berk.)	11 Illinois	10.5 Cornell	11 Cornell
	12 Calif. (U.C.L.A.)	12 Johns Hopkins	12 Northwestern
	13 Stanford	13 Northwestern	13 Calif. (U.C.L.A.)
	14 Johns Hopkins	14 Indiana	14 Indiana
	15 Duke	15 Illinois	15 North Carolina
		16 Minnesota	16 Minnesota
		17 North Carolina	17 Illinois
		18.5 Duke	18 Johns Hopkins
		18.5 Syracuse	19 Duke
		20 Pennsylvania	20 Syracuse

* M.I.T. was not included in the 1925, 1957, and 1963 studies.

sive) that the profession's perceptions of quality are slow to modify. Five of the six schools he designates as "distinguished" also headed Keniston's 1957 ranking; the sixth school (Yale) missed by only one place. Four of the six "distinguished" departments (Harvard, Chicago, Columbia, and Princeton) were among the top seven on Hughes' list forty years ago, and Berkeley alone did not appear on Hughes' eleven- department 1925 honor-roll.

Cartter's results, as did those of earlier inquiries, testify to the close relationship between the overall rank of an institution and that of its individual departments. Good universities usually have good departments; highly regarded departments are usually found at prestigious institutions. Since institutional image changes slowly, departments at top-ranked schools enjoy a built-in buffer against a sudden or severe drop in standing. Conversely, first-rate departments at "lesser" universities face a formidable task in achieving full recognition of their actual quality. In the academic world, too, it may well be that "Full many a flower is born to blush unseen . . ."

Though the leading departments now produce a smaller proportion of the profession than formerly, their collective output remains substantial. Harvard, Chicago, and Columbia accounted for almost 22 per cent of the 1958–65 Ph.D. total, the six "distinguished" departments for 32.4 per cent, and the 18 top institutions (i.e., Cartter's "distinguished" plus "strong" categories) for 53 per cent.

These departments continue to play a predominant part in training those who become the profession's luminaries and dignitaries. Of the nineteen political scientists named in a recent survey as having made the most significant contributions to the discipline after 1945, sixteen held American doctorates. Fifteen of these were taken at a "distinguished" department. The distribution here was six from Chicago,[46] three from Harvard, three from Columbia, two from Yale, and one from Berkeley.

This "old school tie" pattern is no less apparent when we examine the doctoral origins of the Association's officers and council members between 1945 and 1965. Two hundred and seven

[46] For what it is worth, five of the top six positions went to Chicago-trained Ph.D.'s.

persons were involved.[47] American doctorates were held by 191, foreign doctorates by 5, and eleven did not have a Ph.D. Of the 191 American degrees, Harvard, Chicago, and Columbia accounted for 48.2 per cent; the six "distinguished" departments for 61.3 per cent; the top ten departments, 72.3 per cent; and the "distinguished" and the "strong" departments together, 84.8 per cent. At the other end of the spectrum, New York University, American University, Georgetown, Syracuse, and the University of Southern California, now collectively generating some 19 per cent of the discipline's doctors, claim only 2 per cent of the Association's officialdom.

The same configuration occurs among those publishing scholarly articles. Taking two leading journals, the *Review* and the *Journal of Politics,* and using 1953, 1957, 1961, and 1965 as sample years, we find that persons holding doctorates from one or another of the top ten schools authored 80 per cent of the articles in the *Review* and 70 per cent of those in the *Journal of Politics.* Ph.D.'s from these ten institutions constitute, though, barely half of the profession's present membership.[48]

Lastly, persons with "prestige" doctorates have a near-monopoly of faculty posts at the best schools. "Distinguished" departments are manned almost exclusively by graduates of "distinguished" departments. Roughly speaking, the odds are about 10 to 1 that someone on the faculty of a highly rated department took his doctorate at one or another of the top-ranking departments. The same situation prevails at the best colleges.

A number of fairly commonplace generalizations can be drawn from the foregoing data. First, American graduate political science departments are differentiated according to their reputed quality, with a half-dozen or so being recognized as clearly pre-eminent. Second, departmental reputations for excellence (or the lack of it) are slow to change. Third, graduates of the top-ranking departments constitute a statistically disproportionate percentage of (a) those recognized as the discipline's leading intellectual lights, (b) those appointed or elected to official Association position, (c) those writing for the leading scholarly journals, and (d) those

[47] Persons holding office more than once, or holding more than one office, were counted only once.

[48] That is, they constitute half of the members who have doctorates.

holding appointments on the faculties of the leading departments.

From one vantage-point, it seems only appropriate and fitting that the profession's "best" and "most productive" persons should come from the best departments. Still, as we have suggested elsewhere,[49] it is not impossible to draw quite different inferences from these same data.

FOUNDATION SUPPORT: PREFERENTIAL PHILANTHROPY, OR, THE RICH GET RICHER

The second decade of the post-1945 period was one of un-paralleled prosperity for the academic community in general and for political science in particular. Enrollments spurted; jobs were increasingly plentiful; promotions came more readily; and salaries finally caught up with, if they did not outpace, the spiralling cost of living.

An unprecedented flow of foundation funds helped further ease the rigors of scholarly life. Whereas a $10,000 grant was a major event in the 1930's or even 1940's, so modest an amount barely occasioned mention by the late 1950's. Carnegie and Rockefeller multiplied manyfold their support of political science. Of even greater moment was the appearance of a new giant—the Ford Foundation. The lavish beneficence of this leviathan late-comer dwarfed the combined giving of the older agencies. Taking the twenty years as a whole, it would be conservative to say that the Ford complex provided 90 per cent of the money channeled to political science by American philanthropic institutions. Under these circumstances, political scientists would have been less than human were they not tempted to manifest a deep interest in the kinds of research known to be favored by Ford Foundation staff and advisers. This is a point to which we will later return.

Of more immediate concern is the manner in which funds for political science were allotted among the several departments. Taking the years 1959–64, and limiting our attention to grants of $50,000 and up, we get the following distribution:

[49] Somit and Tanenhaus, *op. cit.*, pp. 44–48.

TABLE 4: ROCKEFELLER, FORD, AND CARNEGIE GRANTS
OF $50,000 OR OVER IN POLITICAL SCIENCE AND
RELATED AREAS FROM 1959 TO 1964*

University	Rockefeller	Ford	Carnegie	Total
Harvard	195,000	20,200,000	75,000	20,470,000
Columbia		16,775,679	57,000	16,832,679
Univ. of Cal.	375,000	11,321,700	321,000	12,017,700
Chicago		5,400,000		5,400,000
Johns Hopkins	500,000	3,400,000	250,000	4,150,000
Cornell		3,250,000	600,000	3,850,000
Northwestern		3,500,000	200,000	3,700,000
Michigan	206,800	3,164,500	200,000	3,571,300
Stanford		3,550,000		3,550,000
Princeton	250,000	2,596,000	475,000	3,321,000
Yale		3,000,000	167,000	3,167,000
Indiana		3,023,000	105,000	3,128,000
Univ. of Washington		2,610,400	90,000	2,700,400
Wisconsin		1,900,000	150,000	2,050,000
Syracuse		1,750,000		1,750,000
Duke		1,515,000	65,000	1,580,000
M.I.T.		650,000	715,500	1,365,500
Pennsylvania		1,281,375		1,281,375
Michigan State		1,000,000		1,000,000
Kansas		791,000		791,000
Notre Dame		790,000		790,000
Dartmouth		675,000	100,000	775,000
Denver		650,000		650,000
Oregon		500,000	150,000	650,000
Minnesota		550,000		550,000
Florida		550,000		550,000
Delaware		500,000		500,000
N.Y.U.		168,000	170,000	338,000
Smith		281,000		281,000
Earlham		275,000		275,000
New Mexico		275,000		275,000
Illinois		273,068		273,068
Rutgers		200,000		200,000
Spelman		200,000		200,000
Univ. Alaska		198,000		198,000
Chattanooga		181,000		181,000

* Because of the manner in which the various foundations report the awarding of grants it is impossible to determine in every case exactly which areas of the social sciences received the funds. For example, the Ford Foundation frequently reports that it is providing a grant to a certain university for "non-western" studies. In such cases, since we did not have access to the breakdown of these funds, the whole amount has been included.

Gettysburg	180,000	180,000
Vanderbilt	150,000	150,000
Wilkes	150,000	150,000
Massachusetts	139,000	139,000
Mills	132,000	132,000
Vermont	129,000	129,000
Oklahoma	125,000	125,000
Ohio State	105,000	105,000
Purdue	100,000	100,000
Hunter	75,000	75,000
Missouri	70,000	70,000
Hawaii	68,460	68,460

Three aspects of Table 4 are especially noteworthy. First, the amounts involved. Even in these days of the cheap dollar, the five-year total of a 100 million dollars plus is rather impressive. Next, is the massive predominance of the Ford Foundation. Both Rockefeller and Carnegie are great foundations. Nonetheless, Ford outgave the two combined by a ratio of almost 20 to 1.

Lastly, and perhaps most interesting, is the total which went to each institution. The rank order of dollars received bears a striking resemblance to Cartter's quality rating. Almost half of the total benefactions went to just three of the "distinguished" departments. The six departments honored by this designation were collectively awarded some 60 per cent of the total; the top dozen departments almost 80 per cent. The other thirty-some schools together garnered the remaining 20 per cent.

Only slight departures from this pattern appear when we look at the statistics for the individual foundations. Of the five Rockefeller grants, three went to "distinguished," and two to "strong," departments. "Distinguished" departments alone received 5 million dollars or more from Ford. Of the 18 departments allotted from 1 to 5 million dollars, only five rated below "distinguished" and all five were in the "good" category. The six "distinguished" institutions got almost two-thirds of the dollar sums disbursed, the leading twelve over three-quarters. Carnegie, though comparatively tight-fisted in its handling of "distinguished" departments (they were assigned barely a quarter of the total), nonetheless funneled more than three-fourths of its political science expenditure to the ranking dozen departments.

The conclusions that one draws from these figures depends on one's views about the principles that should control foundation giving. If the primary purpose of a foundation grant is to support the "best" researchers and the "best" instructional programs, then it is only proper that the "best" departments get the lion's share. Nor would the picture alter greatly if one argued that foundations should support the *best* proposals, whatever their source. It is a fact of academic life that foundation personnel and foundation consultants are likely to have been trained at, or affiliated with, the more prestigious departments. In assessing the worth of competing proposals they will almost inevitably find the greatest merit in those emanating from the foremost institutions.

Alternative guidelines have, of course, been suggested. There may be some point to the idea that, within proper bounds, foundation money should go where it is most urgently needed. Closely related is the principle that foundations should use their resources to narrow, rather than to widen, the gap in quality among institutions. On the basis of need, the top ranking schools are certainly least deserving, for, with few exceptions, they are among the most affluent of our universities.[50] By either or both of these standards present practices leave something to be desired.

THE INTER-UNIVERSITY CONSORTIUM FOR POLITICAL RESEARCH[51]

No discussion of the profession's post-1945 history would be complete without mention of two organizations whose interests and functions parallel, albeit in diverse fashion, those of the Association. One is the now-defunct Citizenship Clearing House— National Center for Education in Politics, the other is the exceed-

[50] The relative ease with which outstanding institutions get foundation support reinforces their institutional image, since the funds so secured help strengthen staff and program even more and thus further enhance the reputation for outstanding quality.

[51] Though we are limiting our attention to American developments, some brief mention should be made of the International Political Science Association, founded under UNESCO auspices in 1949. American political scientists played an important role both in founding IPSA and in its early development. This relationship may have cooled a bit recently but the Association still remains a major contributor of IPSA funds. See below, fn. 21, p. 201.

ingly active Inter-University Consortium for Political Research. There is a fascinating historical parallel, too: the former was the natural heir of the Reed Committee on Policy; the latter is a contemporary reincarnation of the Merriam-inspired National Conferences on the Science of Politics. Since the Citizenship Clearing House was a major example of the profession's continued commitment to education for democratic citizenship, we will deal with it at the appropriate place below.[52]

The Inter-University Consortium for Political Research probably constitutes the clearest institutional embodiment of the discipline's behavioral tendencies. Originally organized to "promote graduate training and research in politics," it is now more broadly concerned with promoting "the conduct of research on selected phases of the political process." Toward this end, the Consortium sponsors summer programs for training faculty and students in behavioral research methods, holds conferences of both a training and a research strategy character, serves as a data repository and distribution center, functions as a clearing house for information about research and about data processing developments, processes data on request, and provides technical assistance in handling difficult or unusual methodological problems.

Organizationally, the Consortium is a partnership between a group of American, Canadian, and overseas universities, and the University of Michigan's Survey Research Center.[53] Put somewhat differently, it is a cooperative venture between a number of educational institutions, on the one hand, and a major social science research facility, on the other. The spectacular success of the Consortium in attracting members attests to its standing among behaviorally oriented political scientists. When first launched in 1962–63, the Consortium had 21 cooperating schools. By June, 1966, the number had climbed to 73. Virtually every institution of any graduate standing in political science has joined; no member has yet withdrawn.[54]

[52] Below, pp. 195–99.

[53] In one sense, the Consortium's training program is an outgrowth of summer institutes for training in survey methods first begun by the Survey Research Center in 1948.

[54] Member institutions pay a fee which varies according to the nature of their educational program. A good part of these fees come back to the schools in the form of subsidies covering the cost of participation in summer programs and attendance at Consortium meetings.

171

Several factors have contributed to the Consortium's swift emergence as a major force within the discipline: first, administrative skills of unusual order; second, the rise of behavioralism and the role played by the Consortium (and the Survey Research Center) in furthering the development and application of quantitative research techniques; third, the availability (to the Consortium) of highly skilled Survey Research Center personnel whose competence in sampling, interviewing, data processing, and data analysis are probably unsurpassed elsewhere in the world of social science; and fourth, the ability of the Consortium to secure funding on a substantial scale.[55]

Like the antecedent National Conferences on the Science of Politics, the Consortium has become a rallying point for advocates of a more scientific, quantitatively oriented discipline. Like the National Conferences, it actively promotes this approach. Like the National Conferences, it has attracted to itself most of the leading exponents of the contemporary version of a "science of politics." Organizationally, the similarity extends even further: like the National Conferences, the Consortium formally operates outside the Association while, at the same time, Consortium spokesmen play an important part in Association affairs.

Here, though, the similarity ends. Unlike the National Conferences, the Consortium has its own permanent and highly efficient bureaucracy. Unlike its predecessor, the Consortium has been able to pay its own way. At best, the National Conferences eked out a year-to-year existence; the Consortium gives every indication of being a well-established, continuing operation.

As matters now stand, the Consortium fills an important need within the discipline. Its long-term function, the scope and nature of its operation, and perhaps its very future, it seems reasonably safe to say, will turn largely on the course and fate of the behavioral movement.

[55] The Consortium has received several foundation grants but, perhaps most impressive of all, has been its support from the National Science Foundation. By late 1966 total monies from this source alone exceeded $600,000.

XII
political science as a learned discipline: behavioralism

*P*olitical scientists have quarreled over many matters in the contemporary period but the most divisive issue by far has been behavioralism. If the controversy it has elicited is any measure, this latest quest for a more scientific politics is easily the paramount development in the discipline's entire intellectual history.[1]

[1] A very incomplete list of the more interesting items in the literature accompanying this controversy includes the following:

Arnold Brecht, *Political Theary, The Foundations of Twentieth Century Political Thought,* Princeton, 1959.
David E. Butler, *The Study of Political Behaviour,* London, 1958.
James C. Charlesworth (ed.), *The Limits of Behavioralism in Political Science,* Philadelphia, 1962.
Robert A. Dahl, *Modern Political Analysis,* Englewood Cliffs, New Jersey, 1963.
David Easton, *A Framework for Political Analysis,* Englewood Cliffs, New Jersey, 1965.
David Easton, *The Political System,* New York, 1953.
Heinz Eulau, *The Behavioral Persuasion,* New York, 1963.
Heinz Eulau, Samuel J. Eldersveld, and Morris Janowitz, *Political Behavior: A Reader in Theory and Research,* Glencoe, Illinois, 1956.
Charles S. Hyneman, *The Study of Politics,* Urbana, Illinois, 1959.
Harold D. Lasswell, *The Future of American Politics,* New York, 1963.

Two recent presidential[2] speeches have remarked on the similarities between the post-1945 behavioral movement and the pattern of events which Thomas S. Kuhn has discerned in "scientific revolutions."[3] A "normal science," Kuhn suggests, is characterized by general agreement among its practitioners on the problems which properly concern them and on the concepts and methods whereby these problems are best studied. In his now familiar language, this common set of beliefs constitutes that discipline's "paradigm." Scientific revolutions occur when an existing paradigm gives rise to anomalies (insolvable problems, inexplicable or apparently contradictory findings, etc.) which cannot be handled by the existing conceptual apparatus. Should this happen with some regularity, or should an anomaly occur at a particularly critical juncture, there may emerge a rival definition of concerns, concepts, and techniques. Scientific revolutions can thus be viewed

Harold D. Lasswell and Abraham Kaplan, *Power and Society: A Framework for Political Inquiry,* New Haven, 1950.

Daniel Lerner and Harold D. Lasswell (eds.), *The Policy Sciences,* Stanford, Calif., 1951.

Roy C. Macridis, *The Study of Comparative Government,* Garden City, New York, 1955.

Jean Meynaud, *Introduction à la Science Politique,* Paris, 1959.

Hans J. Morgenthau, *Scientific Man Versus Power Politics,* Chicago, 1946.

Austin Ranney (ed.), *Essays on the Behavioral Study of Politics,* Urbana, Illinois, 1962.

Research Frontiers in Politics and Government, Washington, D.C., 1955.

Herbert J. Storing (ed.), *Essays on the Scientific Study of Politics,* New York, 1962.

Leo Strauss, *Natural Right and History,* Chicago, 1953.

David B. Truman, *The Governmental Process,* New York, 1951.

Vernon Van Dyke, *Political Science: A Philosophical Analysis,* Stanford, Calif., 1960.

Eric Voegelin, *The New Science of Politics: An Introductory Essay,* Chicago, 1952.

Dwight Waldo, *Political Science in the United States of America, A Trend Report,* Paris, 1956.

T. D. Weldon, *The Vocabulary of Politics,* Harmondsworth, England, 1953.

Roland Young (ed.), *Approaches to the Study of Politics,* Evanston, Illinois, 1958.

Robert A. Dahl, "The Behavioral Approach in Political Science: Epitaph for a Monument to a Successful Protest," *APSR,* vol. 55 (1961).

[2] David B. Truman, "Disillusion and Regeneration: The Quest for a Discipline," *APSR,* vol. 59 (1965) pp. 865–73, and Gabriel Almond, "Political Theory and Political Science," *ASPR,* vol. 60 (1966), p. 869–79.

[3] Thomas S. Kuhn, *The Structure of Scientific Revolutions,* Chicago, 1962.

as major scientific advances or as shifts from one paradigm to another.

Whether political science (or any other social science) constitutes a "normal science" in the stricter sense of that term may be a matter of some disagreement. There is also some question whether either traditional political science or behavioralism actually satisfies all the requirements of a "paradigm." Allowing for these objections, the idea of a "scientific revolution" and of a shift of "paradigms" provides a useful framework for the discussion of recent developments within the discipline. From such a vantage point, behavioralism may be treated, if only metaphorically, as an attempt to move political science from a pre-paradigmatic (or literally non-scientific) condition to a paradigmatic stage or, alternatively, as an effort to replace a previously accepted paradigm with one that is more powerful.[4] That the merits of the undertaking are still being controverted may well be due to the difficulty, indigenous to the social sciences, of demonstrating beyond reasonable doubt the superior explanatory power of the new mode of conceptualization. This is the same shoal, it will be recalled, on which the Merriam-led advocates of a scientific politics foundered in the 1920's.

[4] Without arguing for a close similarity between the natural and the social sciences, Truman inclines to the second of these alternatives. As he sees it, the pre-behavioral discipline was characterized by "six closely related features" of "predominant agreement." These six were:

"(1) an unconcern with political systems as such, including the American system, which amounted in most cases to taking their properties and requirements for granted; (2) an unexamined and mostly implicit conception of political change and development that was blandly optimistic and unreflectively reformist; (3) an almost total neglect of theory in any meaningful sense of the term; (4) a consequent enthusiasm for a conception of "science" that rarely went beyond raw empiricism; (5) a strongly parochial preoccupation with things American that stunted the development of an effective comparative method; and (6) the establishment of a confining commitment to concrete description." *Ibid.,* p. 866.

We have, of course, traced in some detail the emergence and persistence of these several traits. On the other hand, we have also noted the recurrent attempts, from Burgess through Merriam, to substitute other paradigmatic elements. For this reason, we would be somewhat more dubious than Truman about the predominance of agreement on these commitments.

In this chapter we will first describe the constellation of beliefs and commitments which collectively constitute the behavioral "paradigm." Next we will summarize the various arguments which have been advanced against behavioralism, or more precisely, against its component doctrines. Third, we will trace the rise of behavioralism from 1945 to the present. Finally will come what may well be the critical question: what has been the impact of behavioralism upon the discipline to date?

THE BEHAVIORAL CREED

Ironically, participants in the earlier stages of the behavioral-traditional debate often disagreed as fiercely over the issues to be disputed as over the merits of their respective beliefs. Several factors contributed to this situation. There was, for example, the almost irresistible temptation to attribute to one's opponent an untenable or extreme position and then to demolish what was, in reality, a straw man. More labor and ingenuity sometimes went into this kind of argumentation than in trying to understand what it was that the other person was actually trying to say. The ensuing logic-chopping, hair-splitting, and jesuitry was worthy of an exchange between medieval theologians.

Further contributing to the confusion was the amorphous nature of behavioralism, especially at the outset. During this initial period, as Evron M. Kirkpatrick has written, "the term served as a sort of umbrella, capacious enough to provide a temporary shelter for a heterogeneous group united only by dissatisfaction with traditional political science."[5] Grappling with this same problem, another commentator, Robert A. Dahl, concluded that behavioralism was no less a "mood" than a doctrinal commitment.[6] It was even possible, as the literature demonstrates, to quarrel over who was or was not a behavioralist.

The root of the difficulty, unquestionably, is the protean nature of behavioralism. It is less a tightly structured dogma than a congerie of related values and objectives. Those who call them-

[5] "The Impact of the Behavioral Approach on Traditional Political Science," in Ranney, *op. cit.*, p. 11.

[6] Dahl, "The Behavioral Approach . . .," *op. cit.*, pp. 766–71.

selves behavioralists often differ over component elements of their philosophy, with few accepting the "package" in toto. Similarly, anti-behavioralists tend not to take common exception to all of the behavioralistic tenets but direct their fire at those particular notions which strike them as particularly wrongheaded. A good deal of the argument thus does not concern itself with the merits of behavioralism per se but only with certain of its ideas and aspirations.

Over the past few years the basic outlines of the behavioral position have emerged with increasing clarity. A number of persons—David B. Truman, Robert A. Dahl, David Easton, Heinz Eulau, Evron M. Kirkpatrick, and Mulford Q. Sibley, *inter alia*—have written thoughtful, dispassionate analyses of the movement. While they do not agree on every point, a basic consensus can be discerned. The succeeding paragraphs summarize and describe what are now generally regarded as the major tenets of behavioralism. Before presenting them, however, it is essential to repeat the previous caveat: not even the most committed behavioralist necessarily holds all of these views. Few, however ardent their desire for a truly scientific politics, would be willing to carry every one of these propositions to its logical extreme. Each statement is thus to be read and understood as if it were qualified by such phrases as "to the degree possible," "wherever practicable," and "other things being equal."

With this proviso firmly in mind, the following can be identified as the key behavioralist articles of faith.

1. Political science can ultimately become a science capable of prediction and explanation. The nature of this science, it is generally conceded, will probably be much closer to biology than to physics or chemistry. Given this possibility, the political scientist should engage in an unrelenting search for regularities of political behavior and for the variables associated with them. He should, therefore, eschew purely descriptive studies in favor of the rigorous,* analytical treatment essential to the systematic development of political knowledge.

2. Political science should concern itself primarily, if not

* This is one of the most commonly employed terms in the behavioralist vocabulary. For those who are uncertain as to its precise denotation, it means exactly what it says it means—rigorous.

exclusively, with phenomena which can actually be observed, i.e., with what is done or said. This behavior may be that of individuals and/or of political aggregates. The behavioralist deplores the "institutional" approach because it is impossible properly to study institutional behavior other than as manifest in the actions and words of those who carry out institutional functions.

3. Data should be quantified and "findings" based upon quantifiable data. In the final analysis, the behavioralist argues, only quantification can make possible the discovery and precise statement of relationships and regularities. Associated with this is the aspiration—and occasionally the attempt—to state these relationships as mathematical propositions and to explore their implications by conventional mathematical manipulation.

4. Research should be theory oriented and theory directed. Ideally, inquiry should proceed from carefully developed theoretical formulations which yield, in turn, "operational-izable" hypotheses, that is, hypotheses which can be tested against empirical data. Since theory must take into account the nature, scope, and variety of the phenomena under study, the behavioralist speaks of "low-level," "middle-level," and "general" theory. The ultimate objective is the development of "over-arching" generalizations which will accurately describe and interrelate political phenomena in the same fashion, to use a threadbare illustration, that Newton's laws once seemed to account for the physical world.

5. Political science should abjure, in favor of "pure" research, both applied research aimed at providing solutions to specific, immediate social problems and melioratory programmatic ventures.* These efforts, as the behavioralist sees it, produce little valid scientific knowledge and represent, instead, an essentially unproductive diversion of energy, resources, and attention.

6. The truth or falsity of values (democracy, equality, freedom, etc.) cannot be established scientifically and are beyond the scope of legitimate inquiry. From this it follows that political scientists should abandon the "great issues" except where behavior springing from or related to these issues can be treated as empirical events (the incidence of a belief in democracy, for example,

---

* Presumably among the undertakings so proscribed would be the perennially popular projects aimed at democratic citizenship or "better minds for better politics."

and the manner in which this belief is reflected in voting behavior would thus be an appropriate subject of study). Needless to say, the contention that political science has no proper concern with moral or ethical questions as such has been one of the most bitterly argued aspects of behavioralism.

7. Political scientists should be more interdisciplinary. Political behavior is only one form of social behavior and the profession would profit tremendously by drawing on the skills, techniques, and concepts of its sister social sciences. Some behavioralists would deny, in fact, that political science constitutes a true discipline in itself.

8. Political science should become more self-conscious and critical about its methodology. Its practitioners should develop a greater familiarity with, and make better use of, such tools as multivariate analysis, sample surveys, mathematical models, and simulation. And, almost needless to say, they should make every effort to be aware of, and to discount, their own "value" preferences in planning, executing, and assessing their research undertakings.

The foregoing represents, we believe, a reasonably complete and accurate catalogue of the intellectual commitments symbolized by the term "behavioralism." While we have grouped them under eight broad headings, these propositions can readily be arranged in some other fashion, with more or fewer categories as desired.

Few, if any, of these ideas are new to political science. There is little in behavioralism that would be completely strange or repugnant to such earlier proponents of a "science of politics" as Merriam, Catlin, and Munro. Or, to go back yet another generation, neither would Lowell, Ford, Macy, and Bentley have found many of these propositions totally novel or unacceptable.

Granting that these ideas can be traced well into the past, there are differences which should not be overlooked. If the basic objectives have not changed radically, the underlying intellectual position is now more systematically developed. The current doctrine is more concerned with formal theory and with fundamental, organizing concepts than was previously the case, although Burgess, Ford, Lowell, Bentley, and Catlin clearly foreshadowed this interest. Lastly, many of the earlier proponents of a scientific politics sought, above all, a political science which could effectively grapple with the practical problems besetting the American democracy. Not for them, certainly, the aseptic aloofness of pure research.

VINDICAE CONTRA BEHAVIORALISMOS

We have described the leading articles of the behavioralist creed. Equity no less than discretion dictates that we now present the relevant countercommitments. Of necessity, only the basic outline of each argument can be indicated. As before, this discussion should be prefaced with the warning that not all anti-behavioralists hold all of these views and that few are inclined to push their arguments to logical extremes. Furthermore, a number of these propositions may well be acceptable to those who regard themselves as behaviorally inclined.

With this in mind, the anti-behavioral brief can be summarized as follows:

1. Political science is not, nor is it ever likely to become, a science in any realistic sense of the term. It cannot become a science for a number of reasons. The phenomena with which political scientists deal do not lend themselves to rigorous study. We cannot treat human behavior, individual or social, with the dispassion needed for scientific knowledge. Neither political science (nor any other social science) is amenable to experimental inquiry. There are too many variables and historical contingencies to permit other than the most general statement of regularities. "Laws" of political behavior cannot be stated for a sentient creature such as man, because he is free to modify his actions in keeping with, or in violation of, such laws once they are made known. Furthermore, though the anti-behavioralist has no objection per se to the use of hypotheses, he argues that rigid adherence to this notion may stifle, rather than advance research. The purely descriptive approach, sometimes the only practicable technique, has a legitimate and an important role to play in inquiry.

2. Overt political behavior tells only part of the story. Different individuals may perform the same act for quite different reasons. To understand what they do, one must go beyond, or behind, observable behavior. Moreover, individuals and groups act

within an institutional or a social setting, and a knowledge of that setting is essential to any meaningful explanation of their behavior. The anti-behavioralist holds that the larger part of political life lies beneath the surface of human action and cannot be directly apprehended.

3. Whatever the theoretical merits of quantification, for most practical purposes it is now and will continue to be an unattainable goal. Quantification requires precise concepts and reliable metrics —and political science possesses neither. Significant questions normally cannot be quantified; questions which can are usually trivial in nature. As for mathematics—well, how can one mathematicise that which is both imprecise and immensurable?

4. While it is desirable that research be informed by theory, the behavioralists' aspirations have far outrun their data. It verges on the ridiculous to talk of an "over-arching" general theory when political science still lacks accepted low- and middle-level formulations adequate to the facts at hand. This preoccupation with general theory tends to block less ambitious but in the long run more productive inquiry. At best, it has led to the proliferation of concepts which cannot successfully be operationalized.

5. Applied research and a concern with questions of public policy are, on philosophical and historical grounds, warranted and desirable. American political scientists have a moral obligation to devote some portion of their energies to civic matters, and, just as pure research often yields findings of practical value, so applied and programmatic inquiry may contribute to the better understanding of political and social behavior.

6. Significant political issues invariably involve moral and ethical issues. Political science has historically been, and must continue to be, concerned with questions of right and wrong, even if these cannot be "scientifically" resolved. Were the discipline to turn its back on such matters it would have little justification for continued existence. Going considerably beyond this, one wing of anti-behavioralism denies that values cannot be demonstrated true or false and that political scientists are necessarily condemned to an eternal philosophical relativism.

7. There are many areas where an interdisciplinary approach may be useful but care must be taken to preserve the identity and integrity of political science. All too often, the anti-behavioralist feels, there has been an indiscriminate borrowing of

concepts and techniques which are simply inappropriate for political inquiry.

8. Self-consciousness about methodology can be, and has been, carried too far. Overly critical and unrealistic standards impede rather than advance the pursuit of knowledge. This same obsession has led many behavioralists, it is argued, to exalt technique at the cost of content. Technical, rather than substantive, considerations have been permitted to set the area of inquiry. In any case, many of these technical innovations are still too sophisticated and refined for the raw material with which political scientists must work. As for "scientific objectivity," there is almost universal skepticism among the anti-behavioralists that it is attainable—and considerable doubt that it is inherently desirable.

Just as behavioralists differ among themselves, so do their opponents disagree with each other on a number of matters.[7] One of these deserves specific mention. Some anti-behavioralists are satisfied with political science as it has been practiced in the past and see no cogent reason for drastic change. While they concede that certain aspects of the discipline could be strengthened, they believe that, on the whole, it has been equal to its chosen task. Other anti-behavioralists are less complacent about the state of the discipline. They admit that political science has yet to accumulate a very impressive body of knowledge and may even feel that it has lost ground to the other social sciences. But however these two groups may diverge in their assessment of what has been accomplished to date, they are in accord on a crucial point: behavioralism is not a desirable or viable alternative to the kind of political science it seeks to displace.

The foregoing analysis obviously leaves a major problem unresolved. Many who call themselves behavioralists refuse to embrace the entire octalog of their faith; few of their opponents would reject all eight out of hand. What combination of beliefs, then, held with what relative intensity, makes one a behavioralist? Which cluster of tenets, scorned with how much severity, makes one anti-behavioral?

There is no really satisfactory answer. Of course, we can recast the question by shifting to a more subjective method of

[7] These generalizations rely heavily on the results of the survey reported in Somit and Tanenhaus, *American Political Science, op. cit.*

classification and have each political scientist fix his own position on the behavioral—anti-behavioral spectrum as he himself defines it. This line of attack is not free of methodological difficulties but it can be operationalized and does have some utility.* It points to what seems to be an inescapable conclusion: whether a given political scientist falls into the one or the other category turns, in the final analysis, on his state of mind rather than on readily applicable objective criteria.

THE RISE OF BEHAVIORALISM

ORIGINS AND CAUSES

Orthodoxy has it that the term "behavioral science," subsequently corrupted to "behavioralism,"[8] was coined by a group of quantitatively oriented, "rigorously" inclined social scientists at the University of Chicago. Anxious to secure federal financing for social science research, but apprehensive that some unenlightened "persons confound social science with socialism," they conceived the term "behavioral science." Though "behavior" had been used before, the then most recent example being Herbert Simon's 1947 *Administrative Behavior,* after 1949 "behavioralism" and "behavioral science" came increasingly to connote the kind of social science espoused by the Chicago group.[9]

In political science, behavioralism was unmistakably a lineal descendant of the antecedent "science of politics" movement. Many of its component ideas had been advanced in somewhat cruder form during the 1920's, and were already familiar to the older members of the profession. If behavioralism has a father, paternity belongs to Charles E. Merriam, who "staked out" much

* For all practical purposes this is what we did in our earlier study, *American Political Science, op. cit.* Although there is no need to summarize those findings here, we might point out that stance on behavioralism (as self-defined) correlated significantly with attitudes toward a variety of other professional issues.

[8] It is interesting to note that the term "behaviorism" was common until the early 1960's, and then gave way to the longer variant.

[9] James G. Miller in *State of the Social Sciences,* Leonard D. White (ed.), Chicago, 1956, pp. 29–31.

of the ground now claimed by it. And if Merriam was the sire, Burgess, Lowell, and Bentley were godfathers to the enterprise.

So much for intellectual genealogy. Now, what was there in the post-1945 climate of opinion that enabled behavioralism to take root so swiftly and to flourish so remarkably? We may be still too close to the event for a definitive explanation but what seem to be the most important predisposing conditions and forces can be tentatively identified. The ensuing list, we should add, is not a rank order.

To begin, there was a widespread dissatisfaction with the "state of the discipline." This stemmed from several sources: the discovery that the talents and skills of political scientists were not highly valued by governmental personnel officers; the disconcerting realization, by those who did spend some time in the public service, of the profound difference between the "accepted wisdom" of the profession and the reality of the governmental process; the inability of traditional political science to account for the rise of fascism, national socialism, and communism, or to explain the continuation of these regimes in power; a growing sensitivity to, and unhappiness with, the basically descriptive nature of the discipline; and a knowledge of apparent advances in other social sciences and a mounting fear that political science was lagging behind its sister professions.

Post-war experiences with technical assistance and economic aid programs contributed to the sense of malaise. The various efforts to export U.S. political and administrative "know-how" forced upon American political scientists a painful awareness that much of their vaunted expertise applied, if at all, only to the type of political and administrative problems encountered in Western, industrialized societies. This discovery provided a powerful impetus to the quest for cross-cultural and trans-national regularities which has characterized one aspect of behavioral inquiry.

The migration of European social scientists to the United States during the 1930's and 1940's also hastened the winds of change. Although few of these scholars were themselves behaviorally inclined, and most in fact hostile to it, they exposed their American hosts to currents of thought (Max Weber, logical positivism, etc.) from which behavioralism was heavily to borrow.

Another factor was the expanding use of public opinion polls and the refinement of survey techniques. These provided instru-

184

ments for developing vast new bodies of data. Research in this area was greatly facilitated by advances in mathematical statistics and the increased availability of electronic computers to perform what had previously been impossibly tedious computations.

Closely related to the foregoing, and making a good deal of this research possible, was the partiality to behavioralism manifested by those who controlled the allocation of research grants. The Social Science Research Council's Committee on Political Behavior, through which considerable money was channeled, was behaviorally inclined. The foundations in general, and the Ford Foundation (with its Behavioral Science Program) in particular, poured huge sums into behavioral projects. On the federal level, access to public funds was largely limited to the social sciences deemed worthy of the appellation "behavioral sciences."[10] Widespread knowledge of this situation, it is safe to say, did not adversely affect conversions to the faith. Even those who had private reservations about behavioralism sometimes found it possible, when research grants hung in the balance, to render at least lip service to the new creed.

THE EMERGENCE OF BEHAVIORALISM

Looking back from our foreshortened perspective, the rise of behavioralism seems to fall into three stages, although not every event can be neatly fitted into this scheme. The three are: from the end of World War II through 1949; from 1950 to the mid-1950's; and from then to the present. In the first period there are only scattered signs of what is to come, like the irregular rumbling of thunder and flashing of lightning in the distance. In the second, the full impact of behavioralism burst upon the profession. In the third, its opponents, though hardly quiescent during the preceding decade, launched a determined, if not desperate, counter-attack.[11]

[10] From political science's viewpoint, perhaps the worst offender in this respect was the National Science Foundation. See p. 154 above.

[11] A somewhat different timetable, we should add, has been advanced by Robert Dahl who argued, in 1961, that the profession had already entered the phase of reconciliation and mutual adjustment. Evidence from a variety of sources, including some rather heated discussions at subsequent Association meetings, suggests that Dahl's optimism was at least premature. Even today, there is little evidence that either side is interested in a ceasefire, let alone an enduring treaty of peace. Cf. Dahl, *op. cit.*

185

POST-WAR TO 1950. During these years the direction in which the profession was moving was yet unclear. While there were signs of a changing outlook, the omens were by no means unambiguous.

As already mentioned, in 1945 the Social Science Research Council established its Committtee on Political Behavior. The Committee promptly underwrote a series of summer institutes aimed at encouraging the behavioral study of politics.[12] 1946 brought a resumption, in the *Review,* of the debate over whether a "non-normative" political science was possible or desirable and, at the annual meeting, a panel on "Beyond Relativism in Political Theory."

These years saw the publication of two books of signal importance—Herbert Simon's aforementioned *Administrative Behavior* and Hans Morgenthau's *Scientific Man vs. Power Politics* (1946). The former looked toward a "science of administration" and, by inference, to a science of politics; the other was a determined assault on the whole idea of a scientific politics, and traced the unfortunate consequences of that notion on American thinking about international relations and foreign policy. As the 1940's closed, there appeared two major studies which were behaviorally inclined—C. Herman Pritchett's *Roosevelt Court* (1948) and V. O. Key's *Southern Politics in State and Nation* (1949). At about this time, too, the "News and Notes" section of the *Review* began to carry a fairly steady stream of items reporting foundation grants in support of behaviorally oriented projects and programs. And, in 1948, the Survey Research Center initiated its annual Summer Sessions for training in survey methods.

FROM 1950 TO THE MID-1950's. If there is a "Great Divide" or a "critical period" in the rise of behavioralism, it probably occurred between 1950 and 1951. Before then, behavioralism was at most a tendency; after that time, it was not only a major movement but one which promised (or threatened) to sweep the discipline. A brief recital of events indicates why these years were crucial.

1950 brought Hyneman's *Bureaucracy in a Democracy,* *Power and Society* by Lasswell and Kaplan, and the Simon, Smithburg, and Thompson text, *Public Administration.* The last-

[12] It was through this Committee that the Council financed one of the first "big" behavioral studies, the Survey Research Center's 1952 presidential election survey.

named, described by its authors as "a realistic, behavioral description of the processes of administration," was a radical departure from previous texts in that field. Lasswell and Kaplan outlined a conceptual and theoretical framework for the study of political behavior, and the significance of their attempt is reflected in the fury of Morgenthau's assault on the book's philosophical premises.[13] Hyneman's distillation of his wartime administrative experiences (given a fifteen page laudatory notice in the *Review*) called, in effect, for a more realistic approach to government and administration. During this year the *Review* carried Bertram Gross' long and nigh-ecstatic commentary on the reissue of Bentley's *The Process of Government;* it also introduced a new feature, a sub-section of "booknotes and bibliography" entitled "methodology and research in the social sciences." Perhaps it was purely coincidental but this was also the first year that a political scientist unmistakably aligned with the profession's behavioral wing (Peter Odegard) was elected President of the Association.

Behavioralism gained additional momentum in 1951. Behavioralists moved into the key Association committees.[14] One issue of the *Journal of Politics* had four essays on "Political Theory and Research." The *Review* published a discussion of "Science and Politics," several articles on power, Oliver Garceau's milestone working paper on "Research in the Political Process" done for the SSRC's Committee on Political Behavior, and a typically Lasswellian piece on "The Immediate Future of Research

[13] In his review, Morgenthau declared that Lasswell and Kaplan: ". . . are among the most gifted representatives of schools which at present ride the crest of the wave. Yet in truth they represent an obsolescent point of view. This book perhaps constitutes the most extreme, and therefore self-defeating, product of the fundamental errors of those schools. It may well contribute to their demise by virtue of its own absurdity. There is already at work—in Chicago as elsewhere—a strong reaction to the 'straightforward empirical viewpoint' of our authors. It is true that Mr. Lasswell and Mr. Kaplan don't know it yet. The research foundations don't know it yet. The professional organizations don't know it yet. But an ever-increasing number of able and vigorous thinkers do know it." *APSR,* vol. 46 (1952), p. 234.

[14] At least four (Laswell, Truman, Speier, and W. T. R. Fox) were appointed to the Committee on Research; another (Bertram Gross) became chairman of the Committee on Politics.

Policy and Method in Political Science."[15] Overshadowing these was David Truman's *The Governmental Process,* which restated and developed Bentley's "group approach." Truman's book was promptly hailed as providing the key to a real "science of politics" by incautious readers who, a few short years later, would accuse him of having promised more than he was able to deliver. On the other side of the ideological fence, there was Eric Voegelin's impressive but less widely read *The New Science of Politics.*

Mention must be made, although reluctantly, of the Association's Committee for the Advancement of Teaching 1951 opus, *Goals for Political Science.* This report, which, as one reviewer said, had "little more than distinguished authorship to recommend it," managed to face in all directions on all issues. Paradoxically, the very triteness and superficiality of the volume made it important. Many readers must have been struck, as was one reviewer, by the frightening possibility that *Goals* reflected "faithfully the state of political science at mid-century" with political scientists "riding off in all directions" and with many of them wondering, while at full gallop, "whether some other direction might not have been better."[16] So unflattering is the portrait of the discipline which emerges from the book, a fact to which the Committee seemed oblivious, that some political scientists may have turned to behavioralism mainly as a reaction against the status quo.

This reaction gained impetus in 1953 when the Ford Foundation underwrote "self-studies" of the behavioral sciences at a number of major universities. The ensuing reports (not to mention the grants themselves) gave additional publicity and respectability to the movement. At the same time, David Easton published *The Political System,* a sweeping critique of contemporary political science in general and of political theory in particular. If Easton did not specifically endorse behavioralism, his call for the development of "systematic theory" and his mordant description of the state of the discipline could only serve to strengthen that cause.

[15] Lasswell and Simon, it might be added, seem suddenly to have been discovered (or rediscovered) by the *Review.* Neither had contributed to the journal from 1946 to 1949; both have pieces in each of the volumes (i.e., nos. 44, 45, 46) between 1950 and 1952.

[16] James W. Fesler, in "Goals For Political Science: A Discussion," *APSR,* vol. 45 (1951), p. 1000.

By the mid-1950's, then, behavioralism had arrived. Behaviorally oriented articles appeared with greater frequency in the journals. Pendleton Herring, one of the original members of the Social Science Research Council's Committee on Political Behavior, was chosen Association President in 1953; Harold Lasswell, *the* behavioralist, became president-elect in 1955; and another member of the original SSRC committee, V. O. Key, was elected to the same office a year later. There was a special panel devoted to "political behavior" at the 1956 annual meeting, and the roster of Council members and Association officials was increasingly studded with the names of persons prominent in the behavioral camp.

By the mid-1950's, beyond doubt, behavioralism posed a threat not only to the predominance of traditional political science but conceivably to its very survival. Perhaps first fully realizing the force of the behavioralist thrust and the possible consequences of its success, the anti-behavioralists struck back in deadly earnest. The result, of course, was the bitter "ideological" warfare which absorbed so much of the profession's energies and attention over the next several years.

FROM THE MID-1950'S TO THE PRESENT. No constructive purpose would be served by chronicling, step by step, article by article, and book by book, the polemics of this decade. There are often lucid and thoughtful contributions but, on balance, the argument is not notably advanced, since the basic positions of the contending parties had already been fairly well developed. Anyone interested in the gory details need only read the *Review,* being sure not to overlook the pages devoted to "Communications" and to book reviews. Those with less time to invest can get a taste of the flavor and level of these exchanges by reading the *Essays on the Scientific Study of Politics* (1962) and the vitriolic critique and counter-critique of the volume which followed in the *Review.*

Fortunately, the decade also witnessed the publication of a number of substantive studies which testified, more persuasively than could any tract, to the merits of the behavioral "paradigm." While it would be pointless to attempt a complete listing, several of the most significant items may be mentioned. In chronological order they were:

189

Morton A. Kaplan, *System and Process in International Politics* (1957); Gabriel A. Almond and James S. Coleman, *The Politics of the Developing Areas* (1959); Glendon A. Schubert, *Quantitative Analysis of Judicial Behavior* (1959); Angus Campbell, Philip E. Converse, Warren E. Miller, and Donald E. Stokes, *The American Voter* (1960); Thomas Hovet, Jr., *Bloc Politics in the United Nations* (1960), Robert A. Dahl, *Who Governs? Democracy and Power in an American City* (1961); John C. Wahlke, Heinz Eulau, William Buchanan, and LeRoy C. Ferguson, *The Legislative System. Explorations in Legislative Behavior* (1962); Gabriel A. Almond and Sidney Verba, *The Civic Culture. Political Attitudes and Democracy in Five Nations* (1963); Karl W. Deutsch, *The Nerves of Government: Models of Political Communication and Control* (1963); Robert E. Agger, Daniel Goldrich, and Bert E. Swanson, *The Rulers and the Ruled: Political Power and Impotence in American Communities* (1964); and David Easton, *A Systems Analysis of Political Life* (1965).

The story of any war usually ends with a statement of who won and who lost or, if the struggle is yet undecided, some indication of the likely outcome. But, as David Truman ruefully observed in his presidential remarks, it is yet too soon to tell how this issue will finally be resolved. It is not too early, however, to take cognizance of the influence which behavioralism has already had on the manner in which the profession pursues its chosen tasks.

THE BEHAVIORAL INFLUENCE

What has been the influence of behavioralism on American political science? The answer is in some ways quite clear. Behavioralism has made the discipline more self-conscious and self-critical. Vast energy has gone into a stocktaking and self-evaluation which, in any case, was long overdue.

Consider also the dramatic changes in vocabulary. An older generation spoke knowingly of checks and balances, *jus soli,* divesting legislation, brokerage function, quota system, bloc voting, resulting powers, proportional representation, pressure group, sovereignty, dual federalism, lobbying, recall and referendum, Posdcorb, quasi-judicial agencies, concurrent majority, legislative court, Taylorism, state of nature, item veto, unit rule, and natural law. From today's younger practitioners there flows trippingly from the tongue such exotic phrases as boundary maintenance, bargaining, cognitive dissonance, community power structure, conflict resolution, conceptual framework, cross-pressures, decision making, dysfunctional, factor analysis, feedback, Fortran, game theory, Guttman scaling, homeostasis, input-output, interaction, model, multiple regression, multivariate analysis, non-parametric, payoff, transaction flow model, role, simulation, political systems analysis, T test, unit record equipment, variance, and, of course, political socialization. It is no longer unusual to find these freshly minted coins of disciplinary discourse dotting the pages of text books written primarily for undergraduates. The vocabulary associated with behavioralism also testifies to the extent that political science has become interdisciplinary, for most of these terms, and the concepts and techniques they symbolize, were borrowed (sometimes rather indiscriminately)[17] from other fields of inquiry.

Another consequence of behavioralism has been a sharply increased attention to research techniques and to analytic theory. Formal courses in methodology, now firmly established in most graduate departments, are now filtering down into the under-graduate curriculum. Further evidence of this interest can be found in the pages of the *Review*. Three two-year periods were singled out and the *Review*'s contents over each of these spans analyzed.* The first period, 1946–48, can be regarded as "pre-behavioral" or "very early behavioral"; the second, 1950–52, coincides with the first real blossoming of the movement; and the third, 1963–65, allows a decade for the behavioral influence to be manifest. The results were as follows:

[17] On this subject, see the essay by Martin Landau, "On the Uses of Metaphor in Political Analysis," *Social Research,* vol. 28 (1961), pp. 331–53.

* Only substantive articles were classified. Communications to the editor and bibliographic essays were excluded. In several instances, very brief "discussion" collections by several contributors were counted as a single item.

TABLE 1: IMPACT OF BEHAVIORALISM AS REFLECTED IN THE CONTENTS OF THE AMERICAN POLITICAL SCIENCE REVIEW

	1946–8		1950–2		1963–5	
	N	%	N	%	N	%
Low level quantitative techniques	15	10.9	15	11.4	19	18.3
More powerful quant. techniques	1	.7	6	4.5	23	22.1
Discussions of scientific method	6	4.3	5	3.8	2	1.9
Analytic Theory	0	0.0	17	12.9	17	16.3
Other	116	84.1	89	67.4	43	41.3
	138	100.0	132	99.9	104	99.9

The most compelling change between 1946–48 and 1950–52 was the increased attention to analytic theory, an important, though certainly not an exclusive, concern of behavioralism. This trend continued upward, at a slower rate, between 1950–52 and 1963–65. Almost equally impressive was the increase in the proportion of articles employing more powerful quantitative techniques.[18] While only a modest change occurred between 1946–48 and 1950–52, perhaps because of the time required for the necessary technological retooling, the 22 per cent figure for 1963–65 leaves no doubt as to what transpired. But the data in Table 1 actually understate the case. The articles falling into the "other" and the "low level quantitative techniques" categories in 1963–65 tended to be more analytical and less descriptive than those which appeared in the earlier periods.

Other signs of the behavioral ferment might also be noted. The political science department reputed to have the most distinguished graduate faculty (Yale) is heavily oriented toward be-

[18] A word may be in order about the criteria used in making these classifications. Articles which made use of only percentages and simple counting, no matter how imaginative the analysis, were placed in the "low level quantitative technique" category. To be included in the "more powerful quantitative technique" category, an article had to utilize techniques assuming ordinal or interval measurement, or to employ tests of significance with nominal data. The "analytic theory" category includes articles which sought to articulate or to appraise some type of conceptual scheme such as group, power, systems, elite, etc.

havioralism. The elected officialdom of the Association has increasingly tended to be composed of persons prominent in the behavioral movement. Recent APSA presidents, for example, include Lasswell, Key, Hyneman, Truman, Almond, and Dahl. When, in 1963, a random sample of the profession was asked to name the political scientists who have made the most significant contributions to the discipline since 1945, seven of the ten most frequently mentioned (Key, Truman, Dahl, Lasswell, Simon, Almond, and Easton) were of the behavioral persuasion. And, as a last item, the fields of specialization regarded as the most behaviorally oriented were also the fields in which respondents to this survey thought the most significant work was being done.

Unquestionably, behavioralism has had a very substantial impact. But—has the behavioral contribution been sufficiently great to constitute an irrefutable demonstration of the efficacy of its "paradigm"? Or, on the other hand, has its payoff been so meager that a contrary conclusion is justified?

For plentiful and imposing reasons, these questions cannot be answered at the present time. If the single most distinguished graduate department is behavioral in outlook, the five next most distinguished are certainly not. Recent presidents of the Association include several distinguished practitioners (e.g., Cole, Swisher, Redford, and Friedrich) who have not been associated with the behavioral movement. Although behavioralism has left its mark on almost every specialization within the discipline, in only a few (such as community politics, electoral behavior, political socialization, and public opinion) have behavioral theories and techniques proved so obviously superior as to recast drastically an area of inquiry. The *Review,* while more behavioral than it was a few years ago, is not overwhelmingly so. The basic undergraduate course in the discipline remains the traditional offering in American government, and the best-selling textbooks for this course are still predominantly pre-behavioral in conception and substance.

The most direct and most convincing evidence, though, is the discipline's own assessment of behavioralism. A random sample of the profession was asked, in 1963, to respond to two propositions (among others). These propositions, and the responses elicited, were:

1. The really significant problems of political life cannot be successfully attacked by the behavioral approach.

Strongly agree	Agree	Can't Say	Disagree	Strongly disagree
14.4%	24.1%	15.8%	31.8%	13.9%

2. Much of the work being done in political behavior is only marginally related to political science.

Strongly agree	Agree	Can't Say	Disagree	Strongly disagree
19.0%	21.8%	10.9%	36.0%	12.3%

One need not resort to elegant statistical analysis of these highly correlated sets of responses to conclude that the discipline had not by then developed a consensus on this general issue. Unless the attitude of the profession has changed drastically in the intervening few years, the future of the behavioral movement continues uncertain.

XIII
extra-scientific responsibilities and activities, 1945–1966

W hatever the impact of behavioralism on other aspects of the discipline, the idea that political scientists should attend strictly to scientific inquiry made very slow headway. As in pre-behavioral days, many continued to devote their energies to questions of public policy. If anything, education for democratic citizenship received greater attention than before, with the Association initially cooperating with the newly founded Citizenship Clearing House and then, after that relationship cooled, launching its own program. Perhaps the major change was the emergence of a viewpoint which questioned the effectiveness, rather than the propriety, of these efforts.

Another development was a broadening interest in the work of foreign political scientists. Although the impulse has been erratic, there has been a definite movement away from the provincialism of preceding decades.

EDUCATION FOR DEMOCRATIC CITIZENSHIP

The data permit only one conclusion: American political scientists, by and large, continue to regard education for democratic citizenship as one of their primary responsibilities. "Amongst political scientists in the United States," reported the (not always infallible) Committee for the Advancement of Teaching, "training for intelligent citizenship is the predominant interest and emphasis."[1] Dwight Waldo, a cautious and reliable commentator, voiced a similar opinion several years later, writing that the most important objective of those teaching political science was "education for citizenship."[2] Numerous presidential speeches and official Association pronouncements sounded the same theme.[3]

The widespread activities conducted by the Citizenship Clearing House—National Center for Education in Politics[4] afforded tangible and impressive evidence of this interest. The CCH-NCEP was noteworthy not only because of what it sought to accomplish but because, it bore, to a fascinating degree, many of the familial characteristics of the Association's once potent Committee on Policy.[5] The resemblances are striking. The two pursued nearly identical goals. During its formative years, the policies and program of the Clearing House were heavily influenced by Thomas H. Reed, the same Reed who, twenty years earlier, had been the Chairman and guiding spirit of the Committee on Policy.[6] Both the CCH-NCEP and the Committee on Policy came to be regarded by some political scientists as a potential rival to the Association itself. Both foundered when the requisite foundation support was no longer forthcoming. The key difference between them was that the Clearing House was organizationally independent, whereas the Committee on Policy was an agency of, and formally subordinate to, the Association.

[1] *Op. cit.* p. ix.

[2] Young, *op. cit.,* p. 96.

[3] See, e.g., *APSR,* vols. 40 (1946), pp. 227; 42 (1948), p. 106; and 44 (1950), p. 160.

[4] Known as the Citizenship Clearing House until 1962 when it became the National Center For Education in Politics. For convenience sake, we will henceforth refer to it either as the "Clearing House" or as "CCH-NCEP."

[5] Above, pp. 97–100.

[6] The best statements of the Reeds' (he was now working together with Mrs. Reed) educational philosophy are contained in the two reports entitled *Evaluation of Citizenship Training and Incentive in American Colleges and Universities* (1950) and the much better known *Preparing College Men and Women For Politics* (1952).

196

The rise and fall of CCH-NCEP can be quickly summarized.[7] In December, 1946, the Association's Executive Council was informed by Dean Arthur Vanderbilt[8] that he had received a grant from the National Foundation For Education to establish a "Citizenship Clearing House" which would help young political science graduates find "opportunities in practical politics." The Council promptly expressed its approval of "any attempt, competently made, to facilitate the transition from the study of political science to participation in practical politics." Noting "with interest" the project described by Dean Vanderbilt, the Council directed the President "to appoint a committee to investigate the whole problem, to advise with Dean Vanderbilt, and to report back."[9]

Pursuant to this resolution, an Advisory Panel on Methods of Encouraging Political Participation was created. The Advisory Panel soon metamorphosed into a Committee on Citizenship Participation in Politics which, with Dean Vanderbilt as a member, joined with the Clearing House in 1949 and 1950 in sponsoring regional conferences aimed at getting political scientists to do more in the way of encouraging students to "get into politics."

Relations between the Clearing House and the Association were reasonably cordial during these early years. CCH-NCEP activities were reported regularly in the *Review* until 1954 and the first Director of the Clearing House, Professor George Williams of the New York University School of Law, served for several years as Chairman of the Association's Committee on Citizenship Participation in Politics. By the mid-1950's, though, the atmosphere seems to have become rather strained. While the *Review* notes a Ford Foundation grant of almost a million dollars to the Clearing House in 1956, there is scant mention of its activities after that, though formal cooperation between the two organizations con-

[7] We are indebted to Professor Bernard C. Hennessy, who served as CCH-NCEP director from 1961 to 1966, for his very helpful comments. See also his *Political Education and Political Science: The National Center for Education in Politics,* New York, September, 1966.

[8] Dean Vanderbilt headed the School of Law at New York University. He was later (1948) to become Chief Justice of the New Jersey Supreme Court. The "inaugural" conference of the clearing house was not actually held until September, 1947.

[9] *APSR,* vol. 41 (1947), p. 121.

tinued almost to the mid-1960's. From the Association's side, the reasons for this coolness are not too difficult to guess. The CCH-NCEP was a potential, if not an actual, rival for the loyalties of that wing of the profession especially attracted by extra-scientific ventures. During the early 1950's, the Clearing House demonstrated a real capacity to obtain foundation support, a capacity embarassingly superior to the Association's. To widen the rift, some influential political scientists, particularly among the behavioralists, had grave reservations about the entire activist thrust.

The decade and a half following the mid-century mark was literally a "boom and bust" period for the CCH-NCEP. A 1950 Falk Foundation grant, the first of what would eventually total almost three-quarters of a million dollars from that source, enabled the Clearing House to set up a national network of "autonomous regional units," to launch a program of summer workshops, and to initiate various "fellowships" in practical politics. Then came the sizable 1956 grant already mentioned and, in 1959, an additional $700,000 from Ford. Two years later, the boom ended when Ford announced a $600,000 "terminal" gift. Efforts to raise money from other sources proved unsuccessful. Its funds exhausted, the CCH-NCEP closed its doors in late 1966. Several of its regional affiliates, however, continue to function.

By this time, the Association had received 3 million dollars from Ford to expand its own work in this area,[10] and the void left by the Clearing House's demise was partially filled. The Association's efforts, however, are directed largely at graduate students, journalists, and professional politicians,[11] whereas the CCH-NCEP aimed primarily at undergraduates. For the present, this latter field lies fallow.

Occasional criticisms of education for democratic citizenship notwithstanding,[12] both the written record and the energies mar-

[10] Above, pp. 153–54.

[11] Important exceptions are the "government" courses offered in the television series entitled "Continental Classroom." These courses, which may be taken for college credit, are co-sponsored by the Association, the National Council for the Social Studies, the American Association of Colleges for Teacher Education, and the National Broadcasting Company.

[12] The author of an article which discussed the manner in which the introductory political science course could be used to indoctrinate students with the "proper" political values was attacked by some of his colleagues, although it was not always clear whether the strictures were aimed at the

shalled behind the CCH-NCEP's and the Association's undertakings suggest that most political scientists would agree with the recent declaration by one of their colleagues that "the first of my obligations . . . is to the principles of the political system under which I have the good fortune to live."[13] Still, in the past decade or so, a new type of dissent has been voiced. A handful of studies have questioned the practicality, rather than the propriety, of the perennial effort to teach good citizenship and to inspire greater interest in personal political participation. Some of these studies have examined educational programs aimed at inculcating "values," others have focused on attempts to evoke political "activism" among college students. All have come to much the same conclusion: there is no persuasive evidence that any of these undertakings achieve their intended ends. In fact, the findings reported in the burgeoning "political socialization" literature suggest quite another conclusion.[14]

The "civic educators" may have thus been outflanked and their citadel brought under attack from an unexpected quarter. Education for democratic citizenship and "better minds for better politics" will henceforth have to be defended not by the cannoneering of moral pronouncements but by the small arms fire of demonstrated results. Whether the position can be held by this means is an open question.

PARTICIPATION IN PUBLIC AFFAIRS

American political scientists have traditionally been engrossed with current political questions. The decision to focus the first couple of post-1945 Association meetings on the problem of government in the post-war world indicated that they intended to

---

error of his beliefs or his folly in stating them for publication *APSR,* vol. 42 (1948), p. 542. The authors of *Goals* also drew some adverse comment for their apparent endorsement of the idea that civic education was a legitimate function, if not an outright duty, of the profession.

[13] Leslie Lipson, *The Democratic Civilization,* New York, 1964, p. vii.

[14] This point is nicely made by Evron M. and Jeanne J. Kirkpartrick in their chapter on "Political Science," in Erling Masser Hunt, *et. al., High School Social Studies: Perspectives,* Boston, 1962, pp. 99–125.

continue so doing. That augury has proved correct. In fact, Dwight Waldo's sampling of the literature led him to conclude that this concern has increased rather than diminished.[15]

But even those who believe that matters of public policy are legitimate objects of attention are not altogether sure that political scientists have been dealing with the right questions. This disquiet was voiced by Arthur Macmahon in his 1948 presidential address when he simultaneously defended the "instrumental outlook" and urged the profession to "lift its sights."[16] Harold Lasswell repeated the admonition two years later, reminding his colleagues that "in the selection of research problems it is important to take the major policy issues of our epoch into consideration."[17]

To date, this has not always been the case. If we take the really "big" issues of the past twenty years—foreign policy, nuclear policy, civil rights (including McCarthyism), the relationship of government to the economy—there is little in the pages of the *Review*[18] which suggests that American political scientists have had much to say about the direction which national policy should take.[19] This discipline may have fallen between two stools. To the

[15] *APRS,* vol. 44 (1950), p. 425.
[16] APSR, vol. 42 (1948), p. 425. An undated, mimeographed, Association listing of "Political Scientists in Elective Office and Appointive Administrative Positions" strongly suggests that this interest has not been entirely academic or literary. The holding of public position is, of course, a long-established practice in the profession.
[17] According to Lasswell, an emphasis on the "fundamental problems of man in society, rather than on topical issues of the moment" is the basic concern of the "policy sciences." Political science belongs among them to the extent that it is "concerned with explaining the policy-making and policy-execution process, and with locating data and providing interpretations which are relevant to the policy problems of a given period." Objectivity, he felt, could be maintained in gathering and interpreting data, even though the actual choice of the problems to be studied was necessarily value-oriented. For one of the fullest expositions of his outlook, see his essay, "The Policy Orientation," in Daniel Lerner and Harold D. Lasswell (eds.), *The Policy Sciences* (Stanford: 1951), pp. 3–15.
[18] It could be argued that the *Review* does not accurately mirror the interests of the profession but the implications of such an argument are so far-reaching that it is best rejected out of hand. Besides, the *Review* is not notably different from the other general political science journals in this respect. It is improbable that all of these are out of step.
[19] As Robert Dahl has observed, political scientists have almost completely ignored problems of government, business, and the economic order. Prominent among those who have had something to say on some of the issues mentioned are Peter Odegard, whose 1951 presidential address

degree that it has scientific pretensions, it may have devoted too much attention to questions of public policy. To the degree that it aspired to a role in the shaping of events, it may have been overly modest in choosing its issues and in making its wisdom available to others.[20]

BROADENING DISCIPLINARY HORIZONS

A modest renewal of interest in the political science of other countries, and especially that of Europe, has occurred over the past two decades. Several factors contributed to this: the convergence of interest in studying party, electoral, and legislative behavior among French, Scandinavian, British, and American practitioners; the participation by American political scientists in foreign aid and technical assistance programs; the availability of exchange appointments and Fulbright fellowships; and the efforts, especially by the behavioralists, to develop models which can be applied to all political societies, advanced or "developing," Western or non-Western.

A more internationally minded outlook has shown itself in several ways. American political scientists played an important role in organizing the International Political Science Association, founded under UNESCO auspices in 1949.[21] Braving the hazards and discomforts of Paris, Rome, Geneva, Brussels, and London, they have also participated—to the maximum degree permitted by foundation subventions—in the International Association's triennial meetings.[22] Americans were prominent, too, in the planning

---

dealt forthrightly with McCarthyism, and Hans Morgenthau, who has occasionally been disenchanted with official foreign policy.

[20] For a thoughtful discussion of this general issue, see Vernon Van Dyke's "Process and Policy as Focal Concepts in Political Research," *Report,* The Laboratory for Political Research, Department of Political Science, University of Iowa, 1966, mimeo, pp. 13 ff., and his forthcoming "The Optimum Scope of Political Science."

[21] The American Political Science Association assisted the International Political Science Association to get grants, initially, from the Ford Foundation and, later, from the Asia Foundation. It also met most of the cost of two International Association Round Table and Executive Committee meetings held in the United States, respectively, in 1957 and 1960.

[22] Americans, it should be added, constitute well over half of the International Association's total membership.

and execution of a UNESCO study of political science around the world. Discussions of French, Swedish, and Japanese political science have appeared in the *Review*,[23] and the "news and notes" pages of that journal abound with items reporting the beginning or completion by American scholars of professorial tours of duty in Europe, Africa, Asia, and Latin America. For the first time in a half-century, the "year abroad" has again become a valued status symbol. Another, and perhaps the most significant, manifestation has been the blossoming of "comparative politics" and "comparative administration" as areas of specialization.

To be sure, it would be easy to exaggerate this resurgence of "internationalism." There was a temporary rift between the American Political Science Association and the International Political Science Association in 1964. Some officials of the latter organization have recently been troubled by what they fear is a renewal of an "isolationist" outlook among their American confreres. Nor do the book review pages of the discipline's leading journal suggest any drastic shift of attitude. Between 1961 and 1965, for example, only two non-English language volumes received extended notice in the *Review,* whereas 12 such books were so treated between 1951 and 1955.

On balance, however, there can be little question that American practitioners are becoming more attentive to scholarship in other countries. The change is long overdue. American political science, as H. B. Adams and John W. Burgess themselves testified, was conceived in the "seminaries" of Europe and it is only fitting that this intellectual kinship be recognized and filial ties acknowledged. Indeed, it will be interesting to observe the consequences of this rapprochement. Both sides, no doubt, will be influenced by the interchange. It may be, however, that just as American political science was once Europeanized, this second encounter between the two will have the opposite result. If so, not only will the original debt have been repaid but, in a curious sense, the discipline's intellectual course will have come full circle.

[23] *APSR,* vols. 51 (1957), p. 511; 44 (1950), p. 977; and 46 (1952), p. 202.

part 5
conclusion

XIV
quo
vadimus

*T*hose who trace the development of a discipline have neither a mandate nor an obligation to venture beyond the present. But, though we hope the preceding pages have not made the fact too painfully apparent, we are, after all, political scientists rather than historians. We have argued, moreover, that certain commitments and problems can be traced through the life-span of the profession; further, that there is almost a cyclical regularity to the manner in which political scientists have become enamoured of, and then disenchanted with, the idea of a scientific politics. The nature of our analysis implicitly urges, and the importance of the subject certainly invites, some attention to the query—*quo vadimus?*

Perhaps the primary justification for what might otherwise appear an act of egregious supererogation rests on the difference between *projection* and *prediction*. In two of the three central concerns around which the previous discussion has been organized (professional growth and extra-scientific responsibilities) the trends seem sufficiently clear to leave little doubt about their direction over the next decade or so. Although we assuredly cannot foretell what will happen in the third area (political science as science) we can anticipate some of the more likely short-run developments. Of course, there is the danger that we have misread current trends or that these will be profoundly altered by future events. Nonetheless, authors must have the courage of their conclusions.

PROFESSIONAL GROWTH

The number of political scientists will rise steadily over the next seven or eight years as swelling college enrollments continue to generate a demand for additional faculty. To a lesser degree, this growth will also be nurtured by the expansion of governmental functions and correspondingly greater opportunities in the public service, particularly in agencies concerned with urban and metropolitan affairs.

These are only two small clouds on this otherwise roseate horizon: the internecine controversy over behavioralism and the threat of outside encroachment. But these are hardly serious dangers. Political scientists have historically demonstrated an enviable capacity to reconcile the near-irreconcilable, and it is nearly inconceivable that the present dispute would be permitted to jeopardize the growth, let alone the existence, of the profession. And, with the exception of some areas of public administration (and perhaps border regions of political socialization), the territory now claimed by political science can probably be held against any external foray.

Barring some cataclysmic upheaval in our educational system, the discipline will become progressively more *academized*. About 75 per cent of the Association's membership hold teaching appointments. As faculties expand, the proportion of academic political scientists will increase, even allowing for greater employment on the governmental side.

With a sellers' market prevailing, doctoral output will continue upward. At the same time, the percentage of political scientists holding degrees from "name" institutions—and it is safe to assume that the composition of this elite group will hold fairly constant—will decline yet further. What effect this will have on the profession's traditionally discriminatory employment practices cannot be foreseen. The most plausible supposition is that the short-term imbalance between supply and demand should make it a shade easier for those coming from less prestigious schools to move into the top-ranked departments.

206

On another point, however, we can speak with some assurance. In the decade ahead the discipline will be no more successful than before in resolving the perennial debate about the content of a "sound" doctoral program. To the list of chronic issues already noted will be added that of the training to be required in statistics, mathematics, formal logic, data processing, and similar technical skills. As in the past, the manner in which these issues are resolved in any given department will hinge no less on the strength of the contending factions than on any general educational principle.

EXTRA-SCIENTIFIC ACTIVITIES AND RESPONSIBILITIES

From time immemorial, the twin tasks of education for democratic citizenship and of active personal participation in political and governmental affairs have absorbed the energies of many American political scientists. It is unlikely that the immediate future will witness any significant change in these longstanding commitments.

Diverse and powerful forces bear upon civic training for the young. Almost all of the publicly supported institutions of higher learning, and a goodly number of the private schools, regularly proclaim this to be one of their paramount objectives. Appeals for financial aid, whether directed at state legislatures or at private philanthropy, place great weight on the presumed relationship between higher education and intelligent democratic citizenship. To renounce this time-honored responsibility would be to jettison a uniquely effective argument for public and private support.

At the instructional level, the burden of transmitting the knowledge and understanding deemed essential for informed democratic participation is usually carried by some type of "required" political science (or government) course and constitutes a major justification for that requirement. These courses are the departments' bread-and-butter offerings. Their reduction or elimination would have untoward and far-reaching consequences.

Only the cynic would deny that college administrators and political scientists devoutly believe, by and large, in the necessity and merits of citizenship education. At the same time, only the naïve would deny a concomitant awareness that any turning away from this noble purpose would present both with serious practical difficulties. Given this happy conjunction of conviction and benefit, a radical break with the past seems most improbable.

Nor is the profession's longstanding concern with immediate political questions and its demonstrated predilection for applied, programmatic research likely to be drastically diminished, not even by behavioralism. Certainly, a plausible case can be made for the proposition that American political scientists should lend their knowledge and talents to the solution of the problems besetting their society. Reformism and pragmatism are writ large in our way of life, and the activist tradition is deeply rooted in the American political and social outlook.

A second factor should also be mentioned here. *Pure* research may be highly prestigious but it is *applied* research which more often commands the truly impressive grants. Society, its faith in science now extending even to social science, is showing a heartening willingness to subsidize academic attempts to find solutions to urgent social problems. Even the most doctrinaire behavioralist will be hard put to resist the reduced teaching loads, attractively furnished offices and private secretaries, expense accounts, travel funds, and all the other perquisites that go with generously budgeted research grants.[1]

POLITICAL SCIENCE AS SCIENCE

The ultimate nature of American political science, we need hardly say, will be profoundly influenced by the fate of the behavioral movement. Though we can only speculate on the eventual outcome, a problem to which we will shortly return, evidence already at hand points to two likely developments in the immediate future. First, the discipline will become more behavioral in tempo. Second, and not altogether paradoxically, the "scientistic" aspirations of behavioralism will become progressively more modest in tone and scope.

---

[1] A reaction against massive expenditures for "pure" research without any immediately visible "pay-off" is already taking place in the hard sciences.

American political scientists today seem to be about evenly divided on the merits of behavioralism, although the division takes a rather curious form. Rather than the normal bell-shaped curve, or even a bi-polar alignment showing two large contesting camps, there is a fairly smooth distribution from one end of the gradient to another, although two small extremist factions do emerge.[2] However these findings are interpreted, it seems clear, as we pointed out above, that the profession has yet to swing decisively one way or another.

Several factors warrant the expectation that in the next few years there will be a trend toward behavioralism and toward a behavioralistically inclined political science. More and more departments have been adding behaviorally oriented persons to their staffs; in rare instances, entire departments have "gone behavioral." These behavioralists have made a heavy investment of time and effort in acquiring their special skills. They will demand the same investment from their own students. Neither those who have already acquired this expertise nor those now in the painful process of doing so will lightly abandon the type of inquiry for which they have so arduously prepared themselves. To the degree that contemporary behavioralism demands far greater technical sophistication than the post-World War I science of politics thrust, it has built into itself a self-perpetuating dynamism lacking in the predecessor movement.

Another factor encouraging a short-run swing toward behavioralism is its success in capturing key positions within the power structure of the profession. An impressive number of those elected to Association office, we have seen, are either spokesmen for, or actively sympathetic to the behavioralist cause. Behavioralists exercise an important, if not a decisive, voice in determining the allocation of foundation and government research grants. Power feeds upon itself—and every profession has its careerists. The "sweet smell of success" will assuredly attract to behavioralism its fair share of academic opportunists. In this sense, behavioralism enjoys a competitive advantage beyond its inherent merits.

This gain in "popularity" will probably coincide with a

[2] Albert Somit and Joseph Tanenhaus, *American Political Science, op. cit.,* pp. 22–24.

narrowing of the distance between the behavioralist and the traditionalist positions on the possibility of a science of politics. Signs of this are already evident. Several eminent behavioralists have of late explicitly disclaimed the idea that behavioralism will lead to a science of politics in the foreseeable future. They argue, rather, that it will result in a *more* scientific and *more* precise body of knowledge than would otherwise be possible. As more behavioralists take up the task of translating theories, models and systems into operationally researchable hypotheses, and of imposing intellectual order upon predictably recalcitrant data, we can confidently expect an increasingly realistic understanding of the problems that must be resolved in making the discipline appreciably more rigorous, let alone in constructing a scientific politics.

But these short-run developments are less important, Keynes' classic rejoinder notwithstanding, than the ultimate future of the profession. The critical question is not where will political science be in 1970 or even 1975 but where—and what—will it be a quarter-century from now?

Whether behavioralism will eventually transform itself into the predominant "paradigm" depends upon a number of eventualities. Once the present flush of enthusiasm has waned, will it be able, given the expertise demanded, to attract and train enough disciples to build itself into something more than a minority movement? Will the behavioralists, who have relied heavily upon national surveys and similar large-scale inquiries for their data, continue to command the massive grants which make this kind of research possible? If not, can they develop alternative, less costly sources of data? Will the theorists and system-builders be able to bridge the yawning chasm between their ideas and the empirical world, a feat beyond their capacities to date? Above all, will the behavioral "pay-off" be sufficiently impressive to win acceptance of its goals and techniques by the main body of American political scientists? Should most, if not all, of these questions be answered in the affirmative, the political science of the late twentieth century will be a vastly different enterprise from that which we have historically known or know today.

If, however, behavioralism cannot satisfy these requirements, what then? A prolonged failure to make good on a fair share of its promises will inevitably provoke a reaction which not even control

210

of the Establishment could withstand. The perceived self-interest of the profession, plus the ambitions of a future generation of Young Turks, would play the same role in such a counter-reformation as they did in the post-1945 revolt against traditional political science. Should behavioralism suffer the same fate as the Burgess-inspired movement of the 1880's and the Merriam-led push of the 1920's, will it leave behind it a discipline profoundly altered and enriched? Or, as has been the fate of similar previous attempts, will its major significance derive from the way in which it has prepared the ground for yet a subsequent effort to build a science of politics—this one, say, another generation or so hence?

XV

1965 —1980:
journey toward an uncertain future

As the first edition of this book went to press in the fall of 1966, the future of American political science seemed roseate. Despite a sharp increase in the production of Ph.D.s (from an average of 155 a year in 1946–50 to more than 300 a year in 1961–65), the new jobs created by rapidly expanding institutions of higher education more than kept pace. In the sellers' market of the 1960's, academic salaries outdistanced inflation and teaching loads declined.

As the ranks of the profession swelled, so did its scholarly output. Books, some now regarded as classics, rolled off the presses in torrents,[1] and journals began to proliferate. Skills in quantitative analysis became a routine aspect of graduate training. Even expertise in mathematical modeling began to develop as major books by economists Downs, Buchanan, and Tullock and Olson, and political scientist Riker perked interest in rational choice theory for explaining collective judgments.

With a changing of the guard at the editorial offices of the *American Political Science Review* in the mid-1960's, that arbiter of respectability abandoned its reluctance to publish research employing quantitative techniques beyond the firm grasp of its general readers; the *American Journal of Political Science* (formerly the *Midwest Journal*) soon followed suit. In 1966, when the National Science Foundation finally added political science to those academic disciplines eligible for support by its social science division, the last bastion of resistance to the legitimacy of the behavioral movement had fallen. By the mid-1960's, then, the dispute over behavioralism seemed to have lost most of its stridency—in part, no doubt, because the expanding academic universe was spacious enough to accomodate political scientists regardless of their methodological and substantive persuasions.

The short-lived tranquility of the mid-1960's was shattered by two cataclysmic external forces: the war in Vietnam and the far-reaching transformation of the academic market which began at the turn of the decade. Frustrations stemming from the Vietnamese quagmire, fed by the latent discontents within the profession, led to major changes in the structure and governance of the American Political Science Association and to a renewed, and even angrier, assault on the behavioralist credo. But the impact of the Vietnamese experience on American political science, significant though it may have been, has already been overshadowed by the consequences of a declining birthrate and of a concurrent shift of student preferences. In the pages which follow, we will trace these and other developments of the past decade and a half.

STRUCTURE AND GOVERNANCE OF THE AMERICAN POLITICAL SCIENCE ASSOCIATION

Hardly had the conflict over behaviorism begun to wane before members of the American Political Science Association were caught up in the swirl of disillusionment that swept through academe during the later years of Lyndon Johnson's presidency. Besides the war itself, there were the revelations about the CIA's exploitation of educators through the use of hidden funds; the growing self-awareness of disadvantaged groups and the bad conscience of academicians regarding them; the events of the 1968 election campaign that culminated in the imbroglio at the Democratic nominating convention in Chicago; and, not least, the explosion of student activism. Within the Association, the Caucus for a New Political Science (henceforth CNPS or simply Caucus), first organized in 1967, served as the rallying point for many of the discontented—and they were legion, as our 1963 survey of APSA members had demonstrated.[2]

The Caucus may have attracted more than its share of Marxists, radicals, feminists, careerists, and rabid antibehavioralists, but its supporters during its most influential years (1968–76) included many visible and highly respected scholars representing a true diversity of outlooks and professional specializations. However they may have differed on other issues, what CNPS members had in common was a desire to convert the Association from a non-partisan group interested in the study of things political into an instrument for facilitating social change.

The annual business meeting in September of 1968 turned nearly riotous as its participants hotly debated the proper role of the APSA. In retrospect, that meeting, which carried on long past midnight, was the moment of crisis. If belatedly sensitized to the need to make the Association more responsive to its general membership and to protect both from the dangers of an unrepresentative group seizing control of a business meeting, the APSA's leaders, and others opposed to its politicization, reacted with vigor and dispatch. The Council quickly (February 1969) established a Committee on Constitutional Revision, and the editors of *PS* stimulated a spirited debate on constitutional reform. By the fall of 1969, Association elections could be easily contested but, if there were competing slates, they had to be submitted to a vote of the entire membership by mail ballot. Subsequent business meetings revised the APSA Constitution to require that, in essence, resolutions and constitutional amendments be approved by mail referendum. In addition, an administrative committee, now composed entirely of elected official, replaced the executive committee.

Other important reforms designed to make the Association more responsive to its membership did not require constitutional amendment. The old bases of committee representation—geography, field of specialization, eminence—were broadened to include race, sex, student status, and even ideology. The council also formed special committees to deal with the problems of women, blacks, chicanos, and other disadvantaged groups. In addition, a policy of easier access to information about Association affairs was implemented. Council meetings were opened to the public, budgets more carefully reported, a detailed listing of endowment holdings published yearly, the annual report of the executive director printed in *PS* well in advance of the annual business meeting, and the preliminary work of the Program Committee published in *PS* in good time for individuals to influence the final

215

product. Elaborate minutes for each Council meeting, including the ayes and nays on each roll call vote, also appeared in *PS*.

Yet another group of "non-constitutional" reforms improved the capacity of elected and appointed officials of the Association to carry out their responsibilities. More orderly and equitable procedures for conducting the somewhat unwieldy annual business meeting were introduced. The Council began to convene more frequently, for a while as often as five times a year. Committees received budgets for conducting studies and holding meetings to prepare their reports; *PS* promptly made these reports available to the membership at large.

As mentioned above, after a sharply fought battle, the 1969 annual business meeting amended the APSA Constitution to transfer the forum for electing Association officials from the business meeting itself to a mail ballot of the membership. Although most Caucus adherents opposed the change, that organization has entered a slate in every election since 1969.[3] During the first five elections, highly visible CNPS candidates often ran well. In 1972, the Caucus candidate for president-elect lost by only 59 votes in a total poll of 6,471; and, in 1974, when to the delight of the CNPS the APSA Nominating Committee selected James MacGregor Burns as its nominee for president-elect, Caucus candidates defeated the official nominees for one vice-presidency, the secretary, and four of the eight Council seats contested that year.

But the CNPS could not muster a majority of voting members at Council meetings and the 1974 balloting marked the apogee of its popularity. Thereafter, as political scientists turned increasingly inward away from problems of the broader society to narrow professional concerns, the Caucus ceased to pose a serious electoral threat.

In contrast to its inability to turn the Association into an instrument for social change, the CNPS's efforts to ease access to participation in the annual program proved successful and enduring. Long-established practice had placed control of the program in the hands of a program committee, whose chairperson was selected by the president-elect and whose remaining members were then chosen by the chairperson. Technically under the supervision of the Council, the program committee was largely a law unto itself, and there was no continuity from one program committee to another. From 1968–1970, the CNPS won the right to organize panels of its own for inclusion in the program. Thereafter, the Caucus (and all other groups seeking to participate) was freely accomodated, if in somewhat pejorative fashion, by an official program book which described its panels in a separate section entitled, "Courtesy Listing of Unaffiliated Groups." By 1979, this special section listed panels sonsored by about three dozen groups.[4] Thanks to these mushrooming organizations and the panels they sponsored, the number of those serving as paper-givers, discussants, etc., climbed to about 50 percent of all registrants at the annual meeting. Of all the CNPS's achievements since 1967, this surely must be the most remarkable—transforming political science into a profession of active scholars.[5]

THE DETERIORATING ACADEMIC MARKETPLACE

The Vietnamest experience, contrary to the best hopes of some radical NCPS members, did not put an end to American political science.[6] Nor, however substantial their effect on the structure and governance of the American Political Science Association, did the political events of the late 1960's and early 1970's have more than a transitory impact on research, graduate training, and even undergraduate teaching.[7]

In contrast, another external force, the deteriorating job market, carried far-reaching implications for all of these. By 1960 the birthrate had already begun to drop. In 1965, as we dutifully noted in the first edition of this book (p. 158), Allan M. Cartter, a leading authority on educational manpower, called attention to the inevitable and devastating consequences of a declining birthrate for the academic marketplace. Preoccupied by the short-run opportunities to expand their departments and training programs, political scientists, like other academicians, were apparently incapable of attending to sucj projections and prophecies. As Cartter complained to the Congress' Joint Economic Committee in 1969, "One can only surmise that old dogmas are difficult to dispel, and that no amount of evidence other than men with Ph.D.'s selling apples on street corners is going to convince some people that market situations are dramatically changing around them."[8]

Two other developments intensified the severity of the problem. In the early 1970's, students began to move out of the humanities and social sciences and into more professionally oriented curricula. Thus, while total enrollments still inched upward, or at worst levelled off, political science departments began to lose, initially, their claim to additional staff and, shortly thereafter, became increasingly hard pressed to justify the "lines" currently allotted to them. Second, although collectively agreeing that "something should be done" about Ph.D. output, the individual departments reenacted the "Parable of the Commons" in their reluctance, with a few exceptions, to cut back drastically on their own doctoral programs. The number of students entering these programs held steady between 1976 and 1979 (the lastest year for which data are now available) and the number of Ph.D.'s produced annually continued to hover in the 850-900 area.

The manifestly deteriorating job situation prompted the APSA to begin collecting systematic data on the supply and placement of political scientists. Conducted by Thomas E. Mann of the Association's Washington office, and reported by him in *PS*, these annual studies yielded some disturbing findings. Of the roughly thousand "firm" candidates for jobs each year from 1972-1977, only 70 percent were placed—and only 50 percent in regular tenure track positions; the ratio of academic to professionally-related nonacademic placements ran a consistent 8.5 to 1;[9] employability varied with subfield, ranging from barely 50 percent in political theory to 80 percent and better in public administration and public policy; an increasing proportion of job applicants (about one-third in 1978-79) were experienced faculty members with little or no prospects for tenure at their home institutions; the creation of new positions dropped below 300 by 1974, 250 by 1975, and 200 by 1978. In 1980, Mann warned, the population cohort from which the overwhelming majority of college students are drawn will begin a fifteen-year decline that will probably reduce college enrollments by some 25 percent—and the number of new jobs will begin to plummet to almost zero.

By 1976 the outlook was already so bleak that the APSA's Committee of Chairmen sounded the alarm. In the only editorial ever published in *PS*,[10] the committee called upon graduate departments to reduce the size of their doctoral programs, apprise applicants of market conditions, and revise their curricula to train students for professionally-related nonacademic positions. Subsequently, *PS* ran a barrage of articles restating the problem, recapit-

218

ulating and refining Mann's data, evaluating the prospects for professionally-related nonacademic careers,[11] and examining the fairly formidable changes that would be required if post-baccalaureate programs in political science attempted to prepare their students to compete effectively with the graduates of schools of law, business and public administration, and public policy.

For all that has been said and written, little has actually been done. As mentioned above, the number of students admitted to doctoral programs has been essentially constant, and doctoral output persists at a level several times higher than the new positions available. And, though the descriptions in the Association's *Annual Guide to Graduate Study in Political Science* suggest that most doctoral programs provide suitable preparation for nonteaching careers in research, administration, and policy analysis, there is scanty evidence that the content of these programs has been substantially altered to meet their stated objectives. Nor are the factors underlying this failure difficult to fathom. The principal reason why Ph.D.'s in political science have difficulty in finding professionally-related nonacademic employment is that prospective employers are not particularly impressed by their theoretical knowledge, substantive expertise, or methodological skills. In the opinion of the Association's Committee on Professional Development, which has wrestled with these concerns since 1977, the kind of training desired by these employers is broadly similar to that currently provided by interdisciplinary programs in public policy and policy science.[12] To achieve this, the passive, slow-paced, theoretically oriented analysis of macro-level problems would have to give way to an action-oriented attack on specific micro-level policy targets. Heavy emphasis, for example, would need be placed on internship training, tools of economic analysis, statistical procedures appropriate for managerial decision making, group problem solving, the timely preparation of memoranda that weigh alternative courses of action, and the design, delivery, and evaluation of services.

Highly trained faculty are essential if these programs are to produce a truly marketable product. Given current and foreseeable budgetary constraints, new faculty could hardly be hired, even if available. The alternative, then, is a far-reaching, strenuous retooling of existing staff. At best, it is doubtful that such retooling would be successful; it is equally dubious that most faculty members would agree to participate, since they would be forced to abandon much of the research and teaching that they, as political scientists, are prepared to do and which they presumably value quite highly. Perhaps, as some seem to feel, the results would be intellectually and professionally invigorating, perhaps not. What is beyond cavil, however, is that the scope and intellectual orientation of political science as we know it would be fundamentally changed.

The prospects of the American Political Science Association are, of course, closely tied to those of the discipline itself. For the Association, too, the 1980's will be a difficult decade. Regular membership oeaked in 1975, has been declining ever since, and will continue to do so as long as the Association's membership remains predominantly (80 percent) academic. Inevitably, shrinking membership and rising costs have generated grave financial problems, and these will become progressively more severe over the next several years.

Both the Association and American political science, we can safely predict, will survive the 1980's. But they will be profoundly changed in the process—and we can hardly be confident that they will necessarily be the better or the happier for the experience.

ASPECTS OF PROFESSIONAL LIFE

THE DEPARTMENTS

That some departments are believed to be better than others, we remarked in the course of our 1964 volume, is less newsworthy than the regularity with which, decade after decade, the same departments are perceived as preeminent.[13] Since then at least three more major studies of departmental reputation have been made— all with strikingly similar results:[14]

TABLE 1 [15]
RANKING OF POLITICAL SCIENCE GRADUATE DEPARTMENTS

Somit Tanenhaus 1963 (1)		Cartter 1966 (2)		Roose & Anderson 1969 (3)		Roettger 1976 (4)	
1	Harvard	1	Yale	1	Yale	1	Yale
2	Yale	2	Harvard	2	Harvard	2	Harvard
3	Berkeley	3	Berkeley	4.5	Chicago	3	Berkeley
4	Chicago	4	Chicago	4.5	M.I.T.	4	Chicago
5	Princeton	5	Princeton	4.5	Michigan	5	Michigan
6	Columbia	6	Stanford	4.5	Stanford	6	Stanford
7	Michigan	7	M.I.T.	8	North Carolina	7	Princeton
8.5	Stanford	8	Wisconsin	8	Princeton	8	Wisconsin
8.5	Wisconsin	9	Columbia	8	Wisconsin	9	North Carolina
10.5	U.C.L.A.	10	Michigan	10	Berkeley	10	Minnesota
10.5	Cornell	11	Northwestern	11.5	Minnesota	11.5	U.C.L.A.
12	Johns Hopkins	12	Cornell	11.5	Rochester	11.5	Johns Hopkins
13	Northwestern	13	Indiana	14	Indiana	13	Northwestern
14	Indiana	14	North Carolina	14	Northwestern	14	Columbia
15	Illinois	15.5	Johns Hopkins	14	Oregon	15	Cornell
		15.5	U.C.L.A.				

The data in column (3) are taken from: Kenneth D. Roose and Charles J. Anderson, *A Rating of Graduate Programs,* Washington, D.C.: American Council on Education, 1980, p. 65. The data in column (4) are taken from: Walter B. Roettger, "The Discipline: What's Right, What's Wrong, and Who Cares?", a paper presented at the 1978 APSA annual convention. This paper will henceforth be cited simply as Roettger. Only the departments rated fourteenth and fifteenth in 1963 failed to make the 1976 top fifteen; only two of the 1976 leaders were absent from the 1963 ordering; the ranking of individual departments over the four separate studies infrequently changes more than a place or two. Whatever the validity of the profession's beliefs, they seem remarkably impervious to change.

At least a dozen departments made determined efforts to attain "major league" recognition during the "golden sixties" by luring from other institutions as many established (and sometimes merely promising) political scientists as was possible. That policy, the data suggest, probably did more to improve faculty salaries than to raise departmental standings. The experience of the departments is similar in this respect to that of the many universities which, following the same strategy, sought to achieve instant eminence.

221

FIELDS

Since changes in popularity among the discipline's several fields are matters of intellectual interest[16] as well as urgent practical concern,[17] they are assiduously charted. Two basic techniques are employed for this purpose—self-report and analysis of "objective" data. In weighing the results of these efforts, we must remember that both approaches have inherent difficulties. Table 2 provides a case in point.

TABLE 2[18]

	Somit/Tanenhaus 1963	Roettger 1976	APSA 1978
	Percent	Percent	Percent
International Relations	22	21	14
Comparative Government	13	17	17
American Government & Politics	18	32	25
Public Administration	13	12	10
Political Theory	13	–	10
Political Philosophy	–	7	–
Political Theory & Methodology	–	3	–
General Politics & Political Processes	11	–	–
Public Law	10	5	5
Public Policy	–	–	13
Methodology	–	–	5

All three studies were based upon self-report and required the respondent either to write in the name of the field with which he/she felt most closely associated or, alternatively, to select that field from a pre-printed list. Although the three rankings are generally similar, they differ sufficiently among themselves so that meaningful conclusions are not always possible. The Somit/Tanenhaus and Roettger statistics, for example, indicate that International Relations has just about held its own whereas the APSA figures suggest a sharp decline. The two later studies also diverge rather strikingly in their percentages for at least two fields.

Holding in abeyance any question of sample accuracy, these differences stem in large measure from the necessity that, sooner or later, those conducting the study impose upon the responses their own notions of how the discipline is "properly" structured into fields. As the three sets of categories above testify, there are various ways of accomplishing this,[19] making direct comparisons often quite difficult.

A second line of attack, in which the same classification problems are encountered, seeks to measure field popularity by using "objective" indicators rather than self-report. The most common technique here is to count journal articles, by field, over a given period of time.[20] But data derived by this procedure have two serious limitations: first, since only a small percentage of the manuscripts submitted are published, such a study may tell us more about editorial predelictions than about anything else; second, since only a minority of the profession actually attempts to publish, it provides no direct measure of the field preferences of the majority.

On balance, therefore, self-report seems the better of the two approaches. If so, we can say with reasonable confidence that American Government and Politics has replaced International Relations as the most popular field within the discipline, that Comparative Politics has gained, and that Public Law remains solidly ensconced in last place, at least among the "traditional" fields. Beyond this, the situation can only be described as unclear.

THE HALL OF FAME REVISITED: EDIFICE OR RUIN?

Few chapters of our *Profile of a Discipline* elicited more comment than "Hall of Fame" in which we identified those political scientists who, in the opinion of their peers, had made the most significant contributions to the discipline in recent years. Not all of the comments, to be sure, were favorable, for reasons which hardly require explication.

Moved, no doubt, by the same masochistic impulse, Roettger replicated our inquiry, utilizing two time periods—1960-70 and 1970-76.[21] The three sets of findings are:

(1) 1945-60 (Somit/Tanenhaus)		(2) 1960-70 (Roettger)		(3) 1970-76 (Roettger)	
Rank	Name	Rank	Name	Rank	Name
1	Key (35%)	1	Dahl (40%)	1	Lowi (18%)
2	Lasswell (32%)	2	Easton (19%)	2	Wildavsky (10%)
3	Dahl (20%)	3	SRC Group (18%)	3	Dye (9%)
4	Easton (18%)	4	Deutsch (17%)	4	Dahl (8%)
5	Morgenthau (18%)	5	Almond (16%)	5	Huntington (7%)
6	Truman (16%)	6	Wildavsky (7%)	7	SRC Group (6%)
7	Strauss (8%)	7	Lowi (4%)	7	Verba (6%)
8.5	Deutsch (6%)	9	Lipset (4%)	7	Sharkansky (6%)
8.5	Simon (6%)	9	Wolin (4%)	10.5	Barber, Deutsch, Left Radicals,
10.5	Friedrich (5%)	9	Huntington (4%)		Riker
10.5	Schattschneider (5%)				

Even a casual examination of these rankings reveals some rather striking features. First, there has been a great deal of "churning." Only three of the persons shown under 1945–60 (column 1) appear on the 1960–70 roster (column 2). This might be explained by the fact that the studies were separated by almost a decade and a half and drew uon different sample populations. However, much the same phenomenon recurs when we look at Roettger's lists, where these conditins do not apply. Four of the names on his 1960–70 honor roll do not make the 1970–76 tabulation —and a fifth barely escapes this fate by being included, along with several others, in a composite last-place ranking.

Even more significant, we would say, is the sharp decrease in the level of recognition. For the 1960-70 period, the top-ranking political scientist was named by 40 percent, and each of the first five by at least 16 percent, of the respondents; for 1970–76, the top-ranked individual achieved only 18 percent identification and, with a single exception, no one else was nominated by as many as 10 percent of those replying.

As is often the case, the statistics lend themselves to almost diametrically opposed conclusions. The apparent disagreement over who have made the most significant contributions to political science can be regarded as a heartening sign of intellectual ferment within the discipline; with equal plausibility, it can also be seen as disturbing evidence that the profession is increasingly unable to agree on the criteria by which scholarly achievement is to be measured. Both views were voiced at a 1978 APSA panel concerned with that perennially absorbing topic, "The Current State of the Discipline." One panelist interpreted Roettger's data as showing a healthy "circulation of elites." Another, a former APSA president, was less enchanted, declaring that ". . . if this particular list of 'significant contributors' is what our discipline is all about, then I would not only want to celebrate its decline but also pray for its early demise."[22] One of these interpretations, we can unhesitatingly affirm, strikes us as much sounder than the other.

GETTING AHEAD

What factors most contribute to academic success? When asked this question in 1963, political scientists gave first place to "volume of publication," fifth to "quality of publication," and last (tenth) to "teaching." Soon after came the student activists who sought not only to reform the world but were also outraged by, and extraordinarily vocal about, the poor teaching to which they were allegedly subjected. In short order, faculty meetings resounded with *mea culpas;*[23] deans and presidents shouldered each other aside in their haste to proclaim their commitment to inspired pedagogy; the American Political Science Association established a committee to deal with the matter; and, in 1972, a journal *(Teaching Political Science)* was founded to forward the cause.

Regrettably, these efforts do not appear to have had an overwhelming impact on the profession's understanding of the importance attacked to good teaching. Posing the same question in 1976, Roettger (pp. 28-29) found that "volume of publication" had fallen to second place (giving way to "school at which doctorate was taken"), that "quality of publication" remained in fifth, and that "teaching ability" was still firmly entrenched in last place.[24]

To be sure, these are only perceptions. Conceivably, good teaching is more highly valued than political scientists seem to believe. On the other hand, there is some circumstantial evidence which suggests that these beliefs are not altogether unfounded. Both political science faculty and students, Ladd and Lipset discovered, are unhappier about the quality of teaching than their peers in other disciplines.[25] Approaching the issue from another direction, Roettger reported that 65 percent of his respondents felt that "doctoral programs in political science stress research training at the cost of preparing effective undergraduate teachers"—as against 56 percent in 1963 (pp. 42–43). And anecdotal information indicates that publication rather than teaching is increasingly stressed as jobs become fewer, and tenure and promotion more difficult to obtain. Here again, however, we must remember that there is no reason to think that political science differs significantly from other disciplines in this respect.

THE JOURNALS

One of the more notable developments in American political science since the mid-sixties has been the proliferation of professional periodicals. In the mid-sixties, someone attempting to keep abreast of the literature would have had to read perhaps five general and a half-dozen specialized journals. Today, the same objective would require perusal of some ten general and at least fifteen more narrowly focused publications.[26]

Two interrelated factors were undoubtedly operative here: the growing number of political scientists and the concurrent tendency toward greater specialization. The latter spawned a felt need for journals catering to specific sub-fields; the former, by enlarging the potential audience, made the new publications financially viable, or at least encouraged such a hope. The creation of journals seemed to accelerate during the early 1970's, suggesting yet a third factor, the pressure for additional scholarly outlets.

The *American Political Science Review* continued to be the profession's most prestigious periodical; the niche immediately below, occupied in 1963 by the *Journal of Politics* and *World Politics,* expanded to include the *American Journal of Political Science,* which jumped from ninth to fourth place. With two other exceptions—the *Administrative Science Quarterly,* which went from fifth to eighth, and the *Western Political Quarterly,* which dropped from sixth to tenth—no other journal moved more than two places (Roettger, p. 19).[27] A 1974 APSA survey reported that, occasional fuming letters to the editor notwithstanding, 70 percent of those queried ranked the *Review* as either "excellent" or "good." The *Review* could also claim to be the publication read "most extensively." Conceivably so. Still, granting that the data are ambiguous,[28] there is reason to believe that this particular rating was surpassed by *PS,* a sister publication devoted primarily to

226

professional news and to research dealing with the practice, rather than the theory, of American political science.

The *Review*'s manuscript rate continued to run around the 90 percent mark, higher than the regional and specialized journals but about the same as the "major" journals in the other social sciences.[29] Another study found, to no one's great surprise, that a disproportionate percentage of the authors appearing in the *Review* held degrees from prestigious departments and/or had appointments in such departments; and that depending on the time period selected, only 2 percent to 5 percent of American political scientists had ever published in the *Review*. The same study concluded that changes in the editorship of the *Review* seemed to be followed by much greater scholarly activity, as measured by publication in the *Review* . . . of the new editor's departmental colleagues.[30] A persuasive argument, surely, for rotating the editorship as often as practicable.

THE ESTABLISHMENT

Earlier in this chapter we described the attempts made by the American Political Science Association to achieve greater openness in its activities and to democratize the process whereby its officers are chosen and policy issues resolved. Unfortunately, these efforts have apparently not improved the manner in which members of the Association view the way in which it conducts significant aspects of its business.

Our 1963 inquiry contained two propositions bearing on this issue: no. 16—"American political science has developed an Establishment which largely determines the character and standards of the discipline"; no. 26—"there has developed an inner group in the American Political Science Association which, in large part, controls the key panel assignments at the annual Association meetings." Affirmative responses to the former were given by 46 percent, and to the latter by 42 percent, of the respondents. Readministering these items in 1976, Roettger elicited affirmative answers of 67 and 42 percent, respectively. Though perceptions seem not to have changed with regard to control of the annual meeting, there has been a sizable increase in the number of those who feel that the direction of the discipline is controlled by some inner group.

Roettger's results are both puzzling and paradoxical. They are puzzling in that other evidence ("Hall of Fame," above, p. 9) suggests that there is considerably less agreement than before among political scientists on the "character and standards of the discipline." They are paradoxical in that two-thirds of the profession now believe that the annual meeting is controlled by some inner group, despite the fact that the Association has, in effect, abdicated much of its previous responsiblity (see p. 4 above) for the number, type, topic, and quality of the panels offered thereat. Perhaps these sentiments have some relationship to the drop in membership which the Association has experienced in recent years. Whatever the underlying factors, they do not augur well.

CAREER SATISFACTION

Any discussion of this topic must begin with a reminder that the 1970's were not vintage years either for higher education in general or for social science in particular. American colleges and universities were hit, early in the decade, by fiscal problems which became progressively more acute; competition for students, bright or otherwise, became increasingly severe; a college degree no longer ensured its recipient a job, let alone a good one; the quality of higher education was subjected to a swelling torrent of criticism; as enrollments ceased to expand, faculty mobility decreased, with new jobs becoming something of an endangered species; and, perhaps not least important, academic salaries fell further and further behind the cost of living. Little wonder that almost every study taken in recent years has reported plummeting faculty morale.

The social sciences had their special tribulations. Research support declined; beginning in the early 1970's, the number of majors shrank, as students, understandably concerned about employment prospect, shifted to the professional schools. Personnel cut-backs, necessitated by shrinking budgets, began to fall on the social science departments with increasing severity and were reflected in the loss of tenure-track, or even the total number of faculty positions. Equally, if not more, demoralizing was a growing sense that the social sciences could offer little to the solution of the nation's urgent social problems, a realization all the more devastating given the exuberant hopes of the 1960's.

Still, allowing for all of this, political scientists seem to be unhappier with their careers than almost any other group of American scholars. Ladd and Lipset[31] found, in 1975, that 59 percent (the highest percentage in academe) of those teaching political science were pursuing, or would "seriously consider an offer" of a nonacademic position (p. 12); and, in another study, that political scientists ranked highest among the social sciences in their negative responses to the query: "if you were to begin your career again, would you want to be a college professor?"[32] These responses parallel those obtained by Roettger (p. 32) in his readministration of our item: "if you were able to start over and pick your profession again, would you still choose a career in political science?" In 1963, 76 percent of the academics said either "definitely yes" or "probably"; the number dropped to 64 percent in 1976.[33]

It is tempting to speculate upon the factors which may have contributed to this malaise: the fact that, according to Ladd and Lipset (1978, pp. 5-6), political scientists are the worst paid of the social scientists; the falling number and quality of students seriously interested in political science as a career (*ibid.*, pp. 8-9); and, unhappiness over the course of recent developments within the profession.[34] Nonetheless, it is imperative to keep the situation, dismal as it may seem, in proper perspective. These have been difficult years, especially for the social sciences. If professional life seems less than totally satisfying, there is little reason to think that the differences in mood and morale between political science and its sister disciplines are more than a matter of modest degree.

POLITICAL SCIENCE AS SCIENCE: BEHAVIORALISM

By the mid-1960's, the behavioral movement had influenced American political science in several obvious ways. Behavioralism made political scientists more self-conscious and self-critical, more attentive to analytic theory, research design, and quantitative techniques. Leading behavioralists such as Almond, Easton, and Truman left little doubt, furthermore, about their aspirations— expectations might be too strong a word—that "system," "group," "power," "functionalism," or some other overarching concept could ultimately provide the foundation for a science of politics. They hoped that at least some important political phenomena could be explained by means of verified, empirical laws embedded in a set of related axioms.

Nonetheless, as we noted earlier (pp. 183–190), behavioralism remained a highly controversial minority movement within the discipline. Whatever the hopes for "peace with honor" evoked by a seeming lull in hostilities during the mid-1960's,[35] the battle broke out afresh as the decade entered its closing years. Profound differences over Vietnam, civil rights, the urban crisis, student activism, and the New Left served to widen and inflame previous disagreements as to the proper practice of political science.

As the "Establishment" paradigm, however slippery that term, behavioralism came under renewed attack from the right, the center, and the left. David Easton's 1969 APSA presidential address contains what is probably the best known single summary of these criticisms, as well as Easton's now-famous plea for a post-behavioral political science committed, *inter alia,* to the reshaping of American society. The term *post-behavioral,* already current within the discipline, had come to identify, of course, not so much a specific time period but a professional orientation basically hostile to behavioralism; other calls for a "new" post-behavioral political science preceded and followed Easton's.

To what extent were the beliefs or the practices of American political scientists altered by the events and the post-behavioral polemics of the late 1960's and early 1970's? Despite all that has been said about the post-behavioral "revolution," there is little evidence that much has changed with regard either to the views of the profession or the manner in which its members pursue their discipline. Political scientists expressed essentially the same opinions about behavioralism in 1976 as they did when initially sounded on this issue in 1963 (Roettger, p. 11). So far as the rank and file of the profession are concerned, Roettger observes, "...there is little evidence that the discipline has become either more or less inclined toward the behavioral persuasion. Indeed, it seems more accurate to say that the same divisions persist...." If there has been any shift, it is probably indicated in the greater proportion of those who now feel that behavioralism is the dominant paradigm (60 percent) compared with the number (48 percent) who associate themselves with that outlook (*ibid.*, pp. 10–11).

Nor does the political science literature of the 1970's seem significantly different from that of preceding years. Granting that these matters do not lend themselves to precise measurement, a careful reading of the books and journals, and of the reports of annual meetings, etc., hardly supports the idea tht political scientists are more democratic, less conservative, less inclined toward pluralism, more committed to social change, more concerned with applied rather than pure research, more policy oriented, more willing to have the Association take official stands on public issues, more radical, more critical of American society, and more Marxist — all planks in one or another post-behavioral platform — than they were ten or fifteen years ago. Behavioralism, as Roettger's study again demonstrated, has yet to command the loyalties of more than a minority within the profession. The practice of political science, however, is still largely influenced by the behavioral paradigm and the post-behavioral "revolutionists" seem to have been no more successful in lessening that influence than were the anti-behavioralists of previous decades.

If relatively impregnable so far to assault from outside, behavioralism has quite recently been subjected to serious challenge from within — a challenge based on the continuing chasm between behavioral aspirations and actual accomplishments. To be sure, the behavioral quest for greater quantification has made substantial headway. An increasing proportion of the articles published in the *American Political Science Review,* the *American Journal of Political Science,* and most of the other general political science journals utilizes increasingly sophisticated statistical and mathematical techniques.[36] On the other hand, relatively little of this work seems to satisfy the key behavioral precept that research be theory-oriented and directed. After a careful study of 180 political behavior studies published in the *Review* during 1968–77, John C. Wahlke concluded that "the prevailing atheoretical character of most political behavior research is indicated by the extent to which concepts and variables are no more than brute-empirical operational definitions virtually devoid of conceptual content."[37] Small wonder, then, that Gabriel Almond's examination of research on voting behavior, political socialization, public policy, and social mobilization turned up nothing remotely resembling scientific laws.[38] And, as the literature testifies, there seems to be an emerging, if reluctant, consensus that efforts to build scientific theories on such successively fashionable concepts as group, system, functionalism, and power have made little headway.[38]

Not only have behavioralists, with the possible exception of rational choice theorists,[40] little to show in the way of progress toward scientific theory, but some of the movement's early leaders have lost enthusiasm for the enterprise. Although Easton's 1969 presidential address did not contend that a science of politics could not be achieved, it surely questions the wisdom of the attempt. Almond, whatever his feelings about the desirability of scientific theories about politics, now apparently considers the goal unattainable. And while Wahlke, who devoted his 1978 presidential address to a scathing critique of behaviorialism's lack of accomplishment, still believes scientific theories both desirable and possible, he is now convinced that meaningful progress will not be made unless the behavioralists overcome the

> two serious conceptual shortcomings which severely hamper their capacity to obtain theoretically (or practically) significant results. One is lack of anchorage in macro-level political theory, i.e., failure to orient research on political behavior by concern for or awareness of any fundamental questions about the state and fate of the polity or the lives and condition of the people in it, or to link up findings about individual behavior to any such concerns, whatever the original motivation for doing the research on it. The other shortcoming is reliance on a deficient general behavioral theory, on what earlier political philosophers would call a flawed conception of human nature and modern biobehavioral scientists would call an inadequate and erroneous model of the functioning individual human organism.[41]

Given these shortcomings, the condition of contemporary political behavior research should be described not as behavioral, not as post-behavioral, but rather as "pre-behavioral."[42] A truly behavioral political science, he argues, would have a much closer working relationship with the biobehavioral sciences (evolutionary biology and ethology in particular but physiology and neuro-physiology as well); would abandon the assumption that attitudes, as measured by verbal self-report, provide a useful explanation of behavior, and would turn, instead, to the study of behavior itself, rather than of the current verbal surrogate.

It is, of course, too soon to judge the impact of these attempts to reshape the behavioral paradigm.[43] Two predictions, however, can be made with some certainty. For the foreseeable future—the next five to ten years—the discipline will continue to be a house divided, with each faction or school practicing and preaching its own version of political science and exhibiting more or (probably) less tolerance toward those holding rival views; second, that this situation will continue to be regarded as acceptable, or even laud-

232

able, by most of those within the profession. For, s one of our senior statesmen remarked a decade ago, "if you don't know where you are going, it is safe to assume that almost any road will take you there."[44]

FOOTNOTES

[1]Heinz Eulau, "Understanding Political Life in America," *Social Science Quarterly,* vol. 57 (June, 1976), pp. 112-154.

[2]More than half of the respondents in the 1963 survey had agreed that "much that passes for scholarship in political science is superficial or trivial" (65.7 percent), that American political scientists are "unhappy about the current state of their discipline" (54.8 percent), and that much research in political science is undertaken "simply because the projects lend themselves to research by a fashionable tool or because financial support can be readily obtained" (78.6 percent). Barely half of the respondents, moreover, felt that political science "has generally competed successfully with the other social sciences in areas of common interest and study" (50.8 percent). Large minorities also believed that the behavioral approach cannot successfully attack "the really significant problems of political life" (38.5 percent), and that political scientists, by and large, "do not devote enough attention to contemporary public policy matters" (34.6 percent). Still others were troubled by what they saw as control of the Association by a small "in-group." See below, pp. 12.

[3]Inclusion by the APSA's official nominating committee for 1970 of two Caucus members as Council nominees prompted some of the CNP's most powerful opponents to form the Ad Hoc Committee for the purpose of defeating the two Caucus members. Eventually, the ad hoc committee came to see its principal mission as preventing the CNPS and the Women's Caucus (which first entered APSA electoral politics in 1970) from defeating the official nominee for president-elect—and in keeping with that mission adopted the strategy of endorsing the entire official slate even when the CNPS members were on it.

[4]Among these groups were the Inter-University Consortium on Armed Forces and Society, the Walter Bagehot Research Council on National Sovereignty, the Committee on Conceptual and Terminological Analysis, the Caucus for Faith and Politics, the Conference Group on Government and the Arts, American Professors for Peace in the Middle East, the Neighborhood Organization Research Group, the Conference Group on the Political Economy of Advanced Industrial Societies, Native American Politics and Political Science, and the Legislative Process, Behavior, and Representation Group.

[5]The CNPS almost made another inadvertent contribution to organization of the annual program. On the only occasion when Caucus members chaired the program committee, some Council members were so upset by the results that they discovered unanticipated merit in the procedures of other scholarly disciplines and sought to transfer much of the responsibility for the annual program from the usual ad hoc program committee to continuing sections of field specialists. Once it had become clear to even the fainthearted that the CNPS no longer posed a threat, interest in continuing sections largely subsided.

[6]See marvin Surkin and Alan Wolfe (eds.), *An End to Political Science.* New York: Basic Books, 1970.

[7]On undergraduate texts see Marc A. Triebwasser, "Politics, Economics, and American Government Texts," *Teaching Political Science,* vol. 4 (1977), pp. 269-78.

⁸Quoted by Marvin Rintala and John Dreijmanis in "The Academic Labor Market: With Special Reference to Political Science." *The Journal of Educational Thought,* vol. 6 (August, 1972), pp. 105-114, at 112.

⁹Very recent data reveals that, in 1978-79, the figure jumped to 25 percent. It will take a year or two before we know whether this was simply a statistical "blip" or actually indicative of a changing pattern.

¹⁰*PS.* vol IX, No 1, pp. 6-7.

¹¹Robert S. Friedman, "Nonacademic Careers for Political Scientists," *PS,* vol. X, no. 1, pp. 14-16; Roy E. Licklider, "A Skeptic's View of Corporate Jobs and New Academic Programs," *PS,* vol. XII, no. 1, pp. 26-29; Jack Walker, "Challenge of Professional Development for Political Science in the Next Decade and Beyond," *PS,* vol. XI, no. 4, pp. 484-90; and Erwin C. Hargrove, "Can Political Science Develop Alternative Careers for its Graduages?," *PS,* vol. XII, no. 4, pp. 446-50.

¹²Walker, *op. cit.*

¹³Regrettably, considerations of space do not permit treatment of a closely related topic—the patterning of departmental Ph.D. output. here we can note only that: some 110 departments in the U.S. are currently authorized to grant a Ph.D. in political science; one-third of the degrees are granted by nine or ten schools; fewer than 40 departments produce 75 percent of the Ph.D.'s; and those departments ranked "distinguished" and "strong" accounted for about 45 percent of the annual output in 1976, as contrasted with 52 percent in 1969, and 59 percent in 1968. See William J. Siffin, "Portents and Prospects: Graduate Study and the Profession," *PS,* vol. X, no. 1, pp. 10-12, and Walfred H. Peterson, "Doctoral Output in Political Science—Tables for 1973-76," *ibid,* pp. 18-22.

¹⁴For yet another rating, with much the same findings, see Everett C. Ladd and Seymour Martin Lipset, *Chronical of Higher Education,* January 15, 1979. There has also been an attempt to rate departments by use of some "objective" criteria—John S. Robey, "Political Science Departments; Reputations versus Productivity," *PS,* vol. XII, no. 2, pp. 202-209. For one reaction, see "Letters to the Editor," *PS,* vol. XII, no. 4, p. 538.

¹⁵The data in column (1) are taken from: Somit and Tanenhaus, *Profile, op. cit.,* p. 34 (Table 3).
The data in column (2) are taken from: Alan Murray Cartter, *An Assessment of Quality in Graduate Education,* Washington, D.C.: American Council on Education, 1968, p. 100 (Table 31).

¹⁶For examples of the quasi-ideological possibilities of field data analyses, see the exchange between Heinz Eulau, "Quo Vadimus," *PS,* vol. II, no. 1, pp. 12-13; and Norman Wengert, "One Swallow Does Not Make a Spring...," *ibid.,* no. 3, pp. 354-55; also Jack L. Walker, "Brother Can You Paradigm?", *ibid.,* vol. V, no. 4, pp. 419-22.

¹⁷For patterns of placement by field, see below, p. 8 and Thomas E. Mann, "Placement of American Political Scientists," *PS,* vol. IX, no. 4, p. 414.

[18]The Somit/Tanenhaus 1963 findings, slightly modified by Roettger, and the Roettger 1976 data are taken from Roettger, p. 21; the APSA 1978 rankings are from *PS,* vol. XI, no. 3, p. 385.

[19]Careful readers of the *Review* and of *PS* will have noticed that the Association itself uses several classifcation schema—one for the information reported above, another for the book review section, a third for data relating to panels and panel attendance at the annual meeting, etc.

[20]Other data that can and have been used for this purpose are number of courses offered, doctoral dissertations, convention panels and attendance thereat, books and book reviews.

[21]Walter B. Roettger, "Strate and Stability: Reputations of American Political Scientists," *PS,* vol. XI, no. 1, pp. 6-12.

[22]Heinz Eulau, "The Unwatered Hinterland of Political Science: Some Comments on the Occasion of a Premature Memorial Service," APSA Annual Meeting, September 1978, p. 6.

[23]At schools wth a strong classical tradition, these were, of course, *meis culpis.*

[24]A 1969 study reported much the same relationship between the importance attached, respectively, to teaching and research. Charles D. Hadley, "Teaching Political Scientists: the Centrality of Research," *PS,* vol. V, no. 3, pp. 264-270. For a somewhat different perspective on "getting ahead," see Lee Sigelman, "How to Succeed in Political Science by Being Very Trying: A Methodological Sampler," *PS,* vol. X, no. 3, pp. 302-304.

[25]Everett Carl Ladd, Jr. and Seymour Martin Lipset, "Us Revisited," a paper presented at the 1978 Annual Meeting of the American Political Science Association, pp. 13-15.

[26]For a listing, see Michael W. Giles, Denita Mears, and Ellie Weinberger, "Journals in Political Science and Related Fields," *PS,* vol X, no. 1, pp. 36-39; and "Addendum," *PS,* vol. XI, no. 1, pp. 34-35.

[27]Another study, though broader in scope, yielded much the same results. See Michael W. Giles and Gerald C. Wright, Jr., "Political Scientists Evaluation of Sixty-Three Journals," *PS,* vol. VIII, no. 2, pp. 254-257.

[28]Thomas E. Mann, "Report on a Survey of the Membership of the American Political Science Association," *PS,* vol. VII, no. 4, pp. 382-385.

[29]Charles Bonjean and Jan Hullum, "Reasons for Journal Rejection: An Analysis of 600 Manuscripts," *PS,* vol. XI, no. 4, pp. 480-483.

[30]Mostofa Rejai and Glenn R. Parker, "Publishing in the Professional Journals: The Case of the APSR," *New Political Science,* Winter, 1974, pp. 10-13.

236

[31]*op. cit.*, p. 12.

[32]Ladd and Lipset, "US: Characteristics of the American Political Science Community," a paper delivered at the 1973 Annual Meeting of the American Political Science Association, p. 70.

[33]Only seven years earlier, at the height of the "golden" (for academics) sixties, essentially the same question evoked a 90 percent affirmative response. Charles D. Hadley, "Teaching Political Scientists: the Centrality of Research," *PS*, vol. V, no. 3, p. 264.

[34]That the political scientists happiest with their chosen careers were in public administration, where the job opportunities were greatest, and in political philosophy, where "scientistic" commitments tended to be uncommon, gves some credence to these explanations (Roettger, pp. 32-33).

[35]With less than total presidential prescience, David Truman expressed his willingness to bet "...on the possibility of a new disciplinary consensus"! "Disillusion and Regeneration: The Quest for a Discipline," *APSR*, vol. LIX, no. 4, (1965), p. 870. Another commentator, no less sanguine, announced that "happily, we are now far along in the task of clearing the air of the often-stultifying smoke produced by the extremist guns in the behavioral-traditional battle." Neil Riemer, *ibid.*, vol. LIX, no. 3, (September, 1965), p. 697.

[36]William H. Riker, "Editorial Comment," *APSR*, no. 68 (1974), pp. 733-734. For an updating and expansion of Riker's findings, we are indebted to the unknown author of a ms. entitled "A Note on Quantification and Multiple Authorships in Political Science," 1979.

[37]"Pre-Behavioralism in Political Science," *ASPR*, no. 73 (March, 1979), p. 19.

[38]Gabriel A. Almond and Stephen J. Genco, "Clouds, Clocks, and the Study of Politics," *World Politics*, vol. XXIX, no. 4 (July, 1977), pp. 489-522.

[39]For an assessment of the attempt to "behavioralize" area strudies generally, and Communist-area studies in particular, see Dmitri N. Shalin, "Behavioral and Post-Behavioral Methodologies in Communist Studies," a paper presented at the 1979 Annual Meeting of the American Association for the Advancement of Slavic Studies.

[40]Conceivably—and there are many political scientists who remain skeptical—William Riker and his students have taken major initial steps down the long road to a scientific theory of political decision-making.

[41]Wahlke, *op. cit.*, p. 24.

[42]If Wahlke is correct, political science may well be the only discipline in which "post" has chronologically preceded "pre."

[43]Wahlke's pleas for a closer relationship between biology and political science will undoubtedly encourage further work in biopolitics, a field now well into its second decade, but the biopoliticians, however pleased by his endorsement, were already converted. Whether others in the discipline are prepared to embrace a more biological approach, or

237

whether many of the behavioralists who are heavily committed to attitudinal research are willing to change their ways, remains to be seen.

[44]Heinz Eulau, *APSR,* vol. 63, no. 2 (1969), p. 433.

NAME INDEX

Adams, Charles Kendall, 40, 47
Adams, Henry Carter, 40
Adams, Herbert Baxter, 25, 30, 31, 32, 34, 36, 37, 38, 43, 46, 47, 52, 58, 69, 89, 202
Agger, Robert E., 190
Almond, Gabriel A., 113, 190, 193
Amos, Sheldon, 29
Alden, George Henry, 41
Allport, Floyd, 126
Anderson, William, 2, 23, 55, 98, 100, 104, 139
Angell, James B., 40
Aristotle, 28

Bagehot, Walter, 32
Baldwin, Simeon, 25, 43, 56
Bancroft, George, 17
Barnes, Harry Elmer, 119
Bateman, Clifford, 17, 18
Beard, Charles A., 67, 75, 98, 115, 119, 120, 121, 139
Bentley, Arthur F., 66, 67, 68, 72, 75, 76, 78, 79, 109, 117, 179, 184, 187
Berelson, Bernard, 7, 38, 160
Beyle, Herman C., 113, 131
Blumenstock, Dorothy, 131
Bluntchli, J. K., 24
Brecht, Arnold, 173
Brown, Bernard E., 3
Browning, Robert, 36
Bryce, James, 56, 66, 69, 70, 71, 72, 78, 80, 132
Buchanan, William, 190
Burgess, John W., 3, 8, 9, 11, 16, 17, 18, 19, 20, 21, 23, 24, 25, 26, 28, 29, 30, 31, 34, 35, 36, 37, 38, 40, 43, 44, 46, 47, 52, 69, 72, 79, 89, 109, 175, 179, 184, 202, 211
Butler, David E., 173

Campbell, Angus, 190
Cartter, Allan M., 158, 163, 165, 169
Catlin, G. E. G., 114, 115, 116, 117, 118, 126, 130, 179
Charlesworth, James C., 173
Cole, Taylor, 155, 193
Colegrove, Kenneth W., 58
Coleman, James S., 190
Converse, Philip E., 190
Cooley, Thomas E., 40
Corwin, Edward S., 119, 120
Crane, William W., 24, 29
Crecraft, Earl W., 98
Crick, Bernard, 33, 45, 70, 72, 104, 162
Curtius, Ernst, 15

Dahl, Robert A., 173, 174, 176, 177, 185, 190, 193, 200
Darwin, Charles R., 29, 124
Dealey, James Q., 41, 64
Deutsch, Karl W., 190
Dewey, A. Gordon, 115
Dicey, A. V., 66
Droysen, Johann Gustav, 15
Duniway, C. A., 41
Dunning, William A., 23, 31, 38, 45

Easton, David, 70, 173, 177, 188, 190, 193

239

SUBJECT INDEX

Americanization of political science, 21, 23, 38, 49, 50, 61-2, 88
American Economic Association, 22, 40, 51
American Political Science Association, 23, 34, 40, 41, 43, 46, 49, 50, 51-62, 63, 65, 76, 77, 79, 81, 83, 88, 91-100, 109, 122, 124, 128, 131, 135, 137, 138, 143, 145, 146, 147-54, 155, 158, 160, 165, 166, 170, 187, 188, 193
American Political Science Review, 52, 53, 54, 61, 62, 68, 69, 84, 93, 94-7, 99, 122, 126, 128, 130, 131, 132, 136, 139, 141, 146, 147, 148, 150, 151, 154-57, 166, 186, 187, 189, 191, 192, 193, 202
Anti-behavioralism, 88, 177, 180-83, 189

Behavioralism, 3, 74, 87, 113, 143, 153, 154, 156, 157, 171, 172, 173-80, 183-94, 208-11

Citizenship Clearing House-National Center for Education in Politics, 170, 196-99
Citizenship training (education), 45-8, 80-5, 88, 99, 128, 132, 134, 135-38, 195-201
Colleges and Universities:
    Alaska, 168
    American, 159, 166
    Amherst, 16, 17
    Berlin, 15, 17

Bowdoin, 60
Brookings Institution Graduate School, 102, 103, 107
Brown, 41, 60, 163
Bryn Mawr, 45, 107
California, Berkeley, 106, 155, 159, 161, 164, 165
California, Los Angeles, 102, 103, 105, 106, 107, 164, 166, 168
Chattanooga, 168
Chicago, 34, 41, 45, 47, 58, 59, 60, 61, 102, 103, 105, 106, 107, 108, 113, 127, 131, 155, 159, 164, 165, 166, 168, 183
Claremont, 163
College de France, 35
Columbia, 8, 11, 15, 17-21, 30, 31, 34, 35, 36, 38, 44, 46, 50, 57, 58, 59, 60, 67, 69, 101, 102, 103, 106, 107, 108, 155, 158, 164, 165, 166, 168
Cornell, 46, 60, 107, 108, 155, 164, 168
Dartmouth, 60, 168
Delaware, 168
Denver, 168
Duke, 163, 164, 166
Ecole Libre des Sciences Politiques, 35
Earlham, 168
Georgetown, 159, 166
Gettysburg, 169
Göttingen, 15, 17
Harvard, 15, 41, 45, 57, 58, 59, 60, 61, 71, 102, 103,